FAMILY HISTORY

FAMILY
HISTORY
digging deeper

SIMON FOWLER

First published 2012

The History Press
The Mill, Brimscombe Port
Stroud, Gloucestershire, GL5 2QG
www.thehistorypress.co.uk

British Library Cataloguing in Publication Data.
A catalogue record for this book is available from the British Library.

ISBN 978 0 7524 5897 7

Typesetting and origination by The History Press
Printed in Great Britain
Manufacturing managed by Jellyfish Print Solutions Ltd

CONTENTS

PREFACE

It is hard to believe that I have been teaching and writing about family history for nearly thirty-five years. I've even managed to do a little of my own family tree. In that time I've found that there are two types of family historians, those who are starting out and those who have gone beyond the basics.

There are lots of books catering for beginners, but rather fewer for those who are, for want of a better term, more advanced. Some tend to be semi-academic or rather dully written. Presumably the authors thought the subject was a serious one, which deserved serious treatment. Well I don't disagree – at least up to a point. However, for heaven's sake, why not try a livelier approach and inject some fun and fascinating facts?

When I edited *Ancestors Magazine* for The National Archives, we carried out research into why people weren't buying the magazine. The greatest obstacle was that people thought it was for advanced family historians. Which was true, but what was worrying was that many of our readers had been doing their family history for years, but still believed they were beginners. In some cases they probably had forgotten more about the subject than I have ever learnt. Perhaps it was some sort of inferiority complex. Stuff and nonsense: you don't have to have a degree or diploma in the subject to be an expert.

So this book is not about the basics. If you are browsing in a bookshop wondering which book to buy for Auntie Beryl who has just begun the family tree, then – much as I, and my publisher, would like to take your money – there are better books out there, such as Karen Foy's *Family History for Beginners* (The History Press, 2011). So we won't be considering the census or civil registration, except perhaps in discussing why they were established in the first place or looking at alternatives.

Nonetheless, if you, or Beryl, has an enquiring mind and wants to know more about your family tree and the huge array of records you can use to find out about the various branches then I hope this book is for you. In it I'll be pushing back the

A 'cartwheel tuppence' from the reign of George III. The penny and tuppence coins got their name from their size and weight. (*www.detecting.org.uk*)

Essex Record Office is one of the many new county archives which have opened in recent years. (*Author's collection*)

barriers, looking, for example, at new ways in which the internet can help your research, suggesting some unusual archives and records which might just transform your research, and looking at variants of family history around the world. Also, some of Britain's top researchers will be contributing their thoughts about how to get the best from the resources at our disposal.

Even so, I am very aware of the subjects that have not been covered, despite having written over 70,000 words. Some, like emigration and immigration, or records relating to the purchase, sale and ownership of land, are covered better elsewhere. I have also avoided extensive discussion about the army and navy, largely because I have written about their records elsewhere.

Surprisingly, finding anything about certain topics has proved almost impossible. Take jury lists, for example, which are often found with electoral registers. Many record offices have a selection of these records. What was the difference between the lists and the registers, and who was entitled to be a juror?

Family history is changing rapidly. New resources are released and new material digitised and placed online almost on a weekly basis. In addition, websites come and go. So far as I can make it, this book is accurate as of 15 August 2011. However, if the website has vanished, or the URL has changed, then Chapter 2 should be able to help.

I conclude, as Daniel Defoe did in his *Tour Through the Whole Island of Great Britain*, that 'all this relates to times past, and is an excursion which I shall atone for by making no more'.

Thanks to the experts who contributed the short essays which are found scattered through the book: Dr Nick Barratt, Ruth Davies, Emma Jolly and Chris Paton. Thanks also to Gill Blanchard and Celia Heritage, to my editors Katharine Reeve and Lindsey Smith, and the team at The History Press for seeing the book through to print, and above all to my wife Sylvia Levi whose labours allowed me to write the book.

Of course, all errors and omissions are mine.

Simon Fowler
Kew, August 2011

Useful Information

This section contains information that will crop up throughout the book and is given here to avoid needless repetition.

Websites

To save constant repetition of URLs in the book here are the main ones you will come across time and again in the text.

i. Commercial data providers

www.ancestry.co.uk	Ancestry
www.ancestry.com	Ancestry (US)
www.rootsweb.ancestry.com	RootsWeb
www.familyrelatives.com	Familyrelatives
www.findmypast.co.uk	Findmypast
www.thegenealogist.co.uk	TheGenealogist
www.genesreunited.co.uk	Genes Reunited
www.origins.net	Origins
www.scotlandspeople.gov.uk	ScotlandsPeople

ii. The National Archives

www.nationalarchives.gov.uk	The National Archives (TNA) main website
www.nationalarchives.gov.uk/documents online	DocumentsOnline
www.nationalarchives.gov.uk/a2a	Access to Archives (A2A)
www.nationalarchives.gov.uk/archon	ARCHON (database of almost all archives in the UK)
www.nationalarchives.gov.uk/nra	National Register of Archives (The National Archives wiki)
http://yourarchives.nationalarchives.gov.uk	Your Archives

iii. Other archives, museums and libraries

www.bl.uk	British Library
www.lma.gov.uk	London Metropolitan Archives
www.sog.org.uk	Society of Genealogists

iv. Other genealogy websites

www.cyndislist.com	Cyndi's List
www.familysearch.org	FamilySearch
www.genuki.org.uk	GENUKI (UK and Ireland Genealogy)

v. Other websites

www.google.co.uk	Google
http://en.wikipedia.org	Wikipedia

Money

Almost nobody under the age of 50 can remember Britain's pre-decimal currency. However, as you will find figures in a wide range of documents it can be useful to know a bit more about it. Before February 1971 the pound was divided into shillings and pence. There were 20 shillings to the pound and 12 pence to the shilling (or 240 pence in a pound). The pound was often abbreviated as l for *libra* (or pound in Latin), the shilling as s (Latin *soldus*) and penny as d (Latin *denari*). In addition, there were a number of other coins, including the guinea (21s or £1 1s), mark (8s 4d), crown (5s), half-crown (2s 6d), florin (2s), groat (4d) and farthing (¼d).

It is impossible to answer the question 'how much was that worth', because we live in a world of unimaginable affluence where items that were once very expensive are now cheap. A book in Stuart England, for example, might have cost an agricultural labourer a week's wages, but now it might take him just two or three hours' work to buy even an expensive hardback. However, if you want rough equivalents The National Archives provides a currency converter at www.nationalarchives.gov.uk/ currency. You can even download this as a free app to your smartphone. The best guide to this complex subject is Lionel Munby's *How Much is that Worth?* (British Association for Local History, 1989).

Dates

The calendar used by our ancestors was slightly different to the one we are familiar with. You may need to be aware of this when looking at old documents. In medieval times it was customary to date documents by the saint's day on which they were signed or came into force. Alternatively, many official documents, including Acts of Parliament, are dated by regnal year; that is the year of the monarch's reign in which the document was compiled. Thus a document of 1600 might be dated 'in the forty-second year of Elizabeth' or something similar. The regnal year begins on the anniversary of the monarch's accession to the throne (in the case of Elizabeth I, 17 November 1558). Sometimes the regnal year is abbreviated to 42 Eliz I, particularly when describing Acts of Parliament. The use of regnal years began to die out in the late eighteenth century, but it was extremely common before then.

In addition, until 1752 the civil, ecclesiastical and legal year began on 25 March, nearly three months later than the calendar year. For dates in the intervening period, the historical year will therefore be different from the civil or legal year. Clearly, for dates between 1 January and 24 March, the civil year is one less than the historical year. To avoid confusion, such dates are often written as 1 January 1750–1 or 1 January 1750/1.

In addition, there were four quarter days when it was customary to settle accounts and many contracts, such as the hire of servants, were often begun then. In England, Wales and Ireland the quarter days were Lady Day (the feast of the Annunciation) on

25 March; Midsummer Day (St John the Baptist), 24 June; Michaelmas (St Michael and All Angels), 29 September; and Christmas Day. In Scotland, the traditional quarter days (or term days) were Candlemas (the feast of the Purification), 2 February; Whitsunday (Pentecost), 15 May; Lammas (Long Mass, or the feast of First Fruits), 1 August; and Martinmas (St Martin), 11 November.

Good introductions to the subject can be found at www.nationalarchives.gov.uk/ palaeography/quick_reference.htm and www.medievalgenealogy.org.uk. A regnal year calculator is available on the Canadian Ancestry Solutions website (www. ancestrysolutions.com), together with a list of saint's days. Even so, the best guide remains C.R. Cheney and M. Jones (eds), *A Handbook of Dates: For Students of British History* (Cambridge University Press, 2000).

Chapter Endnotes

This book has many endnotes. I know that it can be irritating to keep referring to the end of a chapter, but persevere, it is worth it. In particular they provide additional information so you can find out more if you are interested, such as website addresses and books, as well as explanatory material which did not seem suitable to include in the main body of the text.

Finding Records

Once you have exhausted the basic resources of births, marriage and death records, censuses, wills and service records (most of which are now online) the temptation is to assume that there is nothing else available. This could not be further from the truth. There are lots of sources which do not get the attention they deserve from family historians, although it has to be said that on the whole the additional information they provide on individuals may be limited and they can be difficult to use. These sources are what will largely be discussed in this book.

Apart from knowing what is available, the other problem is finding out where they are to be found. After all, there are over 2,000 archives in the United Kingdom. Fortunately, this is much less difficult than might be imagined. Contact details of almost all archive services within the British Isles are on the National Archive's ARCHON database. You can search by name of repository, by place or by county.[1]

There are several national catalogues to the records themselves. The easiest to use, and most detailed, is Access to Archives (A2A), which contains catalogues from over 400 archives across England with individual item descriptions. Unfortunately, many of the cataloguing projects were done on a regional basis, so some areas are better covered than others, although one of the most useful sources for family historians – quarter sessions – is included in its entirety. There are also less complete equivalents for Wales and Scotland.[2]

An alternative is the National Register of Archives (NRA), which provides descriptions of collections held at local record offices. However, unlike A2A, it does not contain descriptions of individual items within collections, although a set of catalogues supplied by local record offices can be found in the Open Reading Room at Kew. The NRA is particularly useful if you are trying to trace records of a particular company, charity or institution, or papers of an individual. For example, it lists some thirty sources for the papers of Neville Chamberlain, ranging from the major collection at Birmingham University to correspondence with politicians of the day and letters to C.J. Wainwright of the Royal Entomological Society. You can search the register by organisation or company, name, family name or place. The National Archives website also hosts several more specialist databases. The Hospital Records Database lists the whereabouts of hospital records, including patient and staff records, and the Manorial Documents Register identifies the location and nature of manorial records, although not everything from the register is online yet, so you may have to use the typescript indexes at Kew. The records noted here include court rolls, surveys, maps, terriers and other documents relating to the boundaries, franchises, wastes, customs or courts of a manor, but not title deeds.[3]

For particular subjects or geographical areas there may be more specialist lists of repositories, where you can find additional information and resources. For archives within Greater London it is worth checking out AIM25, which 'provides electronic access to collection level descriptions of the archives of over one hundred higher education institutions, learned societies, cultural organisations and livery companies'. If you think the information you want is at a university library then the Archive Hub may be the place to try as it has details of holdings of 200 academic institutions. There are also more specialist databases. Genesis is a project which allows users to cross-search women's studies resources from museums, libraries and archives. The Artists' Papers Register describes 'papers of artists, designers and craftspeople held in publicly accessible collections in the United Kingdom and Ireland'. Meanwhile, MUNDUS provides a gateway to missionary collections (both missionary societies and to missionaries themselves). For the army, the Army Museums Ogilby Trust provides details of regimental museums and their archives.[4] Remember that catalogues are unlikely to mention your ancestor by name. That does not, of course, mean that they cannot be found in the records, however.

Many record offices provide online catalogues. Unfortunately they are often fairly daunting to use, requiring a great deal of patience and lateral thinking to get anything from them. In general it is a good idea to consult any help pages available on the website or in the reading rooms. Also, don't forget the chances are that not everything appears on the catalogue (and it may be almost impossible to find out what has yet to be added). In Worcestershire, for example, just over half of the record office's holdings aren't yet available digitally, including most privately deposited material.[5]

Finally, it is important to be aware that, increasingly, records which were either open or would normally be open are being closed for extended periods because of concerns over the protection of information held about individuals, even those who are long dead. In Powys, for example, the Information Commissioner in March 2011 advised that school registers at the local record office be closed for 100 years to protect former pupils. Although at the time of writing the implications are uncertain, the decision may well affect similar records relating to individuals held elsewhere. Such concerns will also restrict material that will appear online. Conversely, however, you may be able to submit a Freedom of Information request to have material released early. There are restrictions on what you can request, but it is an avenue which may be worth exploring if you know exactly what you want. There have been some notable successes in this field. In particular Guy Etchell, a respected genealogical researcher, persuaded the Information Commissioner that the 1911 census should be opened early, which it was in 2009 rather than in 2012, as the General Register Office had argued.[6]

Notes

1   www.nationalarcives.gov.uk/archon.

2   www.nationalarchives.gov.uk/a2a; www.archivesnetworkwales.info; www.scan.org.uk.

3   www.nationalarchives.gov.uk/nra; www.nationalarchives.gov.uk/hospitalrecords; www.nationalarchives.gov.uk/mdr.

4   www.aim25.ac.uk; http://archiveshub.ac.uk; www.londonmet.ac.uk/genesis; www.apr.ac.uk; www.mundus.ac.uk; www.armymuseums.org.uk. Peter Higginbotham also mentions the major sources relating to workhouses at www.workhouses.org.uk.

5   The Annual Report of the Worcestershire Record Office 2009/10, p. 10. Available at www.worcestershire.gov.uk/cms/pdf/2009-10web5.pdf.

6   For more about this see the Information Commissioner's decision notice of 9 April 2011 at www.ico.gov.uk/~/media/documents/decisionnotices/2011/fs_50314844.ashx. Advice about Freedom of Information is at www.nationalarchives.gov.uk/foi/default. htm. It is a simple procedure and well worth trying if you are trying to get to a particular file that has yet to be released. I have successfully applied to have several files released early for clients, most notably a couple of rather disappointing police files about the Croydon airport bullion raid of 1937.

Chapter 1

ADVENTURES IN THE STACKS

T here are a huge range of records available which contain material that might add something to your knowledge of your ancestors and the world they lived in. Many records are well known and well used, like the census or army service records, but most are hardly used by researchers. In this chapter we will look at three different sets of records that may well mention your forebears: council records, records of occupations and records of organisations. I'll almost guarantee that you will find a new lead or two here to follow up.

Council Records

Volumes of council minutes can be found on the shelves in many archive reading rooms. As well as being decorative they are a surprisingly useful genealogical resource, with many thousands of names. You might be able to find material about councillors and council workers, as well as about ordinary citizens who were affected by the decisions made by the council, such as the award of a scholarship to a grammar school or removal to a new flat under a slum clearance scheme. It is a shame that these records are not better known because there is a fair chance that your ancestors will appear in the minutes, or if you are interested in the history of your house there may well be entries about that as well.[1]

The history of British local government goes back to medieval times and the earliest records date from then. In York, one of England's oldest cities, for example:

The civic archives begin with the Henry II charter in 1155. The York Memorandum Book is the earliest record of Council meetings and provides an unparalleled view of life in 14th and 15th century York. From 1476 to the present day we have a record of every single meeting of the City Council in a continuous series of House Books & Minute Books.[2]

Local government was arguably at its most important in the eighty or so years from the 1860s, when councils began to tackle the social evils that lay all around. Public health was improved with the introduction of sewerage and the worst slums were demolished. Schools and colleges were built to provide an education for children. Libraries were opened and trams ventured on the paved and tarmacked roads. The most visible sign of this confidence is the town halls, which still dominate the skyline in many northern cities. Sidney Webb once described the scope of local government by imagining a town councillor who would:

> walk along the municipal pavement, lit by the municipal gas and cleansed by the municipal brooms with municipal water, and seeing by the municipal clock in the municipal market place that he is too early to meet his children coming from the municipal school hard by the county lunatic asylum, and municipal hospital, will use the national telegraph system to tell them not to walk through the municipal park, but to come by the municipal tram to meet him in the municipal art gallery, museum and library, were he intends to consult some of the national publications in order to prepare for his next speech in the municipal town hall ...[3]

Councils varied greatly in size from parishes and rural district councils, which might only have a few thousand people in their area, to the London County Council, which had an economy larger than those of many European states. Powers were shared between rural district, urban district and borough councils, which dealt with most local matters, and county councils, which were responsible for countywide services such as education, roads and libraries. In addition, there were eighty-three county boroughs – mostly large towns and cities – which had all the powers and responsibilities of county councils.[4]

Councils were, of course, directed by councillors assisted by increasingly professional officers such as the chief clerk and medical officer of health. Councillors came from a variety of backgrounds. In the smaller rural councils they tended to be local landowners; in urban areas, a mixture of professional men and tradesmen. An increasing number of women and working-class men were elected, although the Labour Party only became a force in local politics in the 1920s. Even so, local politics remained largely non-partisan. Councillors were also more involved in the everyday running of the council than would be expected today, investigating cases of need and providing help, either from their own pocket or from local charities, where necessary. The best place to research councillors is through local newspapers. It is also worth checking whether the local studies library or record office has collections of election literature, as these can make for fascinating reading.[5]

Manchester Town Hall is perhaps the greatest of all British Victorian civic centres. The architectural self-confidence is also reflected in the historic records. (*Julius Tik/Wikipedia*)

Councils were traditionally run by committees, with a committee for each function – education, public health and so on – reporting to the full council, which only met a few times a year. In addition, there may be ad hoc committees set up to deal with particular problems, such as war relief in the First World War or air-raid precautions in the Second. Discussions at these meetings were likely to be reported by local newspapers, but the decisions themselves, together with any reports from officials or sub-committees requested by the committee, were recorded in the minutes. Until the 1970s, at least, these minutes were printed and bound, generally with one volume a year or one for each quarter. They are also well indexed with the names of individuals or the addresses of properties under discussion. So it is easy to go through them year by year to see whether your ancestor or house appears. The amount of detail varies depending on the size of the authority and the importance of the committee. Minutes of full council meetings are likely to be less informative than those of the committees or sub-committees. Again, the smaller the authority the more likely you are to find out about individual people or properties. Another factor is the type of committee: those which had direct responsibility for staff, such as the Education Committee, might well record the appointment, promotion and resignation of staff. Minutes of other committees could include lists of payments to local contractors, possibly for resurfacing roads or painting council houses.

For example, Twickenham Borough Council's Education Committee agreed on 30 December 1926 to the appointment of Miss Kate Piercy to Trafalgar School Girls' Department as an assistant teacher. They accepted the resignation of Mr W.R. Buxton as a school attendance officer. He had been on a salary of £162 per annum. The other officers were Mr A. Wooldridge on a salary of £150 and Mr H. Winslet, £75 (half time). It was also agreed to recruit a new school attendance officer and general enquiry officer at a salary of £180, 'with an allowance of £4 per annum for the provision of a bicycle'. Mr Wooldridge's salary was to be increased to £160 from April and he was to be offered incremental increases of £10 until his salary reached £200 plus £4 allowance for a bicycle.[6]

As well as minute books there may well be reports, maps and plans, correspondence and photographs. They are more likely to survive for the larger authorities. Hundreds of thousands of files created by the London County Council (LCC) survive, for example, at the London Metropolitan Archives. At the other end of the scale, only four minute books, dating between 1894 and 1934, and a finance ledger for 1930 to 1934 survive at the Essex Record Office for Belchamp Rural District Council, which looked after two-dozen parishes in northern Essex. Such files can cover all aspects of a council's activities, from planning to public assistance via policing and licensing to libraries. They are generally arranged by departments or committees. Online catalogues or the Access to Archives database may be able to help; otherwise you should to talk to staff at the county record office where the records are kept. More recent records may still be with the council itself, so you may need to contact them directly. In addition, files relating to particular individuals, for example applicants for university scholarships, are likely to be closed for seventy-five years or longer, although you may well find a summary in the minutes.[7]

Over the years councils gained new powers (or had them taken away). As the Poor Law withered from the 1890s, in many places the boards of Poor Law guardians became little more than adjuncts of the local council. Thus it is not surprising that when the guardians were finally abolished in 1930, their responsibilities for workhouses were largely transferred to local authorities, where they were renamed public assistance institutions. However, they lost control of the hospitals they had run, often former workhouse infirmaries, to the new National Health Service in 1948. In addition, they maintained local registry offices in association with the Registrar-General and the General Register Office in Somerset House. Councillors also kept a kept a close eye on the police through police committees and were involved in a host of other initiatives set up by central government, such as pension committees which administered the new system of old-age pensions when they were introduced in 1908. All this is reflected in the records.

```
┌─────────────────────────────┐
│      Related Records        │
└─────────────────────────────┘
```

School Log Books and Registers

Some of the most used records at local record offices are school log books and registers. Introduced in 1862, log books are a weekly record of occurrences at the school compiled by the head teacher. Even if the individual child does not feature (and it is unlikely they would unless they were being punished for some misdemeanour) you can get a fascinating glimpse of their experiences, such as school trips, sports days, mass absenteeism during harvest time, when the children would help bring the harvest in, and wakes week, when industrial towns went en masse to the seaside. The arrival and departure of teachers is generally also given and there may be comments about their behaviour. Registers are less informative, being a note of attendance day by day, although occasionally explanations of absence are given.[8]

Some log books or registers may have been retained by the school, so you may have to contact them directly. Records may be closed for seventy-five years or longer.

Electoral Records

Councils were responsible for maintaining electoral registers. These registers are often suggested as a source for family history. However, rather like telephone directories, they generally only confirm what you know already. Occasionally they might provide additional information about how the individual is eligible to vote. This is normally because they were a rate payer or they paid a certain amount of rent each year. Most local studies libraries or archives have runs of these registers back to 1871, when they were first kept, although there may well be gaps. The British Library has sets of electoral rolls from 1948, which are being digitised by Findmypast and should be online during 2012.[9]

Occupations

Of course the majority of our ancestors worked. However, with some exceptions it is very hard to find out very much about their time in the workforce. In part this was because most people were paid cash-in-hand, so the only records which might help are cashbooks maintained by factories, farmers or shopkeepers, and few of these survive. Information about individuals who worked in the large industrial concerns, which employed hundreds of the thousands of our ancestors by the end of the nineteenth century, is also hard to come by. One exception is for railway and Post Office records, many of which are online at Ancestry.[10]

Flora Thompson described how the men of Juniper Hill (Lark Rise) were paid:

> On Friday evenings when work was done, the men trooped up to the farmhouse for their wages. They were handed out of a window by the farmer himself and acknowledged by a rustic scraping of feet and pulling of forelocks ... he was not a bad-hearted man and had no idea he was sweating his labourers. Did they not get the full standard wage with no deductions for standing by in bad weather? How they managed to live and keep their families on such a sum was their own affair.[11]

However, it is possible to find out about those in the services and some trades, like dockyard works and the Metropolitan Police, where records survive because they were being paid from the public monies, which had to be accounted for. As a result, most records we now use to research soldiers or dockyard artificers – certainly for men before the mid to late nineteenth century – relate to the payment of wages and pensions and individual entitlements to them. Army and navy musters, for example, recorded payments to soldiers and sailors together with any deductions taken from their already low wages. In Nelson's navy this might have included 'slop clothes [basic uniform], trusses for ruptures, buying of dead men's clothes, hammocks and wages remitted ashore'. In addition, there are voluminous pension registers recording the payment of pensions month by month. Also, service records contain detailed figures of the exact number of days a man served, and where he served, to aid calculation of the pension to which he was entitled.[12]

Another two exceptions to this lack of information are as follows. Firstly, trades and professions where applicants had to demonstrate their eligibility to join and sometimes pay a fee to maintain their membership, whether they were bakers, barristers or brewers, tend to be recorded. Secondly, a reasonable number of people had to buy a licence in order to undertake particular trades, such as victuallers' licences which had to be acquired by anybody wanting to run a public house. If the landlord kept a 'disorderly house', as the phrase was, then the magistrates could take the licence away. Thus, where they survive the records can reveal something about the individual and his background.

In general the best source for researching occupations may be the census returns between 1841 and 1911, where there should be a description for each man, woman and child. The least detailed entries are for 1841, when only the briefest of entries might be given, with the most informative in 1911, in which you can get a fairly good idea of what each individual did. From 1851, you may come across entries for employers indicating how many people they employed, such as 'Baker (master employing 4 men, 2 women)' or how much land they farmed, such as 'Farmer of 220 acres (employing 11 labourers)'.[13]

Over 1.5 million separate occupations are recorded in the 1881 census for England and Wales, for a population of 26 million, although many represent slight variations. Agricultural worker, agricultural servant and agricultural labourer, for example, were very similar. Also, a few people had a unique occupation, such as the man who claimed to have been a 'retired opium smuggler', but many reflected the specialist nature of particular trades and industries. Potteries around Stoke-on-Trent, for example, employed a huge range of specialists each with their own seemingly bizarre name, from 'ark man' to 'wedger', via the 'glost rubber' and, everybody's favourite, the 'sagger bottom knocker'.[14]

Men and women might well have had several jobs at the same time, which helps to explain why an individual's occupation can change widely between censuses and on certificates. Keepers of alehouses often combined running the pub with work as a small tradesman or carpenter, using earnings from the licensed premises to supplement the family income. Occasionally multi-occupations are given in the census returns. In the 1881 census Matthew Woollard found many combinations, including: 'Publican & Pheasant Breeder', 'Shoe Maker & Coal Merchant', 'Grocer & Chairmaker' and, dubiously, 'Butcher and Rat Catcher'.[15]

There was also a class of people who were at best semi-employed, although it is hard to identify these people from the census. No Victorian town scene was without its half-starved 'idler' trying to make ends meet by looking after horses for an hour or two, carrying bags or wearing a sandwich board while walking the streets. In the *Soul of London*, published in 1905, Ford Madox Hueffer describes one such unfortunate:

> In a patch of shadow left in a vacant space, you will hardly make out the figure of a forlorn figure standing still. With a pendent placard on his chest, announcing one of the ills of the flesh, he offers for sale things you would think nobody would want to buy, or indistinguishable quavers of melody that nobody could stay to hear.[16]

In the early 1890s the social researcher Charles Booth found that about 35 per cent of Londoners fell into the category of the unemployed or semi-employed. Out of the eight classes he identified on his famous poverty map, three had no secure employment. In particular, families in class C were:

> Intermittent earning. 18s to 21s per week for a moderate family. The victims of competition and on them falls with particular severity the weight of recurrent depressions of trade. Labourers, poorer artisans and street sellers. This irregularity of employment may show itself in the week or in the year: stevedores and waterside porters may secure only one of two days' work in a week, whereas labourers in the building trades may get only eight or nine months in a year.[17]

The entry for William Horne 'Butcher and Rat Catcher' in the 1881 census. (*TNA RG 11/1526 f106, p2/Findmypast*)

One of the few records relating to employment that may be available is the apprenticeship indenture, which bound young men (or occasionally women) to a master for a number of years in order to learn a trade. Once they had passed to the satisfaction of the master or the guild which regulated the trade they could ply their trade as journeymen, before eventually becoming masters themselves if they were wealthy or skilled enough. It was a simple system which developed in medieval times and continues to operate, to a degree, today.[18]

Apprenticeships were regulated by the Statute of Artificers of 1563, which forbade anyone to enter a trade without having completed one. They served the purposes of not only teaching a trade, but also of helping to ensure a supply of trained labour and keeping adolescents under control. The statute was revoked in 1814, although the system was already beginning to decline as a result of the Industrial Revolution. The apprenticeship indenture was a legal document that regulated the duties to be performed by both parties and agreed a premium for the master to take on the apprentice, to be paid by the child's parents or, in the case of paupers, by the overseer of the Poor Law. The amount paid varied depending on the importance or skills of the trade, from £3 for farming to £250 to become a stationer.[19] Depending on the trade, the term of the indenture was usually five or seven years. During the time the boy would receive board and lodging, and would agree to keep his master's secrets and obey his commands. In effect he was becoming a member of a new family. In addition, the new apprentice agreed that:

Taverns and alehouses he shall not haunt: dice, cards or other unlawful games he shall not use; fornication with any woman he shall not commit: matrimony with any women he shall not contract. He shall not absent himself by night or by day without his master's leave, but be a true and faithful servant.[20]

Relations between masters and apprentices varied greatly. A very large proportion of boys, perhaps half, failed to complete their indentures for a variety of reasons. Inevitably over such a long period, the boy might change his mind about his choice of career. Plus, apprentices were often treated as little more than slaves, particularly pauper apprentices about whom nobody cared very much. The French traveller Henri Misson, who visited England in the first decade of the eighteenth century, noted: 'An apprentice is a sort of slave, he wears neither hat nor cap in his master's presence … All he earns is his masters.' However, there is always two sides to each story: Daniel Defoe believed that apprentices were getting uppity, writing that they could barely rouse themselves 'to open or shut the shop-windows, much less to sweep the shop or warehouses … and are often pleas'd to come home in drink. Which also their masters have scarce the authority to resent or question them about.'[21]

There is no nationwide record of masters and pupils. The nearest comes between 1710 and 1811, when the government levied a stamp duty on indentures. Lists of the masters and apprentices are at The National Archives, but the records are by no means complete because there was widespread evasion and no duty was paid on indentures involving pauper children. Indexes can be found on Ancestry and Findmypast, which show the master, his trade and the name of the apprentice.[22]

Otherwise, you really have to know the approximate date of the indenture and more particularly where it took place and what the trade the pupil was apprenticed to. In London and other large cities, until well into the eighteenth century, most trades were regulated by guilds or livery companies. The earliest guilds were established in the fourteenth century to regulate trade through price controls and the number of master tradesmen; maintaining a reasonable level so that all could make a reasonable living. They also ran schools and almshouses for members and their families. Apprentices in London before 1800 were almost certainly bound over to a freeman of a livery company. Surviving records of companies are with the London Metropolitan Archives. Here you are likely to find apprentice binding books, which record the details of apprentices, their parish of origin and father's name, together with the freemen who taught them their skills. Also of use are the registers of freemen and other records about the admission of young men to the guild after the completion of their apprenticeship. Many volumes of apprenticeship abstracts between 1442 and 1850 have been indexed by Cliff Web and are now available on Origins. They are also available in a series of booklets published by the Society of Genealogists.[23]

Outside London it is more difficult, but where records for local guilds survive they are likely to be at local record offices. One exception is Sheffield's Cutler's Company in Hallamshire, which has its own records, including apprenticeship records, from the date of its foundation in 1624. In addition, a number of archives, as well as the Society of Genealogists, have collections of original indentures.[24]

Occasionally disputes between master and apprentice came before the quarter sessions, or in London at the Middlesex county sessions or the Lord Mayor's court. Surprisingly few apprentices appeared before the Old Bailey. One case was of Nicholas Bradshaw, who was sentenced to be hung in 1678 for clipping coinage. In sentencing the Lord Mayor told him:

> But the truth of it is, the Apprentices of London have got such a Trade of abusing their Masters by Clipping, and such tricks, which they are encouraged to by a pack of Goldsmiths Men, who are fit for their purpose, that if some of them be not made Examples, it will be the ruine of many. It is a disease that will run through the whole Flock.[25]

The modern equivalent is the royal colleges and other professional bodies protecting the interests of their members, providing continuing training and opportunities to meet and share experiences. Most maintain extensive libraries and archives primarily for members, but often non-members can get access or have research done on their behalf. The Institute of Electrical Engineers, which was founded in 1871 as the Society of Telegraph Engineers, is typical. There is a page about family history on its website, which says:

> The Archives contain many sources for family historians. We have some information on our members, although the amount generally depends on the member and how much they were involved in the Institution. We have information on eminent engineers who left their archives to the Institution and on those who were involved in major engineering developments.

There are membership applications from 1871 to 1901 and printed lists of members thereafter. In addition, there are collections of photographs and papers of individual electrical engineers, including George Vincent Fowler (no relation). What they don't have are many obituaries of members.

Rather more romantic is the Royal Geographical Society, which has splendid premises near the Albert Hall and an excellent library and archives devoted to the exploration of the world from the society's foundation in 1830. The journal contains detailed obituaries of members, many of whom were eminent explorers. Both Livingstone and Stanley, for example, were members (and there are collections of their papers). A key family history resource is the fellowship certificate, which records the date of election and other relevant information about a candidate, together with the names of proposers and seconders, qualifications and addresses. Also, there may be personal papers, records of the expeditions members organised and a large collection of maps, books, photographs and other material.[26]

At times licences have been required for, among others, slaughterhouse keepers and butchers, corn dealers and pedlars, gamekeepers and hackney cab drivers. Where they survive, and survival is patchy, the records are generally to be found in quarter session records at local record offices. You may be lucky to find a recognisance, which is basically a bond that guaranteed that the holder was of good character, or copies of the licence itself. Otherwise, names and addresses might be recorded in a register or even on scraps of paper. They are rarely indexed.[27]

The licences that most often survive are for inns and taverns, which have had to be licensed by magistrates since 1552. Technically, the licences are for premises and not for individual publicans, and it is certainly helpful to know the name of the pub as the records tended to be arranged in this way. In addition, publicans had to declare that they would not keep a 'disorderly house' and prohibit games of bowls, dice, football and tennis. These declarations were called recognisances or bonds. Few records survive from the seventeenth century, but an act of 1753 enforced the keeping of such registers, so most counties have some material from the late eighteenth century. The system fell into abeyance between 1830 and 1871, when all ratepayers were given the right to run beer houses on the payment of 2 guineas for a licence and petty session clerks were no longer required to keep licences. Earlier registers may just give the name of the licensed premises, the landlord and possibly an address. After 1871 they often give the name of the licensee, the parish in which he lived, the inn sign (the name of the pub) and the names and occupations of two guarantors who vouched for the applicant's probity. Within the records there may also be correspondence, copies of bonds and notes that might contain other information. Using newspapers and other sources it might be possible to build up a reasonable picture of a publican's career.[28]

Surprisingly often there are licences for pedlars, sometimes called higglers, peddars, chapmen or badgers, who were itinerant traders that tramped the country with parcels of clothes and other items, calling at farmhouses and cottages. In 1696–97 an act was passed requiring such traders to buy an annual licence at £4 a head. In 1871 responsibility for licensing these traders passed to the police, so later records may be found in police records. Returns for Hampshire, for example, go up to 1961 and include the name of the individual who bought the certificate, where they lived and how much they paid, by which time the fee had been reduced to 5s.[29]

Very little is known about pedlars. Their heyday was undoubtedly in the seventeenth and eighteenth centuries, when the first cheap mass-produced items became available, but by the 1880s they were dying out as it was then much easier for farmers to go into town. Flora Thompson remembered that:

> ... one last survivor of the once numerous clan still visited the hamlet at long and irregular intervals ... An old white-headed, white-bearded man, still hale and rosy,

The IDLE 'PRENTICE Executed at Tyburn.

'The Idle Apprentice', William Hogarth's view of a hanging at Tyburn. (*Author's collection*)

although almost bent double under the heavy, black canvas-covered pack he carried on his shoulders. 'Anything out of the pack today?' he would ask at each house, and at the least encouragement, fling down his load and open it on the doorstep. He carried a tempting variety of goods, dress-lengths and shirt-lengths and remnants to make up for the children; aprons and pinafores, plain and fancy, corduroys for the men and coloured scarves and ribbons for Sunday wear.[30]

Occasionally local councils would obtain powers to license particular groups of people. In 1916 London County Council began to license all private masseurs, in the hope of stamping out what the files euphemistically call 'special treatment'. Over the next forty years or so there are a number of registers listing masseurs, their place of employment and their specialism, such as Harry Lees of the Palace Toilet Saloons, 90 Buckingham Palace Road, who offered massage, manicure, chiropody and high-frequency treatment. Naturally, of more interest are men and women who for one reason or another were rejected. Unfortunately the reasons are rarely given.[31]

Related Records

The Post Office

Even after nearly 400 years the Post Office remains one of Britain's largest employers. Every town had a post office, sorting office and a network of postmen making several deliveries a day to houses and businesses. Until 1981 it had a virtual monopoly over telegraph and telephone services as well. Also, as the Post Office was a government service and had been since the early seventeenth century, it maintained a bureaucratic mentality and the government's dedication to recordkeeping. The Royal Mail still keeps its own records in a fine small archive at the main Mount Pleasant sorting centre in London, where can be found extensive records relating to the appointment and careers of Post Office staff. Of particular interest are the appointment books (in series POST 58), which are also available on Ancestry. The records are, in fact, indexes to the Postmaster General's minute books. They show the point when a person began working or started at a new position, and were kept between 1831 and 1969. The index contains names of individuals, the dates of their appointment and where they were working. Not yet online are pension records or minutes recording the careers of staff, which go back to the seventeenth century. As always it helps to know roughly when your ancestor worked for the Post Office, what he or she did and when they were employed.[32]

One such employee was John William Blackmore, who in 1940 was a mounted postman on Exmoor. He was profiled in a *Picture Post* article in November 1940:

At seven o'clock every morning, in his sister's tight-stocked grocery shop that serves as general store and post office to the tiny village of Withypool, Postman Blackmoor sorts his mail. These days with sparsely inhabited Exmoor packing its scattered villages with refugees from the big cities, Postman Blackmore has twice the number of letters to sort – and twice the number of eager gossips to chat with on his round. He goes on horseback – the only way to get along many of the wild tracks over the bracken-covered hills and to ford the shallow river.[33]

Organisations

These days we tend to forget the wide range of clubs, societies, charities and other organisations that once filled many of our ancestors' lives. Such societies really took off during the eighteenth century, largely as drinking and debating societies, often with strange names. In 1748, among such clubs in London were the Itinerants, the Knights of the Golden Fleece, the Purple Society, Lumber Troop, Catch'embytes, Porcuses and Brothers of the Wacut. Chair or 'cock-and-hen' clubs offered an eighteenth-century version of speed dating. At each end of a long table were chairs for young men and women. As the evening wore on, with the effects of the drink and the singing of bawdy songs, boys and girls paired off and by midnight, when the club closed, none remained. There were also clubs with less frivolous intentions. In 1783, for example, there were hundreds of clubs in Birmingham, most of which aimed to support their members in times of sickness, but there were also rent clubs, book clubs and clock clubs: 'In the breeches club, every member ballots for a pair, value a guinea … this club dissolves when all the members are served.'[34]

The peak of this movement was undoubtedly the twenty years or so before the First World War, when almost every man (and many women), with the exception of the very poor, were members of societies or clubs that catered for almost every taste. In Lambeth, for example, just for members of the Church of England, Jeffrey Cox found at least fifty-seven mothers' meetings; thirty-six temperance societies for children; twenty-five savings banks or penny banks; twenty-four Christian endeavour societies; twenty-one boot, coal, blanket or clothing clubs; and two maternity societies. In addition, the Non-Conformist churches ran similar bodies for co-religionists, such as the Pleasant Sunday Afternoon movement, which provided wholesome entertainment for young men and women; the Boys and Girls Brigades for children; and the societies of St Vincent de Paul, who helped poor Catholics. In turn, the labour movement offered clarion choirs and cycling clubs; socialist Sunday schools; the Woodcraft Folk; and the Co-operative Women's Guild. Secular clubs also proliferated, from cricket and football clubs to fraternal organisations like the Buffaloes or, my favourite, the Ancient Order of Froth Blowers, which aimed 'to foster the noble Art and gentle and healthy Pastime of froth blowing amongst Gentlemen of-leisure and ex-Soldiers'.[35]

Since the Second World War, unfortunately, these clubs have largely withered away, but in many cases they have left records behind which can reflect on our forebears as organisers, as members or, where appropriate, as applicants for help. As always the best way to find out what survives is by using the National Register of Archives (see Introduction). Where they survive, records are generally held locally, but if there is still a national organisation they may have their own archives, such as the National Co-operative Archives at the Co-operative College in Manchester. Alternatively, an archive may collect particular types of records. The Modern Records Centre at Warwick University, for example, has many trade union archives, and in London the Bishopsgate Institute has material from many metropolitan and co-operative radical organisations.[36]

Apart from the churches, the largest membership organisation in Victorian and Edwardian Britain was almost certainly the friendly societies. They were essentially mutual insurance clubs providing cash benefits in cases of injury and sickness, or to dependents on the death of a member. By the end of the nineteenth century every town and village had one or more society. At their peak, just before the First World War, there were nearly 9 million members, overwhelmingly lower middle- and upper working-class men. Societies were either wholly independent or affiliated to larger organisations. Many independent societies date from the eighteenth century, and perhaps catered for a particular group of workers or were controlled or run, to a degree, by local clergymen and other bigwigs. Affiliated societies took off in the 1820s and were popular because they had financial security as the result of being part of a large organisation, such as the Oddfellows or Rechabites. The Ancient Order of Foresters, formed in 1834, was the largest of these affiliated bodies. Many societies engaged in some form of harmless ritual based on Masonic rites, which gave members a feeling of belonging. The big event of the year was generally a parade through the town to the parish church for a service before sitting down to a large dinner. National Insurance from 1911 and the Welfare State and the National Health Service in the late 1940s led to their decline, as the services they once offered were now provided for free by the state. A few societies still survive, however, offering good-value financial services. Only about 5 per cent of records of friendly societies have been deposited in local archives, generally for branches of national friendly societies. This material often comprises odd items, which could lead to difficulties in researching the story of a local friendly society, let alone an individual member. The larger affiliated societies produced regular journals, so if you know that your ancestor was actively involved they are worth checking out.[37]

There is an overlap between friendly societies and the Freemasons, largely because both engaged in elaborate dressing up and the regalia known as jewels (which members seemed to have an almost unhealthy fascination with), appears much the same. However, there are many more records for Masons, and if your ancestor was a member (which they may well have been if they were in trade, local government or the police) then there could be information about them. The Masons have long had an unfortunate reputation for secrecy and an influence that belied their size and importance, which in recent years the organisation has done its best to combat. These fears have, paradoxically, ensured that detailed records of members survive back to the eighteenth century.

Freemasons like to trace the ancestry of their movement back to medieval times, but for all practical purposes they began in 1717, with the formation of the United Grand Lodge in London, which encouraged and regulated local branches. By the end of the eighteenth century there were 500 local lodges across England and Wales. The movement had also spread rapidly to America and British settlements overseas. George Washington was an enthusiastic Mason, for example. A century later most towns of any size had at least half a dozen lodges.

Members came from all social backgrounds and joined for fellowship and friendship. However, there was often a serious motive behind membership: mutual aid. Masons were sworn to help each other. According to one writer in 1726, Masonry is 'no small advantage to a man who would rise in the world and one of the principle reasons why I would be a mason'. Members in personal or financial difficulties could expect help from fellow masons. In Manchester during the 1790s, James Harrison, who was unemployed and living in a cellar with his son, asked another member, a Manchester factory owner James Stewart, for help. Even though he had no work to offer, Stewart paid a man 18s to teach Harrison the spinning trade and afterwards took him into his works to tend a carding machine. Alternatively, Masons looking for work across the country might be issued with certificates of membership so that they would be recognised and welcomed by lodges wherever they went.[38]

Anyone, regardless of creed, class or race, could become a Freemason, provided they were aged 21 or older. Most members have been men, but there are several women-only lodges, notably the Order of Women Freemasons, which was founded in 1935. Anyone wishing to become a Freemason had to join a craft lodge. Within this they could advance by degrees to become a Master Mason and then serve in various offices in the lodge, such as secretary or warden, working up to become Worshipful Master (an annual appointment). Beyond crafts lodges, the ambitious could progress to higher lodges, such as those of Mark Masonry and Royal Ark Mariners.

Most records of the United Grand Lodge of England, which controlled Freemasonry in England and Wales, as well as its related bodies, are with the Library and Museum of Freemasonry. Information about individuals is based on annual returns of members compiled by each lodge and sent to the Grand Lodge. The earliest such returns date from about 1768. These were used to create registers of members grouped by lodge. There is no complete alphabetical index of members. Due to their poor condition, these registers are not available to researchers, although those between 1768 and 1886 are available in digital format and at the library staff will conduct a search for you. Currently this costs £30.[39]

The type of information normally recorded in membership registers are age, address, occupation and date of joining the lodge. The records do not contain any personal details regarding date of birth or marriage, details of family members or change of address. The records of the United Grand Lodge of England cover England and Wales and parts of the Commonwealth. There are separate grand lodges for Scotland, Ireland and individual American states. If you know the name of the local lodge or chapter then you can search the online catalogue to see if there is a lodge or chapter history. The library's website has a number of different lists of lodges and their locations, which may help. In addition, there is a file for each lodge, which may include summonses to meetings and correspondence.

Most lodges maintain their own archives or have deposited them at local record offices. You may find lodge histories, portraits or photographs of officers, and membership books listing addresses, occupations, ages, dates of initiation and notes on death or transfer to other lodges. Also, for much of the nineteenth and early twentieth centuries there are dedicated Masonic magazines, which often contain details of lodge meetings, photographs of individuals, biographical information and obituaries.

Under the Seditious Societies Act 1799, lodges had to register their members' names annually at the local quarter sessions and those that survive are now at the local record office. You may find an annual certificate from lodges signed by the master or secretary, listing all members with details of their residence and occupation. As they are annual, they can help map out an individual's career or changes of address. The other names on the list may be useful too, for people tended to join lodges in which they already had trade, professional and particularly family connections. Indexes to those for Essex between 1799 and 1934 are online.[40]

Old Masons may have left Masonic regalia and papers behind them. My father-in-law was a prominent Freemason in Leeds in the 1950s and 1960s, and my wife eventually inherited boxes of esoteric books on Masonic theory. By the time I came on the scene, however, nobody knew what had become of his regalia, although it may have been returned to the lodge. Nevertheless, you may be luckier. There may be regalia or photographs of Masons wearing aprons, collars, sashes or gauntlets, all heavy with Masonic symbolism. The decorations usually include the lodge name and number. Collars denote office holders and sashes indicate members of higher lodges than craft lodges. There may also be 'jewels' (medals) which denote Masonic rank. Freemason's Hall has a number of displays of memorabilia, some of which are exquisite. There may also be

VANDYKE & BROWN,   LIVERPOOL.

A now long-forgotten Liverpudlian mason photographed wearing his jewels for a *carte de visite* photograph sometime in the 1860s. (*Author's collection*)

papers, travelling certificates allowing Freemasons to attend other lodge meetings or certificates issued to subscribers to Masonic charities, which were generally for schools for the children of Freemasons or to help elderly or sick Masons.

If you donate clothes and books to a charity shop or buy a poppy for Remembrance Day then you are participating in a philanthropic tradition that goes back to medieval times. To the Victorians in particular, most social ills were best cured by a healthy dose of philanthropy. Most towns and villages had a wide range of charities which ran hospitals and dispensaries, educated destitute children, looked after servants and fallen women, and made small payments to the temporarily destitute and their families. In addition, there were national charities with local branches, some of which, like Barnardo's and the RSPCA, remain household names today. In many local charities, subscribers were issued with letters of recommendation (the actual number depending on their level of support) which could be given to supplicants, allowing them to be admitted to a hospital or be given a parcel of clothing.

Charities were particular about whom they supported. They were there to help those who were industrious but had fallen on hard times or street children who could be given new and more productive lives. They also helped those who fitted their own perceptions of the needy, such as aged men and women who had been regular churchgoers all their lives or orphaned children of soldiers and sailors killed in battle. The least deserving were left to the workhouse.

There was an earlier form of charity generally founded by a particular benefactor, such as a local merchant or landowner. The benefaction might take the form of an alms house, a school, scholarships for apprentices or the annual provision of bread or coals to the deserving elderly, sometimes known as dole funds. My secondary school (Newport Grammar in Essex) was originally founded for poor boys of the village by Dame Joyce Frankland in memory of her son, who died after falling off his horse in the village in 1588. The oldest such charities are medieval in origin. In County Durham, Christ's Hospital was established in 1181 by King Stephen's nephew Hugh de Puiset, Bishop of Durham, to care for local lepers. It continued as a lazar house until 1434, when it became an almshouse for the poor brethren of the parish of Thornley, although it did retain space for two lepers 'if they can be found'. Today, it provides sheltered housing and respite care for the elderly.

Surviving records of charities are likely to be found at local record offices, although records for most small charities have long been lost. Charities that are still in existence tend to keep their own archives, which they may be willing to let you consult (generally for a small donation). You may find case reports on individuals (often closed for 100 years or longer) and board and committee minute books, which may include discussions about individual applications. Also useful are annual reports, which tend to be a summary of the year's work as well as a barely disguised appeal for additional funds. Reports for schools may well list prize-winners and indicate what happened to pupils after they left. Also, if you are lucky there may be photographs of premises they owned, staff and the children they helped. Almost always they include a list of subscribers (that is donors) together with the amount they gave. Donations from members of the royal family or nobility are always listed first. In addition, they may well describe some of the cases helped, but the recipients may only be identified by initials.[41]

The small Richmond Philanthropic Society in its report for 1871/72 described the case of:

> EH widow, aged 43, 3 children ... only resources the earnings of her son amounting to 15s 6d a week, suffering from cancer, and has been confined to her bed three months, requires extra nourishment and must have a fire in her room night and day ... Voted £2. £1 the first week for immediate necessities ...[42]

Two key areas in which charities played a major role up to the 1940s were hospitals and orphanages. In many towns, hospitals and dispensaries were run by charities.[43] As well, these hospitals were where you chose to go rather than the workhouse infirmary, which catered for the poor. Even so, most people, if they could afford it, preferred to be cared for at home unless there was no alternative. Admission records survive for many hospitals, although those less than a hundred years old are likely to be closed because of privacy concerns. The National Archives maintains a Hospital Records Database, which will tell you which records are held where.[44]

It might also be worth visiting the Historic Hospital Admissions Project website, which contains databases of admission records to half a dozen hospitals, including Glasgow's Royal Hospital for Sick Children and three hospitals in London: the Hospital for Sick Children at Great Ormond Street, the Evelina Hospital and the Alexandra Hospital for Children with Hip Disease, with nearly 120,000 individual admission records between 1852 and 1914. It also has a collection of articles on the early history of the hospitals, pen portraits of personalities who inhabited them and a gallery of images.[45]

Most records, however, are for children admitted to Great Ormond Street, with material about all 84,000 individual patient admissions from when the hospital opened in February 1852 until the end of 1914, and a further 10,000 admissions to the hospital's convalescent home, Cromwell House, in leafy Highgate. There are entries for children who may have been aged only a few days until they were 16. For children under the care of the hospital's principal founder, Dr Charles West, the admission record is linked to his case notes. Six-year-old Sarah Coulson, for example, was admitted in August 1875 suffering terrible burns. She had made the long, difficult journey to Great Ormond Street from her home in Derby. After treatment she moved to Cromwell House but eight months later suffered a relapse and had to return to the hospital. A year later records show Sarah was back in Cromwell House and her burns had improved. She was finally allowed to go home after her mother pleaded with doctors for her return.[46]

The care of destitute children was also largely left to charities. One of the earliest orphanages was the Foundling Hospital, which was founded by Thomas Coram in 1741 and attempted to look after infants who had been abandoned by their parents for whatever reason. The hospital required that 'All persons who bring children are requested to affix on each child some particular writing or other distinguishing mark or token so that the child may be known hereafter if necessary'. Mothers could return and claim their child any time provided they had the detailed receipt that was issued to them when they handed over the baby. Few, however, did, which is perhaps just as well. During the first sixty years of the hospital's history nearly 20,000 infants were admitted, of whom 60 per cent died.[47] The registers of admission, still with the tokens attached, are now at the London Metropolitan Archives, along with other records of the hospital. They still exert a powerful influence and in recent years have inspired a number of writers, such as Jamilla Gavin and Jacqueline Wilson. They are also being studied by textile historians as they are one of the few sources showing the cloth worn by the poor in the mid-eighteenth century.[48]

A century or so later the problem of destitute children on London's streets had if anything got worse. Their plight moved a number of charities and philanthropists, chief among them Thomas Barnardo, originally an evangelical missionary to the East End, with a flair for publicity. He set up children's homes in the East End with the phrase 'No destitute child refused admission' above its door and provided many other services for poor boys and girls. In the 1880s he claimed that he was offering '600 hot breakfasts daily and 400 hot dinners four times a week' at his own free day school.[49] By the time of his death in 1905, the charity ran ninety-six homes across Britain caring for more than 8,500 children, including a village at its headquarters at Barkingside on the eastern edge of London.[50] The charity now maintains its own archives about the young people whom it helped, which staff will search for you for a fee. Another charity that offers a similar service is Quarriers, which was founded in 1871 as the Orphan Homes of Scotland, to help the poor children of Glasgow. It too set up a children's home at Bridge of Weir in Renfrewshire. It became a self-contained community comprising over forty children's cottages, Mount Zion church, a large school, a fire station, workshops, farms and other facilities.[51]

There were many rivals to Barnardo's, a few of which became national institutions with a network of local branches and homes. Survival of records is patchy, particularly for the smaller local orphanages. Again the National Register of Archives should be able to tell you what, if anything, survives and where it can be found. Remember too that records for individual children under a hundred years old are likely to be closed or at least restricted to next of kin. Hidden Lives Revealed is a fascinating website maintained by the Church of England Children's Society (originally the Waifs and Strays Society) which illustrates the lives of poor children for a century from the society's foundation in 1881. In particular there are 150 case files, out of 22,500 available between 1881 and 1918, showing the conditions that many young people endured and the help that the society was able to provide. Unfortunately the names have been removed so it is not possible to identify individual children.[52]

A small but still important orphanage was run by the Royal Philanthropic Society at Redhill. It was founded in London in 1788 by a group of gentlemen worried by the large number of homeless children who could earn their living only through begging or crime. In 1792 the first central institution of the society was opened at St George's Fields in Southwark. It was intended for the sons and daughters of convicts, and boys and girls who had themselves been convicted of crime. The school moved to Redhill in 1849. Its records, which are remarkably full, are now with the Surrey History Centre in Woking. Of particular interest are the registers of admissions since they give wonderfully detailed accounts of the boys and girls admitted to the institution, including, in some cases, photographs. The information given in the early registers is generally: name of boy; age; circumstances before admission; trade followed, with notes on apprenticeship, behaviour, discharge and later news. In common with many similar institutions, young men were encouraged to emigrate to begin new lives in the colonies. The centre has an online index to the boys who were in the home between 1788 and 1906.[53]

Orphan Names

One problem facing foundling hospitals was what to call the babies who appeared on their doorsteps without any indication of their birth names. Initially they were often given the names of the hospital's governors and benefactors, although this was stopped when the holders of the names came to think that they were connected in some way with their betters. Thereafter babies might be named after the location of the hospital, such as John Holborn, or their position in life, such as Elizabeth Foundling, or even after a fictional character, such as Robin Hood.

Home Children

For nearly a century between 1873 and the late 1960s orphanages sent tens of thousands of children to start new lives in the overseas dominions, particularly Australia and Canada. Some 100,000 children were sent to Canada alone, and about a quarter of all Canadians have a home child on their family tree. As well as populating the empire with sturdy young Anglo-Saxons, the charities argued that the children would have a better chance here rather than in the grim slums of London and Glasgow. Even so it was a cruel system: siblings were split up, the children endured terrible homesickness and many were abused mentally and physically in their new homes.[54]

There is no central register of these children, although Library and Archives Canada has an online index to children who arrived in the country between 1869 and the early 1930s.[55] If you know which ship they were on you should be able to pick up their names, and those of the rest of the part they travelled with which might perhaps include any siblings, in the outward passenger lists, which were kept between 1890 and 1960, and are on Findmypast.

FROM THE EXPERTS ...

The ScotlandsPeople Centre

Chris Paton introduces Scotland's top genealogical resource:

The Edinburgh-based ScotlandsPeople Centre is Scotland's primary research centre for family history. First opened in January 2009, the facility brings together genealogical resources from the National Records of Scotland and the Court of the Lord Lyon, such as vital records, censuses, heraldry records and testamentary material (wills and inventories). Such treasures are accessible for a daily £15 fee. The centre is open Monday to Friday (9 a.m.–4.30 p.m.). It is advisable to book a seat in advance. On your first visit look out for the free two-hour taster session which takes place at 10 a.m. or 2 p.m.

It is worth noting that the ScotlandsPeople Centre and the ScotlandsPeople website are two different ventures sharing the same brand. The centre uses a separate computer system to the website, so some holdings online are not at the centre and vice versa. In particular, the centre has birth, marriage and death records up to the present day, which is not the case online. However, at the time of writing the website has Roman Catholic parish records, which are not yet available at the centre. So do check the centre's holdings on its website before making a visit. If you wish to print records from the databases you will need to pay for credit in advance, and there is an option to save materials digitally on a USB flash drive, again for a fee.

As well as its own databases, the centre allows access to a number of external websites on most of its computers. It is therefore possible to access websites such as Ancestry or Findmypast, although you need your own account as the centre does not subscribe. I often keep the Ancestry census databases open on my terminal as I can search with some fields not available on the centre's own database. Be advised that one thing the centre does not have at the time of writing is WiFi capability.

Prior to a visit, consult the centre's website to see what else is available. There is an extensive library catalogue listing resources such as monumental inscriptions books, a range of microform and printed materials for non-conformist churches not included in the databases.

The National Records of Scotland (NRS) has many additional records, such as kirk session records and sasines, and it is conveniently based at General Register House as well. However, you will need to obtain an NRS reader's ticket, so bring two passport-sized colour photos with you.

Originally from Northern Ireland, but with both Scottish and Irish roots, **Chris Paton** has a postgraduate diploma in Genealogical Studies and runs the Scotland's Greatest Story research service. He regularly writes for all the British family history press and is a tutor for the Pharos online courses. However, he is best known for his Scottish ancestry blog, which contains all the latest news from the British genealogical scene.

Notes

1 The major guide is John West, *Town Records* (Phillimore, 1983), although this is largely about records before the Victorians. Also of use is Evelyn Lord, *Investigating the Twentieth Century: Sources for Local Historians* (Tempus, 1999).

2 Taken from www.york.gov.uk/leisure/Libraries/archives/Items_held.

3 Quoted in Patricia Hollis, *Ladies Elect: Women in English Local Government 1865–1914* (Oxford University Press, 1987), p. 393. This change in local government was sometimes known as municipal socialism, whose most famous exponent was Birmingham's Joseph Chamberlain.

4 A very brief introduction is given in Lord, *Investigating the Twentieth Century*, pp. 8–9. Local government was radically changed in 1974 when the old system was swept away and more equally sized district councils working in partnership with county councils were introduced. The system has been tweaked on several occasions subsequently, particularly in Wales and Scotland. In London, the Greater London Council replaced the London and Middlesex county councils in 1965, working with thirty-two new London boroughs and the City of London. The GLC was then abolished in 1986 and a new Greater London Authority was established in 1998.

5 Patricia Hollis' *Ladies Elect* offers an excellent introduction to the growing role of women in local political life. Local politics and the work of councillors and councils are well described in Winifred Holtby's novel *South Riding* (1936).

6 Twickenham Borough Council Minutes of Proceedings 1926–27, pp. 70–1, at Richmond-upon-Thames Local Studies Library. The school attendance officer was better known as the truancy officer.

7 In addition, access to an increasing number of files and registers even created as long ago as 1900 is being restricted for reasons of data protection.

8 Few records are yet online, although there is a nationwide project to digitise those before 1914. There are several books which describe log books, including Paul Carter & Kate Thompson, *Sources for Local Historians* (Phillimore, 2007), pp. 81–3; Lord, *Investigating the Twentieth Century*, pp. 53–4; and Pamela Horn, 'School Log Books', in Kate Thompson (ed.), *Short Guides to Records: Second Series Guides* (Historical Association, 1997), pp. 25–48.

9 The best guide to registers is Jeremy Gibson, *Electoral Registers 1832–1948* (2nd edn, Family History Partnership, 2008). Before 1872 there was no secret ballot and voters had to cast their vote in public, which were recorded in poll books. Surviving books can be found in a number of libraries and archives (and some have been published by S&N), and are listed in Jeremy Gibson, *Poll Books 1696–1872: A Directory to Holdings in Great Britain* (4th edn, Family History Partnership, 2008).

10 There are a large number of books available to help family historians. A good survey of what is available is provided by Stuart Raymond, *Occupational Sources for Family Historians*

(2nd edn, Family History Partnership, 2010). Both the Society of Genealogists and, to a lesser degree, Pen & Sword also publish a range of guides to researching various occupations. In the remote chance that you know who employed your ancestor, the National Register of Archives (www.nationalarchives.gov.uk/nra) will indicate whether any records survive.

11 Flora Thompson, *Lark Rise to Candleford* (Penguin, 1981), pp. 60–1.

12 Brian Lavery, *Royal Tars: the Lower Deck of the Royal Navy 875–1850* (Conway, 2010), p. 346. Men who served at Waterloo were given an additional two years' service towards their pension as acknowledgement of the contribution to the great victory.

13 Occupations are discussed by Edward Higgs in *Making Sense of the Census Revisited* (Institute of Historical Research, 2005). Joseph Waters of Cottisford was the farmer who employed the men of Juniper Hill, although unfortunately his entry in the 1891 census gives neither the number of men nor the acreage farmed (TNA RG 12/1171, f95, p4).

14 Matthew Woollard, *The Classification of Occupations in the 1881 Census of England and Wales* (Historical Censuses and Social Surveys Research Group Occasional Paper No 1, 1999), p. 1; online at http://privatewww.essex.ac.uk/~matthew/Papers/Woollard_1881Classifications_no%20illustration.pdf. Many definitions are given in Colin Waters, *A Dictionary of Old Trades, Titles and Occupations* (Countryside Books, 2002). The introduction by John Titford should be read by anybody interested in the subject. Potters' occupations are defined in the Potteries Job Index at www.thepotteries.org/jobs/index.htm.

15 Alehouses (or beer houses) had a licence only to sell beer. There was a huge growth in their number after 1830, when the licensing of pubs was relaxed. Woollard, *Occupations*, p. 8.

16 Quoted in Rick Allen, *The Moving Pageant: a Literary Sourcebook on London Street-life, 1700–1914* (Routledge, 1998), p. 214. Peter Ackroyd in his novel *Dan Lemo and the Limehouse Golam* (1994) provides many good descriptions of the quiet desperation of the semi-employed.

17 The Charles Booth Online Archive, http://booth.lse.ac.uk, has copies of the maps and the notebooks Booth and his team used to record their impression of each street they visited. The poorer the residents the darker the colour on the map: those in class A (black) were 'Vicious, semi-criminal'.

18 A brief introduction is provided in David Hey, *The Oxford Companion to Local and Family History* (Oxford University Press, 2008), pp. 263–4. TNA has, for example, a number of indentures for young men who were apprenticed as merchant mariners into the early 1960s in series BT 150–BT 152. These registers should be available on DocumentsOnline.

19 For more about the sorry plight of many pauper apprentices see John Waller, *The Real Oliver Twist: Robert Blincoe: a Life that Illuminates a Violent Age* (Icon Books, 2006), pp. 53–6.

20 Quoted in Peter Laslett, *The World We Have Lost: Further Explored* (3rd edn, Routledge, 1983), p. 3.

21 Maureen Waller, *1700: Scenes from London Life* (Hodder & Stoughton, 2001), pp. 235–6.

22 See series IR 17. The majority of records are for the period before 1774. A dated and very imperfect index to records between 1710 and 1774 is in IR 1.

23 There are also several excellent introductory leaflets about livery companies prepared by the former Guildhall Library Manuscripts Department at www.history.ac.uk/gh/livapp.htm and www.history.ac.uk/gh/livintro.htm. Origins also have lists of 21,500 members of livery companies who signed the Association Oath of 1696, which includes

the majority of members at this time. Most livery companies maintain websites, which include brief histories.

24 Details are at www.cutlers-hallamshire.org.uk with a summary of their holdings at www.nationalarchives.gov.uk/a2a/records.aspx?cat=2655-cca&cid=-1#-1. See also Joan Unwin, 'A Sharp Tale', *Ancestors Magazine* (32), April 2005. Lists of apprentices and their masters between 1624 and 1814 can be found in R.E. Leader, *The History of the Company of Cutlers in Hallamshire* (2 vols, Sheffield, 1905–06).

25 Old Bailey Proceedings, 11 December 1678, www.oldbaileyonline.org.

26 The IEE material is described at www.theiet.org/about/libarc/archives/research/guides-familyhistory.cfm. The RGS work and collections are described at www.rgs.org. I've organised several family history events at their headquarters and strongly recommend a visit. If you have a chance, ask to see the hat Livingstone wore while in Africa (he appears to have had a very small head).

27 Indexes to all quarter session records are online at www.nationalarchives.gov.uk/a2a. Where local record offices have online catalogues it is generally easy to find what is available. Some records have disappeared altogether, such as licences issued to hackney cab drivers in London.

28 The most useful introduction to these records is Jeremy Gibson & Judith Hunter, *Victuallers' Licences* (Federation of Family History Societies, 1997). There are also several online indexes, notably for the Isle of Wight, Warwickshire and Sheffield. See also my article 'Focus on Victuallers' Licences', *Who Do You Think You Are?* (47), May 2011. Paul Jennings, *The Local* (The History Press, 2007) is an excellent history of pubs and the people who worked in them.

29 For more see Diana Mackarill, 'Pedlars', *The Ephemerist* (152), 2011.

30 Thompson, *Lark Rise*, p. 128.

31 The records are at the London Metropolitan Archives. PC/MASS/03/002 contains printed lists of applicants 1916–40. Lees was among the 600 men and women who registered in March 1923. The refusals are listed in PC/MASS/1 Massage licence registration special cases, refusals, etc. See also my article at http://the-historyman.blogspot.com.

32 There is an excellent and comprehensive guide to researching family history at the Post Office archives at http://postalheritage.org.uk/page/genealogy. Records of the telecommunications side of the Post Office, including staff records, are with the BT Archives. For addresses see Appendix 2.

33 *Picture Post*, 9 November 1940. John Blackmore was appointed in 1935.

34 Peter Clark, *British Clubs and Societies 1580–1800* (Oxford University Press, 2000), p. 2; Liza Picard, *Dr Johnson's London* (Phoenix, 2001), pp. 130–1; R.J. Morris, 'Clubs, Societies and Associations', in F.M.L. Thompson, *The Cambridge Social History of Britain 1750–1950* (Vol. 3 *Social Agencies and Institutions*, Cambridge University Press, 1993), p. 399.

35 Jeffrey Cox, *The English Churches in a Secular Society: Lambeth 1870–1930* (Oxford University Press, 1982), pp. 58–9. The froth blowers' aim was to raise money for voluntary hospitals. http://frothblowers.co.uk.

36 If you have trade unionists on your family tree, then you need to consult Mark Crail, *Tracing Your Labour Movement Ancestors* (Pen & Sword, 2009), or at least visit his excellent trade union ancestors and Chartist websites, www.unionancestors.co.uk and www.chartists.net.

37 Extracted from the Annual Report of the Registrar of Friendly Societies, 1913 PP 1914. lix.1. The best guide to their records remains to be Roger Logan, *Friendly Society Records*

(Federation of Family History Societies, 2000). Also of interest is Victoria Solt Dennis, *Discovering Friendly and Fraternal Societies: Their Badges and Regalia* (Shire Publications, 2008). Thanks to Dan Weinbren for help with this section. The exception was the Girls' Friendly Society, which was an Anglican organisation helping young women. The Foresters' records are still with the society in Southampton; see www.aoforestersheritage.com.

38 Quoted in Clark, *British Clubs*, pp. 328–30. Friendly societies and trade unions also helped men tramping the country looking for work in a similar way. See Robert Leeson, *Travelling Brothers* (Allen & Unwin, 1979).

39 See Appendix 2 for the address. Even if you haven't got Masonic ancestors, Freemason's Hall and the museum is a fascinating place to visit. This section is based in part on a family history webpage at www.freemasonry.london.museum/family-history.

40 www.southchurch.mesh4us.org.uk/oaths.php.

41 Liverpool University has a small collection of charity records, with details at http://sca. lib.liv.ac.uk/collections/colldescs/social.html.

42 Simon Fowler, *The Phil: A History of the Richmond Philanthropic Society 1870–1995* (Richmond Philanthropic Society, 1995), p. 29. The society's annual reports and other papers are at Richmond Local Studies Library.

43 Dispensaries provided medical advice and distributed medicines to the poor.

44 www.nationalarchives.gov.uk/hospitalrecords. The database also includes information about staff records.

45 http://hharp.org.

46 The 1891 census indicates that, sixteen years later, she was a waitress in Derby (RG 12/2735 f84). See also www.kingston.ac.uk/pressoffice/latestnews/2008/december/11-Small-and-special-the-lives-of-Victorian-children-revealed.

47 Rules quoted in Picard, *Dr Johnson's London*, p. 78. The history of the hospital and the foundation's impressive art collection is explored at the Foundling Museum. www.foundlingmuseum.org.uk.

48 Records of the hospital are at the London Metropolitan Archives, but are closed for 110 years.

49 He also included a mawkish poem in his plea for money which never failed to touch the hearts of potential donors: 'Do you hear the tear-filled voice/Please I have forgotten the date./Then you'll stay and copy this history page/For half an hour on your slate./Poor child, poor child, the last tears fall;/For that morning mother had said,/As she sent her breakfastless off to school/In the afternoon we'll get bread.' See William J. Fishman, *East End 1888* (Five Leaves, 2005), p. 159.

50 A brief history can be found at www.barnardos.org.uk/barnardo_s_history.pdf. Barnardo was less than popular with his fellow workers in the field – and less successful rivals for funds – who accused him of financial irregularities and other misdemeanours, although eventually he was cleared of all charges.

51 More about Quarriers and their history is at www.quarriers.org.uk.

52 www.hiddenhistories.org.uk. The cards and other material are in the society's maintained Archive and Record Centre at Block A, Floor 2, Tower Bridge Business Complex, 100 Clement's Road, London, SE16 4DG, email: archive@childrenssociety.org.uk.

53 More about the society and a link to the index is at www.surreycc.gov.uk/sccwebsite/ sccwspages.nsf/LookupWebPagesByTITLE_RTF/The+Royal+Philanthropic+School+ at+Redhill?opendocument. A history of the Farm at Redhill is at www.redhill-reigate-history.co.uk/philanth.htm.

54 There are several websites devoted to the subject with advice for people
    researching home children, including http://freepages.genealogy.rootsweb.ancestry.
    com/~tweetybirdgenealogy/homechild.html and for Canada http://freepages.genealogy.
    rootsweb.ancestry.com/~britishhomechildren and www.britishhomechildren.org.
    Wikipedia also has a useful introduction. The best book is Janet Sacks & Roger Kershaw,
    New Lives for Old (TNA, 2008). Also of interest is Margaret Humphries, *Empty Cradles:
    Oranges and Sunshine* (Corgi, 2011).
55 www.collectionscanada.gc.ca/databases/home–children/index–e.html.

Chapter 2

FAMILY HISTORY ON THE WEB

Almost no other hobby or pursuit has been changed as much by the internet as family history, with perhaps only the music and travel industries having been affected more. Cyberspace has totally altered how we find our ancestors as well as the records we use in doing so, and has brought hundreds of thousands of new adherents to the hobby. It is still possible, just about, to conduct research in the old way, recording information painstakingly on filing cards and spending hours peering at out-of-focus microfilm in draughty archives, but unless you have a phobia of computers there is no reason to.[1]

Uniquely, genealogy has proven an ideal partner for the internet, and could quickly and easily take advantage of the new technology, for a number of reasons. The internet made it very easy to share knowledge and resources. Indeed, it was one of the main reasons it grew up in the first place. Culturally, family historians were used to sharing their research and their knowledge of the records. There are now hundreds, perhaps thousands, of bulletin boards, mailing lists and other ways to ask questions and share knowledge. The oldest, like RootsWeb, go back to the very early internet. It helped that family historians were quick to seize on the fact that it now cost next to nothing to communicate with friends and family around the world. This made it easy to find and then keep in touch with relations. Back in September 1997 I was at a meeting in Cornwall where the audience were excitedly talking about how they had just got online and had been emailing distant relations around the world sharing information.[2]

Archives have also seized the opportunity to reach out to a far wider audience than would have been possible twenty years ago, through websites, online catalogues and the placing of digitised material online. The leader in this has been The National Archives, which has had the vision and the leadership to grasp the opportunities that the new technology offered. However, I also remember the suspicion which the

FamilySearch is probably the greatest free resource online.

arrival of the first internet terminal in the then Public Record Office's library caused and the fight that the then librarian had to install it. So everything could have been very different.

Most family history research is now done online using the services provided by companies who have digitised and indexed the key sources for commercial gain. Some 2 million of us visit one of these websites every month. The extent of the demand for such services was shown when the Public Record Office launched the 1901 census online in the early days of 2002, causing the website to crash. It was many months before the service was resumed and questions were asked in Parliament. After a lot of grumbling, the principle that you have to pay to access this material has largely been accepted by family historians, who benefit from ease of access, better indexing and other resources which would have staggered researchers even twenty years ago. However, it may be argued that subscribers pay handsomely for the privilege.[3]

Genealogical research has proven to be a very lucrative business for both the companies and those archives, notably The National Archives, that are licensing material to go online. According to The National Archives' 2009–10 Annual Report: 'We estimate that our publishing partners have invested around £50 million in putting our records online since 2003. And this approach has contributed to a growth in our commercial income of 30 per cent in 2009–10, creating essential funds that we reinvest in our services and facilities.' All in all, The National Archives made roughly £8 million from commercial activities during the year, some of which came from its licensed associates. The commercial market in Britain is now effectively a duopoly between Ancestry (with about half of the total UK market share) and Findmypast (with a third). In addition, there are also a number of smaller companies, notably TheGenealogist, Origins and Familyrelatives, as well as The National Archives' own DocumentsOnline service, but they find it increasingly difficult to compete. The cost of starting up a competitor is so high that this position is unlikely to change. There is, however, fierce competition between the market leaders, which does keep the price down to an extent.[4]

The market leader is clearly Ancestry, which is the British arm of an American company and has a dominant position in the US genealogical market. It has more than 1.6 million subscribers worldwide. Britain is its second most important market after the United States. According to its annual report, filed with the US Securities and Exchange Commission in April 2011, revenues increased from $150.6 million in 2006 to $300.9 million in 2010, an impressive compound annual growth rate of 18.9 per cent. Ancestry's main rival, Findmypast, is one of the brands owned by BrightSolid, which in turn is a subsidiary of D.C. Thompson, the Dundee-based publisher of magazines and comics, such as *People's Friend* and *The Beano*. BrightSolid also runs ScotlandsPeople, Genes Reunited and Friends Reunited. It is difficult to get hard financial figures, but it is clearly a profitable business. A press release on the company's website indicates that there was 'a 23% increase in turnover during the year to March 31st 2010' and gross profits rose by 12 per cent. It is hard to know what proportion of this increase came from its online genealogical interests, but the press release notes that Findmypast managed to pay back a £5 million loan in October 2010 to its parent company for digitising the 1911 census.[5]

FamilySearch

FamilySearch is the largest genealogical website providing free resources. It is based on the collections of the Church of Jesus Christ of the Latter-day Saints (LDS Church or Mormons) at the world's largest genealogical library, the Family History Library in Salt Lake City. There is also a worldwide network of local family history centres (sometimes called family search centres) based in LDS chapels, where you can order microfilm of material from Salt Lake City. The site was recently relaunched with a host of new facilities, which makes it a lot more useful. It has also been redesigned with a clear and open feel. At the site's heart lies the FamilySearch database, which used to be known as the International Genealogical Index (IGI). It includes transcriptions from thousands of parish registers and other sources, as well as family trees submitted by 'patrons' (members of the LDS Church). It is by far the best source for tracing Britons who lived before 1837. However, it is by no means complete nor is it always very accurate. Most importantly of all it is mainly for births and, to a lesser degree, marriages. There are relatively few deaths recorded here. There is a direct link to FamilySearch from the homepage (click on 'advanced search'). The search engine is simplicity itself to use, but you will probably need to use the modifiers of place and dates where possible, otherwise you may come up with tens of thousands of other people with the same name. An alternative to using the search engine is to browse the records, although the selection of records available here at present is patchy. However, some collections do include scanned copies of the records themselves. The collections contain indexes to the various English and Welsh censuses between 1841 and 1901, although to download images you have to subscribe to Findmypast.[6]

Additionally, FamilySearch is more than just the IGI. There are a host of other features. If you want to learn more about the records, there is the wiki, with tens of thousands of entries so you need to be careful about what you ask it. For example, there are 7,500 entries alone for 'Poor Law'. Also, as with other wikis, you can edit the results. Entries will normally give the call numbers for films, which you can order through your local family history centre. You can also download videos for courses that can help you understand the records, although British readers should note that the courses are designed by and for American audiences. If you are interested in giving something back then you can volunteer to index a collection or two of the records.

Using Databases Efficiently

Much family history today is less about compiling pedigrees and charts and more about manipulating databases to provide the information you want. In theory, and on the *Who Do You Think You Are?* television series, it is very easy. Just type in the names you have, and perhaps where they were on census night, and, hey presto, up comes all the data you want back to the Norman Conquest. Unfortunately, it is not as easy as it looks. Even the commercial data providers, who try to make it as simple as possible for their customers, slip up occasionally. Some databases and online catalogues are downright difficult to use, being seemingly designed for the benefit of the staff or the web designers rather than you and me – the end users. Sometimes the site is badly designed and you go round and round in ever-decreasing circles trying to find something which is either not there or is hidden. Or they promise facilities or services which are not available or are of no use.

One problem is that researchers may be required to have a basic knowledge of Boolean logic. This may sound complicated, but it isn't really. The phrase relates to the logical relationship among search terms. The Boole in Boolean is George Boole (1815–64) a self-taught mathematician and logician from Lincoln who became the founding professor of mathematics at Queen's College, Cork, in 1849 and whose life work lay in the relationships between objects. According to I. Grattan-Guinness' biography of Boole in the *Oxford Dictionary of National Biography*: 'Boolean logic is the basis for the design of all modern computers since the ultimate components of these devices were capable of storing just two values (equated with true and false) and their circuitry calculates the basic Boolean operators over these two values.'[7]

These principles, sometimes called differential operators, Boolean logic or Boolean search, lay at the very heart of the construction of databases and accessing their contents. We don't really need to think about this when we use Google or Bing, for instance, because they are clever enough to know what we are likely to be looking for. Google is by far the largest search engine: in Britain nearly 80 per cent of searches online are made using it. In the US, where Yahoo remains popular, it is about 60 per cent.[8]

George Boole (1815–64) was the mathematician and logician who worked on the relationships between objects, which lay behind much of early computing. (*Kieran McCarthy*)

If we are looking for webpages about Horatio Nelson, we type his name into the search box, and then up come nearly a million results. Then chances are that we'll find what we want in the first few entries. In theory these are likely to be the ones that Google thinks are most relevant. However, commercial companies are adept at using what is called Search Engine Optimisation (SEO) to push their products higher up Google's ranking, knowing that few people will go beyond the first page of results. Type in 'cheese and onion crisps' and you'll find that most entries are for Walker's Crisps, Britain's largest crisp manufacturer, who clearly have taken advantage of SEO so that other companies do not appear above them.[9]

These points, taken predominantly from the BBC website, may help you get the best out of Google:[10]

- **Use multiple words**. For example, entering just the word 'Nelson' will return hits on the naval hero, the towns in New Zealand and Lancashire, and New Zealand wines. Instead, if you type in 'Nelson Admiral Horatio' your top hits will be specifically for Britain's greatest naval hero.
- **Specify words**. Putting a plus sign (+) in front of a word will ensure you only see pages that include that word. Putting a minus sign (-) in front of a word will

eliminate pages with that word. Searching on 'Nelson +Portsmouth -Victory', for example, will get a page of links to sites which mention Nelson in Portsmouth, but not HMS *Victory*.

- **Put phrases in double quotes.** The search "Horatio Nelson" will come up with references to that phrase, otherwise you might find sites devoted to the town or the New Zealand province.

- **Use unusual words.** Everyone's first instinct is to type in the most common words associated with the topic they're interested in. However, to find the most relevant pages, your best strategy is to type in words that are commonly associated with your topic, but that rarely appear together in other contexts. An example here might be the word 'midshipman', relating to Horatio's early career, or 'barrel of brandy', referring to how Nelson's body was stored and transported to Greenwich.[11]

- **Search within your results.** If you get a huge list of results, some of which are relevant, click on 'Search within results' at the bottom of the page and add new search terms to thin out the list you've already found.

- **Use personalised settings.** Click on 'Search settings' or 'advanced search' at the top, right corner of the Google homepage and set the language(s) you want to use, the number of hits to appear on a page and other elements.

- **Read the help files.** Every search engine has carefully written pages to help you search more effectively.

In addition, there are a number of words and phrases – known as Boolean operators – which will prove of use when interrogating particular search engines and most online databases, including The National Archives' Discovery and many local record offices' online catalogues. They do vary slightly between databases, but there should be a help page which explains any local conventions. They are always written in uppercase letters.[12]

The words and phrases include:

- **AND**: used to join words or phrases when both (or all) the terms must appear in the items you retrieve. So it produces results which have both search terms in the answer, such as 'Horatio Nelson'. This is the default search, so when you type Horatio Nelson into Google it will interpret the request as being 'Horatio **AND** Nelson'.

- **NEAR**: a very powerful operator which allows you to find phrases that are near each other but not adjacent. 'Horatio **NEAR** Nelson' turns up results where the words 'Horatio' and 'Nelson' are, say, in the same phrase but not next to each other, such as 'Many boys were named Horatio after Lord Nelson'. This can be a surprisingly useful search picking up entries that you might otherwise not find. You can also use **NOT NEAR** to ensure any phrases or words are well separated.

- **NOT**: used to exclude a particular word or combination of words from your search results, such as 'Nelson **NOT** Horatio' to find references just to the Lancashire town. You can also use the minus sign: 'Nelson –Horatio'. If you are retrieving many records that are unrelated to your topic, try using the **NOT** operator to eliminate a word. This should be done cautiously, because as well as deleting the unwanted items, such a search will also eliminate records that might discuss both the relevant topic as well as any unrelated topics, such as Horatio Nelson in Nelson.
- **OR**: used to join synonymous or related terms, this instructs the search tool to retrieve any record that contains either (or both) of the terms, thus broadening your search results. The **OR** operator is particularly useful when you are unsure of the words used to categorise your topic or if information on your topic is even available. Also, if you are retrieving too few records, broaden your search by adding a synonym with the Boolean operator **OR**. It is similar in many ways to **AND**, but can be used to find similar subjects, such as 'Horatio Nelson **OR** Admiral Nelson'.[13]
- It is also possible to perform complex searches in which more than one Boolean operator is used. To do this, enclose the terms connected with **OR** within brackets. The first phrase in brackets will be searched first. For example: '(admiral **OR** Horatio) **AND** (Nelson **OR** Victory)' may well turn up different results to '(Nelson **OR** Victory) **AND** (admiral **OR** Horatio)'.

None of the commercial data providers, such as Ancestry and Findmypast, use Boolean operators, at least not at the front end of their search operations. They assume that it will just confuse users. Even so, searching their databases is not always straightforward, but there are a few strategies you can use to get round this. The most important of these is to remember that 'less is more'. You can input too much information in the hope that it will narrow the search dramatically. However, this can instead just confuse the search engine. Depending on what you are looking for, just completing an additional box or two might be sufficient. The gender box is normally useless so don't tick this. Instead, if you are allowed, insert an unusual keyword, such as place of birth 'Leamington Spa' or service number '1456/20' as well as 'Paul Belcher', for instance, which will help the search engine to narrow down the search (in effect, it is doing a Boolean search for all Paul Belchers who are connected with Leamington Spa). If you want to know more, each provider offers useful help pages to send you on your way.[14]

Of course, it may not always be the data provider's fault. Your ancestor's name could have been originally recorded wrongly, or they could have given the wrong place of birth and this is what the transcriber noted down. They could hardly have done otherwise. So before you start complaining, check your research. However, if you do spot a mistake, report it. All the companies allow you to do this and will change their indexing accordingly if they agree with you. When the 1911 census was first released by Findmypast, I reported the fact that the Welsh politician Aneurin Bevan's forename had been wrongly transcribed and the data was swiftly corrected.

For researchers, one of the most interesting online developments in recent years has been the growth of federated search, or the ability to search across a number of databases at the same time for individuals or subjects. This can be a valuable tool, but its usefulness is very much dependent on the skills of the researcher and the ability of the search facility to filter your search so that you can find what you want easily and accurately. Perhaps the most important such site for historians is Connected Histories, which is not really a website in the conventional way but a search engine that goes through a number of separate databases devoted to British history between 1500 and 1900 all at the same time. The databases here are a mixture of free resources and subscription sites. As of autumn 2011 those available on the site were: British History Online; British Museum Images; British Newspapers 1600–1900 (subscription); British Library nineteenth-century books and pamphlets (subscription); Charles Booth Archive; Clergy of the Church of England 1540–1835; DocumentsOnline (part pay to view); the History of Parliament; House of Commons Parliamentary Papers (subscription); John Johnson Collection of Printed Ephemera (subscription); John Strype's Survey of London 1720; London Lives 1690–1800; Origins (subscription); Old Bailey Online.[15]

The National Archives' Discovery Service

In the spring of 2011, The National Archives began rolling out a new and much-improved catalogue called the Discovery Service, which will eventually replace the old catalogue. It is radically different to the old catalogue in what it can do and how it looks. You can continue to search the catalogue by keyword or by reference, but now there should also be links to the material on DocumentsOnline (and some other online providers with images from The National Archives' collections) and clearer information about those records that have yet to be released to the public. There are more and clearer filters, which allow you to break down your search more easily by time period (i.e., 1770–99), type of record (roll) or by collection (C 54). It also encourages you to use Boolean operators to narrow down your search yet further. There are some interesting features, such as being able to link places mentioned in the catalogue to their location on Google Maps.[16]

Genealogy Search Engines

Over the years there have been various attempts to construct search engines which will only search genealogy websites. None have been particularly useful or lasted for very long. One of the latest, Mocavo, may be more successful. It searches hundreds of thousands of genealogy websites, looking for the words that you specify. Sites searched include thousands of genealogy message boards, society webpages, genealogy pages uploaded by individuals, state historical societies, family societies, Find-a-Grave, the Internet Archive, the Library of Congress, several sites containing scanned images of old photographs and tens of thousands of distinct sites with transcribed records of genealogical interest. Although most sites searched are American, it also looks at non-US resources. I found three British sites which mention my Paul Belchers of Leicestershire, two of which were new to me. However, it did not search the databases of the big genealogy providers or archives like The National Archives catalogue. In May 2011 Ancestry launched a similar search engine which also searched across genealogy websites, not just those maintained by Ancestry. You can also nominate sites for inclusion.[17]

Unusual Resources from the Commercial Data Providers[18]

Each of the commercial data providers – Ancestry, Findmypast and the like – offer much more than just the census and other major sources. There are also a number of small collections of miscellaneous records. Often they are either scans of reference books, such as the *Army* and *Navy Lists*, or small datasets, like indexes to parish registers or a small series of records. Occasionally there are indexes or transcripts of larger record sets, such as registers of convicts or lists of passport holders. However, this material is rarely exclusive to just one site.

Ancestry has a huge number of datasets large and small. Indeed, they probably have more than all their rivals combined. Their holdings are listed in the online card catalogue, which at time of writing had details of 951 separate datasets, most but not all related to British family history. There are filters to help you find what you want or you can type in the subject or keyword. There are also other ways to uncover what is available, particularly from the homepage.

One of the best resources here is the National Probate Calendar. Ancestry's set of the calendar provides a detailed index to all wills proved in England and Wales from the beginning of the modern probate system in 1858 up to the end of 1946. If you

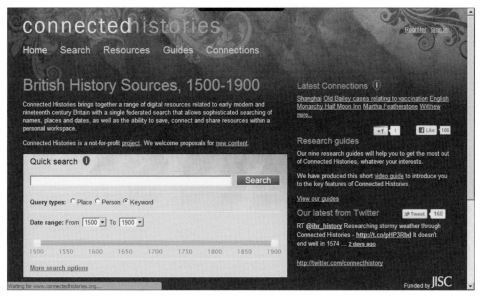

The homepage of Connected Histories, a site which allows searches of selected disparate databases at the same time.

are researching ancestors who lived a hundred years or so ago, entries here can be very informative as they give the deceased's occupation, value of the estate, who the executors were and their relationship to the testator. Additionally, it was not only rich people who made wills: there are many entries for plumbers, publicans and labourers.

Another interesting dataset is the British telephone directories, first published in the 1880s for a century. Most people did not have a phone up until the 1960s so their use is limited, but occasionally they might confirm where somebody lived. Years ago I wrote an article on Darby Sabini, Britain's interwar criminal mastermind, who operated out of a house in suburban Hove, where he had a phone put in as early as 1930 – presumably so he could easily communicate with subordinates in London's gangland.

There are also a number of datasets relating to convicts. The most important of these records are the criminal registers (1791–1892), which list everybody accused of a crime, with details about the defendant, the crime they were accused of and their trial and sentence (if convicted) or other outcome, although there is a better free index provided by the State Library of Queensland. These records may lead to other datasets available on Ancestry, such as transportation registers of convicts sent to Australia between 1788 and 1868, prison hulk registers and letter books, 1802–49, which list prisoners kept on board former naval ships in the Thames and elsewhere. Most were due to be transported to Australia but by no means did everybody make the journey.[19]

There's relatively little military material (and a lot of it, such as the Waterloo medal rolls and Du Revigny's roll of honour, can also be found elsewhere), but an unusual collection is that of the licences issued by the Royal Aero Club to pilots between 1910 and 1950, which include details of most of the men who flew aircraft during the early years of the Royal Flying Corps, until the corps started to provide its own training in 1916.

Findmypast has surprisingly few unusual or unique sources, those that they do have were inherited from the Federation of Family History Society's old Familyhistoryonline website. The federation's contribution is particularly useful as it contains many detailed (and accurate) indexes compiled by local family history societies to birth, marriage and death indexes, census books and parish records. A recent addition has been the Society of Genealogists' indexes, such as the Teachers' Registration Council, which has details of nearly 100,000 men and women who taught in England and Wales between 1870 and 1948. Registration, however, was not compulsory, so many teachers never bothered. A unique, if rather disappointing, resource is the register of passport applications, which lists everybody who applied for a British passport between 1851 and 1903. Unfortunately, only the names of the applicants are recorded. Passports were mainly only required for travel to European countries, but not British colonies, the dominions or, indeed, the United States. Also disappointing are the Business Index, which includes material of various kinds about local businesses, and the Worldwide Army Index, which lists men and their regiments at the time of the 1861 census.[20]

There is also a unique collection of records for the Boer War, based on official casualty rolls, medal and muster rolls, and memorials, which can be very useful if you are researching somebody who lost their lives on the South African *veld*. An attractive resource is the *Irish Memorial Records of the Great War*, which was published in the 1920s describing all Ireland's war dead. Each page is handsomely illustrated.

TheGenealogist has very few unique datasets, apart from the Non-Conformist Parish Records. Instead there are a reasonable number of sources generally taken from books, many of which originally appeared on discs published by S&N (TheGenealogist's parent company), including a range of parish register transcripts and *Army* and *Navy Lists*. Unique sources are small collections of poll books (which record how each elector voted in elections before 1872 when the secret ballot was introduced) and school histories containing lists of old boys and girls, sometimes with brief biographies showing their later careers.

British Origins specialises in the less common records, generally those created before 1837. It is also leading the National Wills Project, providing a central source for pre-1858 wills that at present are hard to use because they are scattered across many archives. The information largely comes from published transcripts and abstracts of records. As well as material for London, there are several indexes to marriages in Dorset and Surrey, as well as a selection of indexes and abstracts to wills proved at ecclesiastical courts, including the Prerogative Court of York. Indeed, Somerset is well represented as there are also electoral registers for the county between 1832 and 1914.[21]

The National Archives' page on Flickr showing a few of the archives' images.

The smallest of the data providers, Familyrelatives, specialises in providing access to directories, including incomplete runs of *Army* and *Navy Lists*, and professional directories for medicine, as well as a selection of school records listing alumni. Unfortunately, there are many gaps in coverage, so there is less here than meets the eye, and most of the records can be found on other sites. Of particular interest is the 1873 Return of Landowners, with names and addresses for every landowner and tenant and the estimated yearly rental valuation of all holdings over 1 acre. Some 320,000 names are to be found here. Similar surveys are on TheGenealogist.

There are several smaller sites which provide access, for a fee, to resources on their site. The largest (and potentially the most expensive) is the Original Record. It allows you to type your ancestor's name into their library of scanned books, directories and indexes to see whether they appear in them, varying from lists of Old Etonians to early Tudor taxpayers in Sussex. Each search gives you a snippet from the original source. A similar service is offered by Genhound.[22]

In Scotland, the major site is ScotlandsPeople, which includes all the major sources for Scottish research. Probably the most unusual source here is the Catholic parish records, although the information which can be obtained from them is fairly spartan. Also worth looking out for are the minor records in the statutory registers, which record the births, marriages and deaths of Scots overseas or in the armed forces.

As the name suggests, Military Genealogy could be useful if you are researching ancestors who served in the forces. There are ten separate datasets mainly for men in the First World War, but covering other conflicts as well. However, the datasets are all available on other sites, notably Findmypast.[23]

Ireland for a Fee and for Free

Ireland was once among the laggards in putting resources online, but she has made great strides in the past few years. Much of the material now available is free as digitisation projects were largely funded by the state rather than the private sector as in Britain. Unfortunately, digitisation will not bring back the records which have been destroyed – a problem that presents particular challenges for Irish researchers – such as those lost during the Four Courts fire in 1922, which saw almost all of the archives of Public Record Office of Ireland go up in flames. It also does not help that the censuses between 1841 and 1891 were pulped for the war effort in 1916.

In particular, The National Archives of Ireland (NAI) has put the 1901 and 1911 censuses online (these are, for all practical purposes, the only surviving Irish censuses and are almost identical to their English or Scottish equivalents); the Irish Libraries Council has included a superb version of Griffith's Valuation, including links to maps of the period so you can see exactly where your ancestor owned property on its Ask About Ireland website. The valuation was conducted between 1847 and 1864, recording anybody who owned more than an acre of land. As such, it is a surrogate for the 1851 and 1861 censuses as it lists all landowners except the very poorest. The Ask About Ireland website also has many other useful genealogical resources. FamilySearch has indexes to Irish birth, marriages and deaths from when civil registration was introduced in 1864 up to 1958. Additionally, the websites of both the NAI and the Public Record Office of Northern Ireland (PRONI) have selections of databases relating to records in their care. Also, the NAI offers links to almost all websites you might use in your Irish research.[24]

There are also several commercial sites. Irish Origins, part of the Origins network, has copies of Griffith's Valuation, indexes to Irish wills, surviving papers from the 1851 census for Dublin, tithe defaulters and some military papers and emigration records. The Ulster Historical Foundation has material for the six counties, and the Irish Family History Foundation has parish register indexes (about 80 per cent of surviving Catholic registers are to be found here) and other material. However, none of these have very much content to offer and in the long term they are likely to be swept aside by the Findmypast Irish site, which was launched in early 2011. A rather different emphasis is at Past Homes, which sells copies of the first-edition, 6in-scale Ordnance Survey maps, which show Ireland as it was before the famine. However, caution perhaps needs to be exercised with regard to the accuracy of these maps. A recent historian of the Ordnance Survey has described the survey's early years in Ireland as 'a colourful saga of imperialism, translation, cultural nationalism and local attempts to sabotage the map-makers' measurements'. Putting this to one side, Ordnance Survey Ireland also offers a number of maps for free, both of the modern Republic and the twenty-six counties as they looked in the 1890s.[25]

Social Media

The World Wide Web offers a lot more than just the chance to visit websites and check your email. In recent years social-networking sites like Twitter, LinkedIn and Facebook have become all the rage. Family history is being affected by the social media revolution, although perhaps less than you might think. In part it is a case of perception: social media is often portrayed as being only for the young and also these services are not thought of as being useful for the pursuit of genealogy. As family historians we already have tried and tested ways to share information through emails, websites and mailing lists. There's been a huge amount of hype over all this and lots of silly things said, particularly by journalists who should know better, but basically social networks are new or alternative ways of communicating or sharing information. Debbie Kennett's book *DNA and Social Networking: a Guide to Genealogy in the Twenty-First Century* (The History Press, 2011) covers all this in great detail and specifically for family history research.

Social media is an umbrella term for all of the activities that come together in an online utility that uses multiple communication mediums of words, pictures or videos, primarily or partly supplied by users. This includes message boards, blogs, wikis, podcasts, pictures and video. Examples of social media applications are Wikipedia (reference), LinkedIn (for business people), Google+, Twitter and Facebook (social networking), YouTube (social networking and video sharing) and Flickr (photo sharing). There are also 'social networks', which are a social structure made of nodes (individuals or organisations) who connect in a virtual community. They provide a collection of various ways for users to interact, such as chat, messaging, email, video, file sharing, blogging, discussion groups and so on. Services here include MySpace, Friends Reunited and Facebook. The term also describes technologies that promote social interaction, networking and information sharing. It is one of the most positive and potentially most important aspects of the internet. Posting customer reviews on Amazon, sharing photos on Flickr or maintaining a Facebook profile are all examples of social media in action. The downside is that interesting arguments and points can be lost in a torrent of occasionally uninformed comments. The American lawyer Mike Godwin observed in the early days of the internet that 'As an online discussion grows longer, the probability of a comparison involving Nazis or Hitler approaches 1'. This has become known as Godwin's Rule.[26]

Some museums and archives have started using these tools to publicise their collections and to try to reach new audiences. The National Archives at Kew is a leader in this and they have a presence on most social media networks. If you are interested, the website Common Craft explains some of these concepts in a series of short informative videos, fortunately in plain English. More detailed analysis of the main social-networking sites can be found on Wikipedia. Facebook is by far the largest company: over half a billion people have joined since it was set up in 2004. It can be used to tell friends about what you are doing, but there is a lot more besides. Users can create profiles with photos, lists of personal interests, contact information and other personal details. Communicating with friends and other users can be done through private or public messages or a chat feature, so you can keep followers up to date with your genealogical research on a regular basis. Users can also create and join interest groups and 'like' pages. There are a number of groups on family history, as well as on individual surname interests. For instance, if you are interested in the surname Pomeroy there is a group in Facebook to join. Two other interesting pages are for *Your Family History* magazine and the 2011 census family history section. As this chapter was being written, Google launched its social-networking service Google+ as a possible rival to Facebook. Initial reactions have been mixed, but undoubtedly there is potential here for family historians to come together to share information and resources.[27]

The media has been full of Twitter-related stories since the social-networking phenomenon burst on to the scene a few years ago. Subscribers can post messages of 140 characters or less, generally on their lives or commenting on the events of the day to followers who sign up to receive an individual's tweets. You can see what people are tweeting through a search engine. The excellent Genealogy in Time website has a genealogy Twitter reader, which allows visitors to see what is being discussed of a genealogical nature. Even stopping by for a minute or two can give a real sense of the huge variety that is genealogy today. You could use Twitter to communicate your family discoveries or sign up to receive tweets from museums and archives. During the summer of 2010 The National Archives began a daily Twitter feed that includes summaries and links to Cabinet papers relating to that day in 1940 onwards (currently tweeting 1942 in 2012). The result was a fascinating day-by-day insight into the war from the War Cabinet's point of view, using real documents. At present, Lothian Archives are exploring their nineteenth-century Poor Law records through the eyes of 'Councillor Alexander Smith; Poor Law Inspector for West Calder Parish. I decide upon lives brought to the point of dependence by illness and injury.' The Twitter feed provides a semi-regular update in real time of cases and notes as recorded in the West Calder Poor Law records. The address, if you wish to follow, is @PoorInspector.[28]

Since it was founded in 2004, users on Flickr have added some 4 billion images, mainly photographs. Individuals and archives have posted old photographs and you can search by subject – although how successful this is depends on how the user decides to tag their images. There is much intriguing material here. Archives and museums are increasingly using the site to display some of their treasures. The National Archives, for example, has a page with images from its collections. Other archives are also posting material, including the British Postal Museum and Archives, and Tyne and Wear Archives, who have put up emotive photographs of child criminals taken between 1871 and 1873, as well as photographs showing the construction of the Atlantic liner *Mauretania*.[29]

YouTube has made available millions of video clips online. The range is phenomenal, from the earliest days of cinema (check out the film of people walking on Brighton beach in 1896) to the present day. There are a few videos that people have posted about their family trees or about how to research them, and archivists have made guides about using their record offices, although it has to be said they are a tad dull. In addition, FamilySearch has recently posted a number of videos about researching genealogy which are certainly worth exploring, even if their choice of background music leaves a lot to be desired.[30]

If you want to search on all of the various social media at once the Who's Talkin website allows users to check subjects across various social media, including blogs and individual tweets. Their search and sorting algorithms combine data taken from over sixty of the internet's most popular social-media gateways.[31]

Privacy

With all of these sites be careful what you put up about yourself. Do not post any information about a living relation (particularly without their permission) or a recently deceased family member in case their identity is stolen or misused. In general it is not a good idea to put up anything really revealing about people who died, say, less than 100 years ago.

Blogs

Related to social media, blogs are basically websites which are updated regularly with news and views provided by the individuals who maintains the sites. They can be a form of online diary. It is easy to comment on individual postings, so there can be a dialogue between the poster and the visitor. Many are excellent, a few are very dull, but most are a good way of keeping up to date with what's going on in the family history world and learning about history in general.

Blogs can be divided into those that pass on news – generally recycling news from other sources, but occasionally there can be original news stories, interviews etc. – or those that relate to the blogger's own interests and views, which can be shared with family and friends. They can also be a good way of posting stories about the research you are undertaking and the interesting things you have found. If you like what you read you can often sign up to the RSS feed for the site, where you will be notified of new postings to the blog. Unfortunately, blogs can sometimes be hard to find and fans tend to pass on the ones they like by word of mouth, but over 1,600 blogs are listed at Blogfinder, of which about a hundred cover the British Isles. In a similar vein are Alltop and Blogcatalog, but again the majority of sites listed are American.[32]

To my mind the finest family history news blogs include Dick Eastman's Genealogical Newsletter, which has been around since before blogging was even thought off. It is the most comprehensive news blog of them all, with news from both sides of the Atlantic. The best British equivalent is provided by researcher and writer Chris Paton. His emphasis is on Scotland and Ireland, and he often breaks stories before anybody else. John D. Reid's blog from Ottawa has a lot of very interesting postings on British and Irish records. He is a bit more critical than either Chris Paton or Dick Eastman, which can be refreshing. Both the major data providers have blogs, which include stories about new databases and products, competitions and other ways of interaction with users. Of the two, I think Ancestry's is the better, but there is no reason why you shouldn't visit both regularly. I also have my own blog, History-Man. The content does vary somewhat, but you might find it of interest. A number of archives also have blogs and it has become popular for archivists working on cataloguing projects to maintain a blog where they can feature interesting finds.[33]

In cataloguing the Hicks Beach papers at Gloucestershire Archives, for example, Karen Cooke found among the papers of Jane Martha Hicks Beach a long list of mid-nineteenth century jokes and riddles which might help while away the evenings and amuse the children. Some don't translate too well, given that they're now over 150 years old, but some are still surprisingly funny – or at least groan-inspiring! They include:

What is Majesty deprived of its externals?

Why is a man going to put his father into a sack like a man travelling to a certain great Eastern city?

Pray ladies tell me if you can …
Who is that highly favoured man
Who though he marry many a wife
May yet live single all his life?

Of what colour are the wind and the storm?[34]

There are also many blogs devoted to aspects of history in general, which can make fascinating reading. Audrey Collins is The National Archives' family history expert and she maintains an intriguing Family Recorder blog specialising in the history of vital statistics and the census. To give you an example of what else is available, I also recommend the Property Historian on researching houses and businesses; Joyful

Molly on women at the end of the eighteenth century; Lee Jackson's Cat's Meat Shop about Victorian London; and the Scottish Military Research Group's Scottish Military blog. You can subscribe to receive regular updates or just call by when the mood takes you. Some bloggers like to put up pages from diaries or letters on the day that they occurred. There are a number of such examples, the best known of which probably is Samuel Pepy's diary. Ones I have come across recently are Ruby Thompson's diary of her experiences as an ordinary housewife during the Blitz, Harry Lamin's letters home from the Western Front during the First World War and the missionary George Thomas Howell's adventures in China.[35]

If you want to do your own blogging there are several pieces of software which can help, such as Wordpress and Blogger. The important thing to remember, however, is to have something interesting and original to say, and to regularly update your site, ideally at least weekly. Otherwise nobody will visit it.[36]

Web 2.0

What is unique about the internet is the ability of users to contribute, amend or critique websites (something which is sometimes referred to as 'Web 2.0'). The best-known example is Wikipedia, with 14.6 million registered users who have contributed nearly 4 million articles to the site, which in turn are read by 400 million people every month, making it the sixth most-visited website worldwide. This is the most successful example of the wiki, defined by the *Cambridge Advanced Learners' Dictionary* as a 'website which allows users to add, delete and edit the contents, or the program that makes this possible'. Wikis have been introduced by a wide range of other bodies that have provided wikis which welcome contributions and can be edited by registered users, including The National Archives' Your Archives, the Learn Pages on FamilySearch and the Families in British India Society (FIBIS) with its FIBIwiki. The great advantage is the expectation that users at The National Archives and elsewhere are more knowledgeable about the records than the staff and that they are willing to share their knowledge. In practice, the number willing to do so is quite small and of course the quality of the contributions does vary.[37]

If you are looking to find people who are researching other branches of your tree (and people who aren't) you should sign up to as many of these sites as you think worthwhile. You should also remember that although 60 million family trees may sound a lot, it only covers a fraction of the families (let alone individuals) who ever lived since the arrival of the written record.

There are several, generally American, sites that are trying to harness the power of social networking for genealogical purposes with the slightly scary intention of creating the 'the big single tree of everyone'. One such is Geni, where, with the basic free service, users add and invite their relatives to join their family tree, which

Geni compares to other trees. Matching trees are then merged into the single world family tree, which currently contains nearly 100 million ancestors and living users. The WorldConnect project at RootsWeb is a database of family trees submitted by thousands of family historians. It is the single largest such collection on the internet, with over 580 million names. Submission is easy – all you have to do is create and upload a GEDCOM file. My Heritage is a family oriented social-networking service and genealogy website, which is largely free. It allows members to create their own family websites, share pictures and videos, organise family events, create family trees and search for ancestors.[38]

The British market leader has long been Genes Reunited, which encourages members to work together to build their family tree by posting details of individuals on the website which can be shared with other members. Over 515 million names are listed on the site. The basic site is free – you can create your own family tree and send messages to people with whom you think you share common ancestry – but if you want more you can pay for additional resources and facilities. The major commercial websites also encourage subscribers to create their own family trees and to link into their databases. Ancestry provides a particularly good service and you don't even need to subscribe to use it, although of course they encourage you to do so. The software will even identify which records they have about your ancestors, and which other members have used the same records as you have recently. Findmypast and TheGenealogist also offer similar services based on their databases.[39]

There are other ways to share your historical knowledge. Sites such as Connected Histories and London Lives 1690–1800 encourage users to save and share the results of searches, although it is actually quite a cumbersome process and few people at the time of writing have done so.[40] Some online catalogues also allow you to do this, including The National Archives catalogue and the new Discovery service.

Another initiative, although it is not exactly new, is to encourage users to index records. Most family history societies have run indexing projects – the largest such project involved thousands of volunteers indexing the 1881 census in the late 1980s. However, although some societies are still engaged in indexing projects, the emphasis has largely moved online where there is a huge potential number of volunteers. It is also easier to send out material to be inputted and checked. Ancestry, for example, are getting subscribers to index a number of fairly difficult records through its Ancestry World Archives Project, including railway staff registers, eighteenth-century apprenticeship records and land records. By mid-2011, some 76,000 volunteers had come forward to index 71 million pages. FamilySearch also has a number of similar projects on the go, including parts of the US 1920 census, the 1930 Mexican census and parish registers from Cheshire. Indeed, volunteers here are tackling projects in countries across the world from Bolivia to Ukraine. There are a number of smaller, more specialist projects. In its Living the Poor Life project, The National Archives recently indexed correspondence between nearly two-dozen Poor Law unions across

Old Weather offers an interesting way of indexing records collectively.

England and Wales, with Whitehall using volunteers from local and family history societies. Further projects are under way. One of the most interesting is Old Weather, where volunteers extract data from the navy's ships' logs for the early years of the twentieth century and thus help with research into climate change. The logs contain detailed observations on meteorological conditions taken every few hours. One of the scientists behind it, Clive Wilkinson, explains:

> The Old Weather project isn't about proving or disproving global warming. We need to collect as much historical data as we can over the oceans, because if we wish to understand what the weather will do in the future, then we need to understand what the weather was doing in the past.[41]

Not all archives contain paper, of course. There are also sound, film and television archives which might contain an interview with an ancestor or perhaps show a fleeting shot of them in a crowd. Older readers will remember newsreels, short programmes of news stories, which were shown alongside feature films in the cinema. There might be a dozen stories in a fifteen- or twenty-minute presentation, some covering the news of the day, but many others were light-hearted pieces. Newsreels were first shown in Britain in 1910 and ceased in 1968. They were at their most influential between the arrival of sound in the early 1930s and the mid-1950s, by which time most households had a television. They have been well indexed and, more remarkably, you can view them online.[42]

Many of the stories feature ordinary people. A not untypical story featured the old people of Bradford Abbas in Dorset in a piece of eighty seconds, circulated by

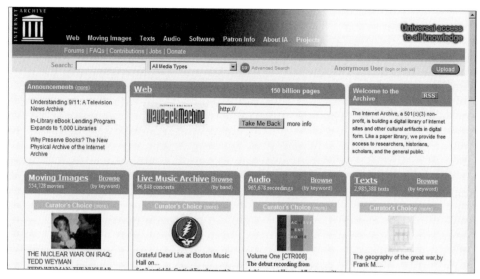

The Internet Archive contains many snapshots of websites which no longer exist, plus much more besides.

Movietone on 4 November 1935. Other items included items about the general election which was then under way, the Italian invasion of Abyssinia, the latest fashions and a soccer match between Aston Villa and Grimsby Town. In the film, Bradford Abbas was called 'the village that never says die' and it featured Mrs Parsons, aged 90, and her daughter, aged 70, leaving the post office after collecting their old-age pensions. Also shown was a group of old friends, George Cheney, aged 89; James Higgins (also 89 'but his beard needs trimming'); Samuel Ring (89); Thomas Coombes (91); and young Sidney Parsons (82), playing up to the camera in the village pub.

There is also a network of national and regional film archives, which are open to the public, although it is essential that you make an appointment in advance. The National Film Archive (NFA), based at Berkhamsted, Hertfordshire, is run by the British Film Institute and has the national collection of films and videos. Unfortunately there isn't an online catalogue to their holdings and if you want to see a film you need to make an appointment.[43]

Another source of moving images is YouTube, which has made available millions of video clips online. Apparently thirty-five hours of new material is added every minute. The range of material is phenomenal, from the earliest days of cinema to the present day, from contemporary film clips to modern researchers' help guides.[44] There is always the chance of finding your ancestor in this footage. My mother's parents were two of the millions of people murdered by the Nazis. Through German records, we know that they were at Theresienstadt (now Terezín) in Czechoslovakia (now the Czech Republic). It was designed to be a model camp which gullible visitors were shown around as proof that the concentration camps were really much like a stay at Butlins; the truth, of course, was very different. In 1943 the Nazis made a propaganda film showing the 'wonderful' conditions to be found at Theresienstadt. Although it was never released commercially, clips are occasionally shown in television programmes about the Holocaust. A few years ago I was watching one such programme when I was sure that I spotted my grandmother – a woman who appeared to look identical to my mother with many of the same mannerisms – working in the kitchens. It is a moment I will never forget. Much of the footage has been placed on YouTube and although I have yet to find any shots of the kitchens, she probably appears in another clip watching a young woman knit.[45]

It is much harder to find television and radio programmes, some of which, like *Nationwide* on television and *Down Your Way* on wireless, made a point of interviewing local people. A few years ago the BBC, who have always dominated broadcasting in Britain, announced plans to put the bulk of their old programmes online, but nothing seems to have been heard of the project for a while. The British Library Sound Archive provides public access to BBC radio programmes, many of which are indexed through the Sound Archive's catalogue.[46]

Oral history interviews can bring alive historical events as well as everyday experiences that otherwise would have been forgotten, which is why they have been used extensively by authors like Max Arthur and Martin Middlebrook in their best-selling books on the two world wars. The Sound Archive also houses Britain's largest collection of oral history recordings, which include some 33,600 oral history recordings, of which around 800 are available online, including interviews with Jewish survivors of the Holocaust, British scientists and the George Ewart Evans collection of interviews with agricultural workers made between 1956 and 1977. There is also the National Life Stories project which was established in 1987 to record first-hand experiences of as wide a cross-section of British people as possible. As a result, recordings form a unique and invaluable record of people's lives in Britain today.[47]

For men and women's experiences of the two world wars and other conflicts of the twentieth century then you may need to turn to the Imperial War Museum's Sound Archive. Details of many of the people whom they have interviewed over the years are available in the museum's online catalogue, which also provides links to a selection of clips you can listen to online. In addition, many record offices have small collections of oral history interviews with local residents, either as part of wider projects or donated by individuals.[48]

Missing Websites

A staggering 250 million websites have been created since the internet went public in 1995. However, websites can die or stagnate, either because the webmaster loses interest or something better comes along. In general it is the small sites, created and maintained by amateurs, which have a short lifespan. While revising a section of my military history on the internet book, which was published in 2007, I recently found that roughly a third of the sites were no longer functioning, including several key sites which contained resources unavailable elsewhere. Plus, many, many others, although still existing, clearly had had no additional data added in the four years since I had previously visited.[49]

It wasn't just the smaller one-person-operated sites that were affected. Take the lottery-funded New Opportunities Fund which spent £55 million setting up 155 websites between 1999 and 2004. The fund had grandiose aims:

> through the digitisation awards by the fund, people in every walk of life in communities across the UK will be able to connect to almost limitless gigabytes of resources ranging from the treasure-store collections of leading museums, galleries and libraries to priceless archives of film and the arts. The funding will help give people access to the full tapestry of UK society past and present … even allowing people to take virtual walks through local and national heritage locations.

However by 2009, twenty-five of these had vanished and a further eighty-three had had no new material added for some time.[50]

Fortunately, if you want to use a website which no longer exists there are various ways to access it. The cache link underneath each description on Google and Bing will take you to the page (generally the site's homepage) as it looked when they last indexed it. In addition, there are several web archives whose intention is to preserve websites, both current and defunct. The largest and best known is the Internet Archive, which preserves snapshots of websites from across the world since about 1998. It is, however, by no means complete, either in the range of websites preserved or the snapshots taken of individual sites. There are also two such archives in Britain. The National Archives preserves websites created by government, both national and local. Meanwhile, the British Library's UK Web Archive covers the rest. Started in 2004, it contains websites that 'publish research, that reflect the diversity of lives, interests and activities throughout the UK, and demonstrate web innovation. This includes "grey literature" sites: those that carry briefings, reports, policy statements, and other ephemeral but significant forms of information.' As well as websites, it includes related items such as podcasts. It is easy to search either by website or by a phrase.[51]

Notes

1 Even so I have to say when I go to record offices I'm always surprised how well used the microfilm and microfiche are, even when the records have long appeared online.
2 Most mailing lists, bulletin board, etc. are listed at www.genuki.org.uk/wg.
3 Take for example the US deluxe membership of Ancestry, which is $155 per annum, roughly equivalent to £100. Membership of the British equivalent is a third more at

£155. If you are in London you can get round this by using the resources for free at TNA and the Society of Genealogists. In addition, many local libraries subscribe to Ancestry.

4 TNA, Annual Report with Resource Accounts 2009–2010 (The Stationery Office, 2010 HC95), pp. 5, 12. The report is online at www.nationalarchives.gov.uk/documents/annualreport0910.pdf. Over the next four years TNA expects that income may double again; see *For the Record For Good: our business plan for 2011–15* (2011) at www.nationalarchives.gov.uk/documents/the-national-archives-business-plan-2011-2015.pdf. Rough figures and a discussion of the market is given in the Office for Fair Trading report 'Anticipated acquisition by Brightsolid Group Limited of Friends Reunited Holdings Limited' (ME/4212/09) at www.oft.gov.uk/shared_oft/mergers_ea02/2009/Brightsolid__FriendsReunited.pdf. See also the Competition Commission report into the acquisition of 18 March 2010, which covered much the same ground, at http://www.competition-commission.org.uk/rep_pub/reports/2010/fulltext/555final_report_excised.pdf. You can get a rough idea of the numbers of unique visitors to these websites (and indeed most others) from Google Trends at http://trends.google.com.

5 Annual Report for 2010 filed on 12 April 2010, p.5, www.sec.gov/Archives/edgar/vprr/11/9999999997-11-008725. The income overwhelmingly came from subscriptions (roughly $282 million out of a total revenue of $301 million). Of this, $41 million came from subscribers in the United Kingdom (p. 39): www.brightsolid.com/news/recent-news/brightsolid-reports-increase-in-turnover-as-growth-continues. No doubt returns filed with Companies House in Edinburgh might be more revealing.

6 www.familysearch.org. Details of local family history centres are available on FamilySearch. British ones are also listed at www.londonfhc.org. Deaths are not included largely for doctrinal reasons. For deaths try the National Burial Index, which is published by the Federation of Family History Societies, parts of which are available on Findmypast or on CD in many libraries and archives. The third edition, published in 2010, is the most comprehensive (see also Chapter 5). Find out more at www.ffhs.org.uk/projects/nbi/nbi-v3.php. As the name suggests, the IGI contains worldwide records, but is particularly strong in North American and British material.

7 I. Grattan-Guinness, 'Boole, George (1815–1864)', *Oxford Dictionary of National Biography* (Oxford University Press, 2004). See also the entry for him on Wikipedia. His wife and five daughters were considerable scientists in their own right.

8 A mind-blowing 34,000 searches per second. For more statistics see http://techliberation.com/2011/05/18/some-metrics-regarding-the-volume-of-online-activity/#_ftn4.

9 The first non-Walker's entry is for the Irish crisp company Tayto, halfway down the second page. See also the delicious column by Craig Brown in the *Daily Mail* www.dailymail.co.uk/debate/article-1236426/CRAIG-BROWN-Crunch-time-cheese-onion-crisps.html. The search was current on 10 May 2011. If you are interested there's a *New York Times* article by Eli Pariser on the dangers of search engines filtering what we read at www.nytimes.com/2011/05/23/opinion/23pariser.html?_r=2&hp.

10 Based on an article at www.bbc.co.uk/webwise/guides/narrowing-search-results. Google's own advice is at www.google.co.uk/support/websearch/bin/answer.py?answer=134479&hl=en-GB.

11 Read more at www.thegreenwichphantom.co.uk/2008/02/nelsons-secret-room/.

12 If you use Boolean operators in foreign-language databases, the operators are likely to be in that language. Searching Google.de, for example, you can use berliner UND luft to find German sites which mention Berlin's unique atmospheric phenomenon.

13 Most of these operators, but not NEAR, are simply explained at http://internettutorials. net/boolean.asp and www.uleth.ca/lib/guides/research/display.asp?PageID=35.

14 I have never understood why Ancestry include a race/nationality box, as this information is almost never recorded in British records. The one exception I have come across is a list of civilian internees in Ruhleben camp during the First World War which indicates which merchant seamen are coloured (TNA MT 9/1094). (Thanks to Sarah Paterson for this snippet.)

15 www.connectedhistories.org.

16 http://discovery.nationalarchives.gov.uk/SearchUI.

17 www.mocavo.co.uk; www.ancestry.co.uk/websearch.

18 This section is based on my article in *Family History Monthly* (193), August 2011.

19 www.slq.qld.gov.au/info/fh/convicts.

20 Very expensive if you use the pre-paid vouchers rather than have a subscription.

21 For further information about these records see Chapter 5.

22 www.theoriginalrecord.com; www.genhound.co.uk.

23 www.military-genealogy.com.

24 www.census.nationalarchives.ie; www.askaboutireland.ie/griffith-valuation/index. xml; www.familysearch.org; www.nationalarchives.ie; www.proni.gov.uk; www. nationalarchives.ie/genealogy/links.html.

25 www.irishorigins.com; www.ancestryireland.com; www.rootsireland.ie; www. findmypast.ie; www.pasthomes.com; http://maps.osi.ie. Curiously, Ancestry does not have a dedicated presence in Ireland. Rachel Hewitt, *Map of a Nation: a Biography of the Ordnance Survey* (Granta, 2010), p. 240.

26 http://en.wikipedia.org/wiki/Godwin's law. A list of other not always entirely serious laws relating to debate online can be found at www.blameitonthevoices.com/2009/10/ internet-rules-and-laws.html. There's also a *New York Times* article on family history and networking at www.nytimes.com/2011/05/19/technology/personaltech/19basics. html?_r=1&scp=5&sq=Social+Networking&st=nyt.

27 For a not entirely serious view of social media and its users, see the videos by Graham Murkett, aka 'Somegreybloke', at www.youtube.com/user/somegreybloke (or at www. somegreybloke.com). If you want to know how to use this technology there's an excellent blog entry at http://blog.helpfultechnology.com/2009/01/how-to-get-started- in-social-media. www.commoncraft.com; www.facebook.com; www.facebook.com/ group.php?gid=134391596605309&ref=search; www.facebook.com/yourfamilyhistory and www.facebook.com/2011CensusFamilyHistory?ref=ts; www.myspace.com. A useful guide to Google+ is at http://googleplusforgenealogists.com. You can sign up for Google+ at https://plus.google.com/up/start/?et=sw&type=st.

28 www.twitter.com; www.genealogyintime.com; http://search.twitter.com; www.twitter. com/ukwarcabinet. (Thanks to Chris Paton for the West Calder tip.)

29 www.flickr.com; www.flickr.com/photos/nationalarchives; www.flickr.com/groups/ archivists/pool/35141800@N08; www.flickr.com/photos/twm_news.

30 www.youtube.com/familysearch.

31 www.whostalkin.com. In addition, there are smaller more specialist sites, such as Friends Reunited (connecting school and work colleagues), LinkedIn (for professionals, though a few family historians, mainly professional researchers, use it) and Mumsnet (for mothers and politicians trying to be human).

32 http://blogfinder.genealogue.com; http://genealogy.alltop.com; www.blogcatalog.com.

33 http://blog.eogn.com; http://scottishancestry.blogspot.com; http://anglo-celtic-connections.blogspot.com; http://blogs.ancestry.com/uk; http://blog.findmypast.co.uk; http://the-historyman.blogspot.com. If you want to comment on this book or point out any inaccuracies this is probably the best way to contact me. Another useful source is the Genealogy in Time website, www.genealogyintime.com, which includes regular updates about new releases of records online.

34 Answers at http://staldwynarchive.blogspot.com. It has to be said that you can see why wireless and then television became so popular so quickly.

35 http://thefamilyrecorder.blogspot.com; http://www.propertyhistorian.com/wp; http://joyfulmolly.wordpress.com; http://catsmeatshop.blogspot.com; http://scottishmilitary.blogspot.com; http://www.pepysdiary.com; http://womanlondonblitz.blogspot.com; http://wwar1.blogspot.com; http://chinainterlude.blogspot.com/.

36 http://wordpress.org; https://www.blogger.com.

37 For a definition of Web 2.0 see www.jisc.ac.uk/whatwedo/topics/web2.aspx. http://en.wikipedia.org/wiki/Wikipedia:About. Adia Edermarian, 'The Saturday interview: Wikipedia's Jimmy Wales', *The Guardian*, 19 February 2011. http://en.wikipedia.org/wiki/Wikipedia:Don't_abbreviate_Wikipedia_as_Wiki. The word *wiki* comes from Hawaiian, meaning quick. Other websites in this paragraph: http://yourarchives.nationalarchives.gov.uk; www.familysearch.org/learn; http://wiki.fibis.org.

38 www.geni.com; http://wc.rootsweb.ancestry.com; www.myheritage.com.

39 www.genesreunited.co.uk. Genes Reunited is owned by Findmypast and has a range of databases that are identical to those on Findmypast. http://trees.ancestry.co.uk. With Findmypast it may be better to post your family tree on Genes Reunited.

40 www.connectedhistories.org; www.londonlives.org.

41 Annabel Reeves, 'Introducing … The World Memory Project', http://blogs.ancestry.com/uk/2011/05/03/introducing%E2%80%A6the-world-memory-project. https://indexing.familysearch.org/newuser/nuhome.jsf?3.7.11; www.nationalarchives.gov.uk/news/483.htm; www.oldweather.org.

42 You can search details of 180,000 stories which were filmed between 1910 and 1983 at http://bufvc.ac.uk/newsonscreen/search. Two of the major makers of newsreels, British Pathé (www.britishpathe.com) and Movietone (www.movietone.com), have made their clips available online free of charge. Both websites are extremely easy to use, and you can search by name as well as by place or topic.

43 Links to UK film archives are at http://bufvc.ac.uk/faf and a catalogue to many of their holdings at http://unionsearch.bfi.org.uk. More about the National Film Archive (NFA) is at www.bfi.org.uk/nationalarchive. Much of their material can also be accessed at the BFI Library in London, and several hundred clips from films are at www.youtube.com/bfifilms, where there is some fascinating material, including films taken during Scott's last expedition to the South Pole. A small selection of the Imperial War Museum's Film Archive of military films is at www.youtube.com/ImperialWarMuseum.

44 http://techliberation.com/2011/05/18/some-metrics-regarding-the-volume-of-online-activity/#_ftn4.

45 Martin Gilbert in *Holocaust Journey: Travelling in Search of the Past* (Phoenix, 1998), p. 85, says that 139,654 men and women and children arrived at Theresienstadt between 1941 and 1945, of whom 33,430 died there, including my grandfather. My grandmother was murdered at Auschwitz. There are two major online databases which list the victims of the *Shoah* (Hebrew for Holocaust). The major source is the Israeli memorial to the

Holocaust Yad Vashem's Central Database of the Victims of the Shoah at
www.yadvashem.org/wps/portal/IY_HON_Welcome. For German victims (including
my grandparents) the German Bundesarchiv maintains a book of remembrance at
www.bundesarchiv.de/gedenkbuch, which can be searched by name and gives date and
place of birth, the camps they were in and date of death.

46 More about the Sound Archive is at www.bl.uk/reshelp/findhelprestype/sound/index.
html.

47 http://sounds.bl.uk.

48 The IWM Sound Archive catalogue (as well as that for film) can be found at www.
iwmcollections.org.uk.

49 Data correlated from Hobbes' Internet Timeline www.zakon.org/robert/internet/
timeline/#Growth. The first and oldest continuously operating website was created as
long ago as 1990 by Tim Berners-Lee at http://info.cern.ch. See also the useful Royal
Pingdom blog at http://royal.pingdom.com/2008/04/04/how-we-got-from-1-to-162-
million-websites-on-the-internet. It is not known what proportion of these sites
is deceased.

50 Full details are at http://web.me.com/xcia0069/nof.html. Thanks to David Thomas for
this information. Sites which have disappeared include Westminster's Ten Generations
(which received nearly £500,000 in grants) and Arts Explorer (£360,000).

51 www.archive.org; www.webarchive.org.uk; definition at www.webarchive.org.uk/ukwa/
info/about.

Chapter 3

PRINTED SOURCES

Some of my favourite sources are printed, partly of course because they are much easier to read. More importantly, they can provide unique insights into your ancestors and how they lived, which cannot be discovered from primary sources or written records. In some cases it is really only possible to find about individuals from these sources, which makes it all the more surprising that they are so little used by family historians. Yet the chances are that somewhere on your family tree there are people who appear here. In particular, they are worth checking if your forebears were in the armed forces, criminals, experienced an unusual death or held any official position, from workhouse master to local politician.

Newspaper court reporting, for example, is likely to provide a better idea of the trial of an ancestor than the official records, which will largely be concerned with the organisation and the result of the trial rather than how it was conducted. Of course, the exact amount of newspaper coverage depends on the crime. The more sensational or intriguing the crime, the more likely the papers were to feature it.

Moreover, the stories may well provide an insight into the lives of ordinary people which otherwise might not appear in the records. In its account of the great Sheffield flood of March 1864, the *Illustrated London News* wrote:

We might cite from the local narratives a great many anecdotes of this kind, which are no less painful and distressing. On the other hand, they record as many wonderful escapes. There were some houses, for instance, in one of which a man named Thomas Wilkinson lived. He 'had been in a flood before,' and when he found the house nearly submerged he got on to the roof. A light cart floated near it, and he got into it and held on by the windows until he was rescued. Whilst in that position he kept up a conversation with the persons in the other house, and advised them to 'hold on' in the garret in which they had sought refuge.

Near these houses the body of a man was found in a tree, and another was jammed between part of a haystack and the side of a cottage. In one of the small cottage houses lived a family named Dean. In one of the upper rooms two little boys were in bed, and they were awakened by feeling the bed floating about. One of them, by pressing against the ceiling, prevented the bed from touching, and so saved himself from being suffocated; but his brother jumped out and was drowned in the chamber.[1]

Until recently these records were difficult to use. You had to know what you were looking for and might have to travel hundreds of miles to find newspapers or directories. Now an increasing proportion of printed sources are online and much more is in the pipeline. Within a few years the majority of British newspapers published before about 1900 will be available in digital form, as well as a good proportion of books published up to the 1930s. There are tangled copyright issues which prevent more recent books and newspapers being republished online, although of course an increasing proportion of new books are also being published in a digital format.

Books

Books are, of course, the printed word encapsulated. Apart from reference books (see below), it is worth looking out for biographies, autobiographies, diaries and memoirs which tell the stories of individuals in their own words. As Professor Asa Briggs noted: 'Diaries, no matter with what centuries they are concerned, are among the most valuable sources for the historian, and of equal value whether or not they were originally intended for eventual publication.' However, it has to be admitted memoirs and diaries can often be surprisingly boring – often it seems that the more interesting the world the writer occupied, the more tedious the book. There are few if any decent memoirs, for example, of the late Victorian and Edwardian music hall and theatre, a period which had a large number of charismatic performers, impresarios and hangers-on. Even so there are many fine books, that bear reading time and again, from Pepys' diaries of the 1660s and the fifteenth-century Paston letters, right up to the diaries of Alan Clark and Chris Mullin offering revealing accounts of politicians on the edge of political power under Margaret Thatcher and Tony Blair.[2]

The best diaries and memoirs are those by men and women with a natural journalistic talent, an eye for the unusual and amusing, and perhaps a feeling that they have written as much for themselves as for the general public. Over the years I have collected a fair number of these books. My favourite is probably Kilvert's diary, which was written by a country clergyman, the Rev. Francis Kilvert, who had ministered to parishes on the Welsh borders and in Wiltshire before his premature death, at the age of 38, in 1879. They were edited and published by the poet William Plomer, who wrote that 'Like most diaries, it was largely trivial and of ephemeral significance, but unlike most diaries it was the work of a writer of character and sensibility'. It is a record of the people he met (particularly young girls for whom he had a particular and slightly unhealthy fascination), the countryside he lived in and the changes which his parishioners were experiencing. 'Why do I keep this voluminous journal?' Kilvert once asked himself. 'Partly because life appears to me such a curious and wonderful thing that it almost seems a pity that even such a humble and uneventful life as mine should pass all together away without some such record as this …'[3]

On 6 February 1871 at Clyro, Radnorshire, he wrote:

> I looked out at dawn. The moon was entangled among light clouds in the North and made a golden maze and network across which the slender poplars swayed and bowed themselves with a solemn and measured movement in the west wind. The afternoon was so beautiful that I waked over to Broad Meadow to see old David Price again. David Price's young good-humoured slatternly wife opened the door to me. The old man was in bed and weaker than when I saw him last. Price said, 'One day a lady was walking on a hill in Flintshire when she met Prince Caradoc who wanted to be rude with her but she spurned him. Whereupon he drew his sword and cut off her head. And a monk coming by at the moment clapped her head on again and she lived fifteen years afterwards.'[4]

The biggest library collections in the British Isles are at the copyright libraries: the British Library, Oxford's Bodleian Library, Cambridge University Library and the national libraries of Scotland, Wales and Ireland, who have the right to demand a copy of all books published in the United Kingdom and the Republic of Ireland. Of these, the British Library, with over 14 million books and nearly a million newspapers and journals, is the largest and most important. They are all open to the public and, with the exceptions of the university libraries in Oxford and Cambridge, welcome family historians.[5]

Of course you will need to abide by the rules. At the Bodleian new users must swear an oath:

> I hereby undertake not to remove from the Library, nor to mark, deface, or injure in any way, any volume, document or other object belonging to it or in its custody; not to bring into the Library, or kindle therein, any fire or flame, and not to smoke in the Library; and I promise to obey all rules of the Library.[6]

Most library catalogues are available online and they are the best way to find out whether they have the book you want. There is an international catalogue, Worldcat, based in the United States, which may tell which books are held where, certainly within the Western world. In Britain, the British Library's integrated catalogue

Inside one the British Library's reading rooms at St Pancras. (*British Library*)

lists all but the most recent of the books accessioned by the library. You can also search all of the British Library's other catalogues from the homepage of its website. Unfortunately, the website was relaunched a couple of years ago and is now markedly less useful than it was before, so it can be an exhausting process to find what you want. If you just want to check a reference or roughly see what is available on a particular topic, then Amazon is probably the best place to go. It is certainly far easier to use than any library catalogue and should list all books published in the UK over the last decade or so. All you have to do is to resist buying anything![7]

If you are looking for a particular book, you shouldn't need to travel. Your local library should be able to get you almost anything through the Inter-Library Loan Service for a few pounds. Alternatively, you might be able to pick up the book second hand. The internet and rising high-street rents have all but destroyed the specialist second-hand bookshops (one of my guilty pleasures). Instead, dealers have retreated online and so it is now easy to buy old books on the internet. I use Abebooks which includes the inventories from hundreds of different booksellers worldwide. It is simple to use and the service is pretty efficient, but it is all very clinical with nothing of the romance of a great book found by chance.[8]

Recently, new innovations in e-reader technology have opened up a new avenue for reading material that once could only be accessed on paper. An ever-greater number of books can be read and downloaded from the internet, either on to your computer or specialist readers like the Kindle and iPad as ebooks. Early evangelists for the internet argued that it would develop into the world's greatest library. In some respects this has happened, though free material tends to be before 1937 due to copyright reasons. To a certain extent, Google led the way with their online Google Book service, the aim of which was to digitise all of the books in the great libraries of the world. Although the company has been somewhat thwarted by copyright issues, Google has still managed to digitise many millions of titles, which are now readable on the Google Books site. For newer books and titles where the copyright is uncertain you may well only find a snippet view. However, the books which you can use include old journals and newspapers, directories and transcriptions of old records or county histories.[9]

The best way to find books is through the Internet Archive, which allows you to search over 2 million digitised books – including those originally scanned by Google, Project Gutenberg and other projects – by keyword and download them in various formats. The quality of reproduction is also excellent, although the indexing can leave something to be desired. As these books have been scanned using OCR (Optical Character Recognition) technology it is easy to search texts for words and phrases within individual books. In addition, Connected Histories has 65,000 nineteenth-century books and many pamphlets from the collections of the British Library which are also worth checking out.[10]

At present it is inevitably a hit or miss process, however. For example, there are many published transcripts of parish registers or vestry minute books, all of which are name-rich sources. The Internet Archive, for instance, has the parish register for Richmond, which was originally published by the Surrey Parish Register Society in 1905 as volume 5 of its series of parish registers for the county. Also available is volume 7, for Addington, but none of the others. Turning to the Royal Navy, there are only odd volumes of the *Navy Lists* for the nineteenth century, although to an extent this is less of a problem because the commercial data providers have the occasional volume on their websites.

Newspapers

Of all the new resources that have become available online in recent years, probably the most remarkable are newspapers. Censuses and parish registers, registers and service records were already well known and in many cases well indexed. Newspapers, with the exception of *The Times*, were really terra incognita for family historians. We knew that there might be stories about our ancestors but the amount of effort required to track them down was disproportionate to the results, largely because they were not indexed. *The Times*, however, had a comprehensive quarterly index known as *Palmer's Index*, after Samuel Palmer, a London bookseller who first compiled it. Originally it indexed the newspaper between 1790 and 1905 in 450 quarterly issues, with 3.7 million references. It was continued up to the mid-1980s and can still sometimes be found in reference libraries.[11]

tion will be given by applying to Mr. W. Fry, Mr. J. Mallard, and Mr. W. Jacks, Assignees, at Bristol: Mr. Isaac Cooke, attorney-at-law, Bristol; and of Messrs. Skinner and Dyke, Aldersgate-street, London. Particulars also may be had at the Place of Sale.

GENTEEL TAVERN and INN,
Within five miles of Town,
To be Sold by Private Contract,
By Messrs. SKINNER and DYKE,
And possession given in the middle of April next,

A VERY OLD and GOOD ACCUSTOM-ED TAVERN, very desirably situate, extremely roomy and convenient, and in compleat repair, and held for a term of 23 years at a very easy rent, near fifteen hundred pounds having been expended within the last ten years in buildings and improvements. The Proprietor is induced to relinquish the business from the recent loss of his wife.

Every Particular may be known by applying at No. 15, Mark-lane; or to Messrs. Skinner and Dyke, Aldersgate-street, any morning before Eleven o'Clock.

CAPITAL QUAY, LOWER THAMES-STREET.
To be Sold by Private Contract,

Advertisements and entries in personal columns are a resource which will become better known once newspapers are available online. This is an advertisement for the sale of a pub which appeared on the front page of the *Morning Post* for 13 March 1798. *(TNA TS 11/5512)*

The first newspapers were published in the seventeenth century, but the early ones have little hard news as we would recognise today, and what there was tended to be lifted from other newspapers. Readership initially was small, and largely from the middle and upper classes. However, the habit caught on and papers would be read aloud in inns and coffee houses or passed from reader to reader. At the beginning of the nineteenth century it was reckoned that sixteen people read each copy of *The Times*.[12] Nevertheless, among the gossip and now almost forgotten innumerable political scandals there is much about ordinary people and the lives they led. Then, as now, there was a huge appetite for the sensational and the unusual.[13] Often enough the names of the individuals are not given or are only alluded to (which suggests to this cynical observer that in some cases, at least, the stories are made up), as in a story that appeared in *The Weekly Journal*, or *The British Gazetteer*, on 17 September 1726:

Ashby de la Zouch, (in Leicestershire) Sept. 5. We had a wedding last week at our church which occason'd no small diversion in these parts, viz. Little John, a pensioner of Blaffarby Parish was married to Little Nan, a pensioner of Ashby Parish; the former was above 90 years of age and the latter near as old, but in stature both together could measure but two yards, i.e. three foot apiece: The Earl of Huntingdon and several persons of distinction in company with his Lordship had the curiosity to view the bridegroom and bride a few days after the nuptials, and were pleased to give them money: 'Tis reckoned a contrivance of some waggish officers of Ashby Parish, to get rid of their female pensioner; for Little John was order'd to carry home his wife to his own parish soon after.[14]

Problems with Newspapers

No source is perfect. For all their unique value, newspapers are frankly some of the least reliable sources you will come across. In part this is because they make many mistakes or assumptions, whether it be spelling names and places wrong, or accusing individuals of crimes or activities they never committed. Years ago I used to help out in the Public Record Office's press office. The press officer was always in a state of despair because the journalists and their subeditors always insisted upon referring to the 'Public Records Office'. Even today they often get the relatively simple name The National Archives wrong or even omit mention of the archives altogether. If you read a daily newspaper the next time there is a story about a new release of records you will see what I mean!

As such, where possible you should try to corroborate stories. With the many online databases this is becoming increasingly easy to do. On 20 November 1701, for example, the London newspaper *The Post Boy* printed the following notice:

Lawrence Corbett, aged about 50, of a little stature, thin faced, of a palish black complection black eyes, and squints a little, who lately lived at Hodgsdon, was about a year and half since tried at the Old Baily for a burglary, and hath been since a prisoner in the Fleet; on Saturday last the 8th instant cheated Mr. Wil. Warham, a goldsmith, at the Golden Cup in Sheer-Lane near Temple Bar, of one dozen of silver spoons, weighing 23 ounces, 10 penny-wt. which is about 2 ounces a piece, the workman's Mark Da. Whoever discovers the said Lawrence Corbet, so that he is apprehended, or the spoons seiz'd, to the above William Warham, shall have 2 guinea's reward.[15]

Unfortunately, the Old Bailey Proceedings database suggests that Lawrence Corbett was never tried at the court.[16] Does this mean that the newspaper made a mistake or did William Warham supply the wrong information? We will of course never know.

Newspapers also have an irritating habit of not following up stories, either because there isn't room or perhaps the conclusion might actually be several years later and the editorial staff had forgotten the original story, so you may never find out what happened in the end.

Lastly, newspapers pander to their readers and reflect their prejudices. Particularly during the Victorian period the readership was likely to be middle class (or have middle-class pretensions) and be fairly conservative, which means that many articles have a veneer of sentimentality and assume that the working classes, the Irish and negroes were childlike at best and feckless at worst. This doesn't matter if one is only reading a few articles, but it needs to be taken into consideration if you are planning to use newspapers a lot in your studies.

The national collection of newspapers is held by the British Newspaper Library, which is part of the British Library. It has copies of almost every newspaper published in the British Isles, together with most magazines and journals. There are examples of 52,000 titles from mass-circulation titles such as *The Times* and *Daily Mirror* to *Athletic and Cycling Truth*, which was published in Birmingham between January and June 1898, and the *Blackburn Mercury and North Lancashire Advertiser*, for which only a few copies survive between May and August 1845. Originally based at Colindale in north London, the Newspaper Library is moving to the British Library's outstation at Boston Spa near Leeds during 2013. A catalogue showing what exactly the British Library holds is on the website.[17] At the time of writing, the timetable for the move to Leeds is not known, but no doubt information will be available nearer the time through the appropriate websites.

Copies of local newspapers can also often be found at local record offices or at central libraries. Very few are yet online nor are there many indexes to their contents. This is a huge problem because newspapers contain so much information in every issue that it is next to impossible to find the story you want, with news items, editorial comment, financial and sports pages, and letters, together with pages of small advertisements for sales, theatre shows and lost dogs. They are almost always produced on microfilm, which can be quite tiring to use. However, this is changing thanks to the British Library, who are engaged in a massive project to digitise and make its newspapers available online. A selection is already available at http://newspapers. bl.uk/blcs. At present the site contains examples of some fifty digitised newspapers and magazines published between 1800 and 1899, including many local papers.

Newspapers showed how influential they could be during the Jack the Ripper case in 1888, which was followed by readers around the world in graphic detail. This gory page comes from the *Illustrated Police Gazette* of 27 October 1888. (*British Library*)

This is nothing compared to what is planned for the next decade. In May 2010, BrightSolid (owners of Findmypast) signed an agreement with the British Library to digitise 40 million newspaper pages and put them online over the next ten years. By 2013 some 4 million pages will be uploaded at www.britishnewspaperarchive. co.uk, roughly double the number already available. Initially the plan is to focus on newspapers published before 1900 and will include titles from Birmingham, Derby, Manchester, Nottingham, Norwich, Leeds and York, along with local titles from London boroughs. Another source will be county newspapers, which provide an unrivalled picture of provincial life spanning the whole of the nineteenth century and supplementing resources already available online such as the UK census.

Along with out-of-copyright material from the newspaper archive, BrightSolid and the British Library also intend digitise a range of material in copyright (roughly everything since 1900), with the agreement of the relevant rights holders. This copyrighted material will be made available via the online resource, providing fuller coverage for users and a much-needed revenue stream for the newspaper companies co-operating with the project.[18]

Even the 2 million or so pages available through the British Newspapers 1800–1900 collection and the 1 million pages of the related seventeenth- and eighteenth-century Burney collection newspapers has revolutionised family history. Realistically, for the first time it is possible to use these papers to complement other records and so build up a rounder portrait of our forebears, with information that would not be possible to obtain elsewhere. For example, stories about four of my Paul Belcher ancestors appear in half a dozen different newspapers. Only once, however, could it be said that they stepped into the limelight. In May 1854, as Rev. Paul Belcher was announcing the banns for an unfortunately unnamed couple at Heather parish church, the father of the bride objected: 'I forbid the banns in this church and everywhere else becos hers too young and hers robbed me.' This story was picked up first by the *Derby Mercury* and then by other papers across the country. Indeed, this is a problem with the site; there is a lot of repetition as newspapers constantly use and reuse stories which originally appeared elsewhere.

If you are lucky, your local library may be a subscriber so you can use it at home for free (see box opposite). Free access is also available at The National Archives and of course at the British Library. Otherwise you have to pay for access. At the time of writing it costs £6.99 for a day's access or £9.99 for seven days. It is easy to search by name or place. You can do a preliminary search for free which will produce short extracts that contain just enough information to confirm whether the story is about your ancestor or not.

The Americans seem to appreciate the genealogical value of old newspapers rather more than the British, particularly as many Americans of all backgrounds have their obituaries published in local newspapers. This tradition is much rarer on this side of the Atlantic. As a result there are a number of US specialist sites which are indexing large numbers of newspapers, including on occasion English or Scottish ones. One such commercial site is at http://newspaperarchive.com, which has a range of unusual newspapers and journals to try out. For obituaries there are number of sites available but www.footnote.com is one of the best. Ancestry too have scanned in a number of early newspapers, including a number of issues of the *Edinburgh Evening Courant* and *The Times* before 1833, but their holdings are far from complete. They also have an obituary index at www.ancestry.com/search/obit/?uk&dbid=8960. If you have a worldwide subscription you can search their collections of obituaries in the US and elsewhere.

Other Newspapers Online

The full searchable archives of several national papers are also available online. Generally you pay for a day's or week's access to all of the newspaper's archives:

- http://archive.guardian.co.uk – [Manchester] *Guardian* (and *Observer*)
- http://archive.timesonline.co.uk – *The Times* (and *Sunday Times*)
- www.ukpressonline.co.uk – *Daily Mirror/Daily Express*
- http://archive.scotsman.com – *Scotsman*
- www.irishtimes.com/search/archive.html – *Irish Times*

You might think that your ancestors would never appear in a national newspaper, but until well after the Second World War they included lots of local stories, such as announcements of births, marriages and deaths or court appearances. So if your people came from Manchester and the north-west it is well worth checking the (Manchester) *Guardian*; for London and the Home Counties look at *The Times*; and in Edinburgh and the Lothians, the *Scotsman*. The indexes are easy to use and are free.

It is also worth looking out for *The Times* digital archive, which is a rather more primitive version of the current *Times* online archive, although it includes exactly the same material. A number of local libraries subscribe to the archive.

Magazines

The late nineteenth century saw the rise of popular magazines meeting the demand from an increasingly well-educated population. The first and one of the most important was the *Gentleman's Magazine*, which was first published in 1731 containing a heady mix of news, bad poetry and essays on local history and antiquities. It includes many obituaries, and details of baptisms and marriages which were likely to interest its middle-class readership. Most of the important stories of the day are reported, yet often they are only mentioned in passing. The issue for August 1776, for example, reprints the American Declaration of Independence, perhaps the most important single document of the eighteenth century. Yet, it is included next to an article about 'Prince Ivan Alexis Knoutschoffschlerwitz', a 'Russian newly arrived in London' who offered 'his services to the ladies in the important business of their hairdressing' and provided a cure for baldness for gentlemen who 'cannot submit to the gothic taste of covering their pates with wigs'.[19]

Also of use may be company magazines and journals, which were published for staff of a particular firm or factory. They often contain items about promotions, marriages, retirements and obituaries of colleagues and former colleagues. Railway staff magazines are particularly useful, because they supplement the rather meagre staff records. There are likely, for example, to be articles about the retirement of individual railwaymen, their promotion or transfer to other stations, and perhaps about their hobbies and outside interests. They begin in the 1880s with the arrival of mass literacy and cheap printing and are still produced today. Railwaymen's families may also be mentioned. In December 1915, at the height of the First World War, Mary and Nellie Dale, daughters of the stationmaster at Pilmoor, wrote to the *North Eastern Railway Magazine*: 'We have collected over £12 for

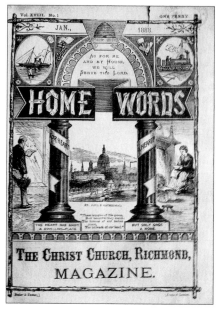

Parish magazines are another underused source. They contain details of all baptisms, marriages and funerals with news about local church activities. (*Richmond Local Studies Library*)

the British Red Cross Society North Riding Branch Guisborough and with the assistance of our parents are trying to arrange a jumble sale for January next.' Among the items to be sold was a fragment of a German shell which fell in Hartlepool.[20]

If you have ancestors who served in the army from about the 1890s to the 1960s then it is worth tracking down the regimental magazine – the regimental museum should have copies and there may be runs at the National Army and Imperial War museums in London. They may be doubly useful if you are unable to find a service record for your forebear. They record the arrival and departure of soldiers, promotions, awards for shooting, as well giving an insight into life in barracks or overseas. *The Snapper* was the regimental magazine for the East Yorkshire Regiment. The issue for April 1911 includes a report from an officer at their base at Fyzabad near Lucknow: 'The hot weather which only seems to have left us a few weeks ago, is again upon us, and early hours punkhas, mosquitos, brain-fever birds and sleepless nights, make us yearn for cooler climes.' Several soldiers were awarded the Second Class Certificate in Education, including Privates M. Sutton, C. Sherwood, H. Harrison and W. Salmon. There are also plenty of advertisements catering for the leisure activity of most soldiers. E. Dyer & Co. of Lucknow 'can guarantee a perfectly pure and wholesome beer … under the most careful supervision of English trained brewers'.[21]

Very few family historians seem to know about parish or church magazines. This is a pity as they contain details of baptisms, marriages and funerals at the church. In addition, the magazines often provide background about ancestors' lives within the church and often everyday life in local communities. The first copies were published in the 1850s and 1860s. Initially they were an evangelical initiative in order to keep the Church in touch with communicants and perhaps the wider public as well. The editorial in the first issue of the *Richmond Parish Magazine* said that its intention was to meet the 'great want of information about church and parish matters amongst us, and especially among the less educated people'. By the end of the century most Anglican parishes had a magazine. Often they came as an insert within a centrally published magazine, such as *Home Words for Heart and Hearth* or *The Evangelist Monthly*. Non-Conformist, Roman Catholics and Jewish communities also produced similar magazines.[22]

Inevitably their contents vary depending on the enthusiasm of the editor, usually either incumbent or a volunteer from the parish, and the time available to them. At the very minimum you should find details of forthcoming church services and lists of baptisms, marriages and funerals conducted in the previous month. There should also be notices of forthcoming social events, such as summer fetes, church suppers and magic lantern shows for children. Most issues will include an editorial from the parish priest often reflecting on local or national issues. There may be reports on local events and the activities of affiliate societies, annual accounts provided by the churchwardens or clubs and societies, details of appeals, and the activities of parishioners perhaps away on missionary work in Africa. Mention might also be made of children who had been awarded prizes for scripture at Sunday school. In 1884, Appleby Magna's magazine said that the following 'Girls and Infants' had won prizes: 'Fanny Garratt, Annie Wyatt, Alfred Insley, James Gresley, Aaron Chandler, Harry Garratt, Philip Booton, Nellie Clark.' Sometimes the contents just reflect the interests of the editor. There may be pieces about local history, oddities and even family history. Around the start of the twentieth century Headley's parish magazine included a selection of pedigrees for notable local families. Runs of parish magazines, or indeed just the odd copy, can sometimes be found at local record offices and local studies libraries. Nearly 1,800 collections are listed on the Access to Archives database, but it is likely that there are others which have yet to be included. Otherwise the best bet is to approach the church itself, where there may be bound sets kept with the parish records.[23]

Few magazines are yet online, although some extracts from the *Gentleman's Magazine* between 1731 and 1868 can be found at Ancestry.co.uk and many volumes have also been scanned into Google Books. Odd issues of the *Illustrated London News* are being added to TheGenealogist. The Internet Library of Early Journals has scanned images of six important eighteenth- and nineteenth-century journals and a further six nineteenth-century journals, including the *English Woman's Journal*, are also available in full. A number of other magazines, including the *Illustrated London News*, have been digitised by academic publishers and may be available at university libraries and larger public libraries, such as the London Metropolitan Archives.[24]

Published by Authority

The *London Gazette* is the oldest daily paper in Britain and has been published by the government since November 1665, circulating a wide range of official notices and legal information. There are also Belfast and Edinburgh gazettes. Initially the *Gazette* contained news stories, including accounts of the Great Fire of London, and classified advertising – most famously King Charles II inserted a small advertisement seeking the return of a lost dog:

> Lost in St. Jameses Park Novemb 15 1671 about eight of the Clock at night, a little Spaniel Dog of his Royal Highesses. He will answer to the name Towser. He is Liver Colour'd and white spotted, his Legs speckled with Liver Colour and White, with long Hair, growing upon his hind Leggs, long ears, and his under Lip a little hanging; if any can give notice of him, they shall have five pounds for their pains.[25]

For family historians the *Gazette* is an important source for researching ancestors who became bankrupt as it contains official notices relating to the winding up of companies, payments of creditors etc. Probably more people will be interested in the military side of the *Gazette*, for it prints details of the appointment and promotion of army, navy and RAF officers (including those in the reserves and militia, and imperial forces), as well as employees in HM dockyards, senior civil servants, diplomats and colonial administrators. Information given includes full name, rank (if appropriate) and unit, department or colony and the job title.

The *London Gazette* is also where details of the award of gallantry medals to individuals (such as the Victoria Cross, George Cross, Military Cross or Air Force Cross) are included. Occasionally a citation is given, explaining in general terms how the medal was won. The individual's full name is given, regiment, ship or unit, rank and, where appropriate, regimental number is also given. The citation for Sergeant Harry Hampton of the 2nd King's Liverpool Regiment, who won the Victoria Cross during the Boer War, reads:

> On the 21st August, 1900, at Van Wyk's Vlei, Sergeant Hampton, who was in command of a small party of Mounted Infantry, held an important position for some time against heavy odds, and when compelled to retire saw all his men into safety, and then, although he had himself been wounded in the head, supported Lance Corporal Walsh, who was unable to walk, until the latter was again hit and apparently killed, Sergeant Hampton himself being again wounded a short time after.[26]

The *Gazette* also includes details of men and women honoured in the New Year's and Sovereign's Birthday Honours Lists, often with a brief note about why the award is being made, such as 'for public service' or 'for services to the confectionary industry'.

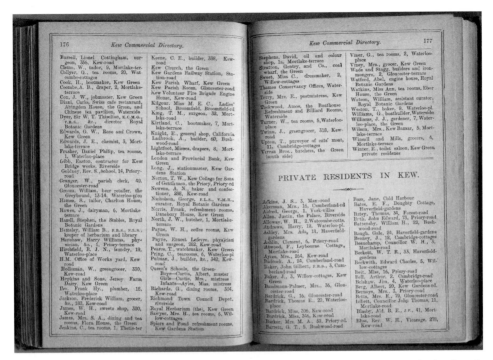

Kew was still just about a separate village in 1901 and so has a separate entry in the local trade directory which was published by the *Richmond and Twickenham Times*. (*Author's collection*)

Lastly, it includes despatches submitted to the government by commanders after battles or campaigns, describing the major events that had taken place. They would usually include the names of those officers and other ranks who the commander particularly thought worthy of mention. Today a 'Mention in Despatches' is still the lower form of gallantry award. On 22 June 1815, an 'extraordinary' issue was rushed out containing the despatch which the Duke of Wellington wrote after victory over Napoleon at the Battle of Waterloo. He lists the officers who were killed or wounded, including the Earl of Uxbridge who, 'after having successfully got through this arduous day, received a wound by almost the last, shot fired, which will I am afraid deprive His Majesty for some considerable time of his services'. [27]

The online *London Gazette* is in theory fully searchable, but the indexing is quite hit and miss, so you may well need to hunt down a set of the originals to double check. Both The National Archives and the British Library should be able to help here. [28]

Directories

Directories provide lists of names of individuals listed by street or by trade. They can be useful in tracing ancestors' movements across town or changes in their occupations, so may supplement census returns or provide clues to a family's fortunes between the censuses. If your ancestor ran a pub, the directory should give you its name and address. This can help in using records of victuallers' licences, which tend to be arranged by the name of the pub rather than the publican. They can be useful in dating photographs, as many Victorian and Edwardian photographers did not stay in business for very long, and as most photographs or small *carte de visites* contain the name and address of the photographer it should be easy to see when a particular studio was in operation. However, as with all records, there are problems. Generally only the (male) householder is given. Paupers and the labouring poor are ignored and often the directory is a year or two out of date.

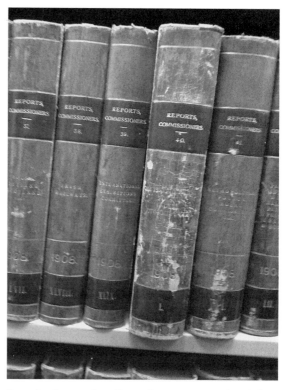

Bound volumes of parliamentary papers on the shelves at the National Library of Scotland. They contain a vast amount of information about Britain and the British from the early eighteenth century. (*National Library of Scotland*)

Trade and court directories begin in the late eighteenth century, but are most useful for the period between about 1850 and 1939. The first nationwide survey was John Wilkes' *The Universal British Directory*, which was published in five volumes between 1790 and 1799. However, it was more practical (and profitable) to prepare directories for individual towns and districts. The first series was undertaken by James Pigot between 1814 and 1853, after which the firm was taken over by Francis Kelly, who had begun by publishing directories of the metropolis. Kelly's became the best-known series of directories, although there were several other national publishers, such as William White. The Post Office also published detailed series of directories for London and other large cities. In addition, there were many smaller publishers of directories and a number of local newspapers also got into the business as well.

There are, in fact, several types of directory, the most important of which is the *General Trade Directory*. It often comprised the following sections: a trade section with the names of persons engaged in each trade; an alphabetical list of people together with their occupations, possibly with a separate list of 'private residents' (that is the professional and upper classes); and a classified alphabetical arrangement of streets, containing the names and occupations of householders. The other major directory was the *Court Directory*, which usually lists prominent residents and tradespeople locally. Again this is often accompanied by a street directory.

Before the entries for each town or village there is normally a descriptive essay, describing the size and population at the last census, local history, the natural history and natural features, industry, half-day closing, market days and postal arrangements. In more detailed local directories there may also be details of political and sporting clubs, local charities and almshouses, and lists of councillors and local officials. This can prove an invaluable insight into how the district was administered and an introduction to the local economy.

The University of Leicester has digitised many directories. They begin in the 1750s, but are most comprehensive for the 1850s, 1890s and 1900s. You can search by location or by decade.[29]

The commercial data providers have also made a number of city and county directories available online. In particular FamilyRelatives has a set of Pigot's trade directories from the 1830s. In addition, Ancestry also offers a complete set of telephone directories from the 1880s, although these aren't much use until the 1960s when for the first time most households began to have a phone.

Google Books has a selection of directories, such as *Gore's Liverpool Directory* (1766) and those by Baines and White. Extracts from street and trade directories relating to pubs and licensed victuallers for places in London and the south-east are at http://deadpubs.co.uk.

Most local studies libraries and record offices will have runs of directories for their own areas. The Guildhall Library in the City of London has a fine collection of trade directories and you can search its catalogue online. There is also a downloadable leaflet about directories and their importance for family and local history at http://tinyurl.com/5nnzs6. The Society of Genealogists also has a nationally important collection of local directories.[30]

In addition, there were and continue to be professional directories, listing all practitioners, the most famous of which is *Crockford's Clerical Directory*. A typical biographical entry for a clergyman, for example, may include where they studied, when they obtained a degree and a work history of where and when they performed their clerical duties. As with many professional directories, those listed may be actively working or have retired, although this is normally indicated. Again the commercial data providers have a small selection of such books; the best collection is offered by Familyrelatives, although TheGenealogist also has a large number of professional directories, and Ancestry and Findmypast have small collections.

The older universities and public schools often publish directories of former students or alumni. You can do a quick search for Cambridge and Oxford alumni before 1900 at Ancestry. Entries may include details of notable accomplishments, occupation, birth date, birth place, other schooling, spouse's name, parents' names, siblings and other miscellaneous information. There's a free alternative for Cambridge, enhanced to include women students, at http://venn.csi.cam.ac.uk/ACAD/intro.html, although it is incomplete and clearly still a work in progress. Familyrelatives has a set of records for Oxford graduates before 1886. In Scotland, details of men and the few women who graduated from the University of Glasgow before 1896 are at www.universitystory.gla.ac.uk/alumni.

Copies of professional and alumni directories can be hard to track down, although the Society of Genealogists has a good selection, particularly for schools and universities. If you are researching a professional man it is worth seeing whether there is a professional body, such as a royal college or institution, for their library or archives are likely to have sets of directories and more besides. However, there may well be a charge for non-members.

Official Publications

Official publications, often called parliamentary papers or occasionally blue books (so called because they originally had blue covers), are hardly ever used for family history, but there is a surprising amount about individuals and more about the world they lived in. These records contain much of the information needed by Parliament to conduct its business. They begin in the mid-eighteenth century. A wide range of official publications are still published today, although they were perhaps at their most informative from the 1840s to the 1890s.

There are several types of record which might be of use, such as reports and papers of royal commissions and other inquiries. These were set up by government to investigate some problem or concern or other. For example, between 1832 and 1908 there were several royal commissions and other inquiries into the condition of the poor. The 1832 commission investigated the mounting concerning over the rising cost of the Poor Law, although the 1905 commission could not agree on how the system established by the first commission could be replaced or humanised. In most cases royal commissions interviewed many witnesses and experts in the field and this evidence is published. On occasion this can be very graphic. In 1842 a royal commission chaired by Lord Shaftesbury investigated the employment of women and children in coal mines. They interviewed a number of women and children, whose evidence still shocks today.

Patience Kershaw, aged 17, told the committee:

My father has been dead about a year; my mother is living and has ten children, five lads and five lasses; the oldest is about thirty, the youngest is four; three lasses go to mill; all the lads are colliers, two getters and three hurriers; one lives at home and does nothing; mother does nought but look after home.[31]

All my sisters have been hurriers, but three went to the mill. Alice went because her legs swelled from hurrying in cold water when she was hot. I never went to day-school; I go to Sunday-school, but I cannot read or write; I go to pit at five o'clock in the morning and come out at five in the evening; I get my breakfast of porridge and milk first; I take my dinner with me, a cake, and eat it as I go; I do not stop or rest any time for the purpose; I get nothing else until I get home, and then have potatoes and meat, not every day meat. I hurry in the clothes I have now got on, trousers and ragged jacket; the bald place upon my head is made by thrusting the corves; my legs have never swelled, but sisters' did when they went to mill; I hurry the corves a mile and more under ground and back; they weigh 300 cwt.; I hurry 11 a-day; I wear a belt and chain at the workings, to get the corves out; the getters that I work for are naked except their caps; they pull off all their clothes; I see them at work when I go up; sometimes they beat me, if I am not quick enough, with their hands; they strike me upon my back; the boys take liberties with me sometimes they pull me about; I am the only girl in the pit; there are about 20 boys and 15 men; all the men are naked; I would rather work in mill than in coal-pit.

Mr S.S. Scriven, the assistant commissioner who interviewed her, said she was 'an ignorant, filthy, ragged, and deplorable-looking object, and such a one as the uncivilized natives of the prairies would be shocked to look upon'.[32]

As well as royal commissions there are many parliamentary select committees which also conducted inquiries and interviewed witnesses. One of the best known of these inquiries examined the scandalous conditions in Andover workhouse in 1846, where the food provided to the inmates was so poor that they were forced to eat the marrow from the bones they were supposed to be crushing. Charles Lewis, one of the paupers in the workhouse, was cross-examined in June 1846 by Thomas Wakely, an MP on the committee:

9841 Have you often seen them eat the marrow? – I have

9842 Did they state why they did it? – I really believe they were very hungry

9843 Did you yourself feel extremely hungry at that time? – I did, but my stomach would not take it

9844 You could not swallow the marrow? – No

9845 Did you see any of the men gnaw the meat from the bones? – Yes

9846 Did they use to steal the bones and hid them away? – Yes

9847 Have you seen them have a scramble and quarrel amongst the bones? – I do not know that I have seen them scramble, but I have seen them hide them

9848 And when a fresh set of bones came in, did they keep a sharp look-out for the best? – Yes

9849 Was that a regular thing? – While I was there.[33]

Other useful records may be annual reports prepared by government departments and agencies. Those produced by the Public Record Office, for example, contain much about the accessioning of records and their cataloguing, as well as statistics about the numbers of readers, documents produced and so on. There are also a huge range of individual returns made to Parliament, normally at the request of an MP on a wide variety of subjects. Often they are for a single year or for a few years, such as returns of 'the number of coroners in each county of England and Wales; and number and dates of contested elections for coroner since 1st January 1800', found in the papers from the session of 1837–38.

It can be hard to track down sets of official publications. Many university libraries will have sets, as should the largest reference libraries. The Parliamentary Archives are also a good place to try. However, almost all of them have been digitised and published in the House of Commons Parliamentary Papers by PROquest. This service is not available online, but can be consulted at The National Archives, the British Library and in other large libraries.

Online Databases for Free

One of the things I have long gone on about is the number of online resources available through your local library to subscribers. I now very rarely borrow books from my local branch, but I do make use of their databases. What is available varies from library service to library service, but they all should subscribe to the *Oxford Dictionary of National Biography*, *Who's Who* and *Who was Who*, all provided as part of a package from the Oxford University Press. The library service in Richmond, where I live, is more generous than most and also includes British Newspapers 1800–1900 and *The Times* Digital Archive, as well as a number of non-history resources varying from help for small businesses to the *Oxford English Dictionary*. Links and more information can be found on council websites: search under libraries, reference services, online reference services or virtual reference services.

If you are an academic or work at a university, college or quasi-academic institution you may have access to the ATHENS service, which provides access to many history databases, including the House of Commons Parliamentary Papers, DocumentsOnline and British Newspapers 1800–1900. Your library should be able to advise on what is available to subscribers.

FROM THE EXPERTS ...

The Statistical Accounts of Scotland

Chris Paton introduces an important background resource for Scottish genealogy:

The Statistical Accounts of Scotland are remarkable documents recording the most intricate details of parish life. On three separate occasions in the last two centuries a national account has been drawn up comprised of entries from each Scottish parish. They record details such as the parish's history and antiquities, the workings of the parochial economy, the names of principal landowners, the religious denominations adhered to, the schools in existence and much, much more. Consulting the records does not just provide a flavour of the place where your family once lived – at times, they may actually help to break the brick wall at which you may well find yourself stuck.

Although there have been three statistical accounts, for family historians the first two have a particular significance, as they pre-date the advent of civil registration in 1855. The original, known as the Old or First Statistical Account, was drawn up under the direction of Sir John Sinclair of Ulbster between 1791 and 1799, with the entry for each parish written by the resident Church of Scotland minister. When published, the first volume or series was not arranged in any particular order, so it starts with Jedburgh in Roxburghshire, Holywood in Dumfriesshire, Portpatrick in Wigtonshire, and so on. The Second Statistical Account was recorded between 1834 and 1845, and was this time collated under the auspices of the Church of Scotland's general assembly. This series was published county by county, with the parishes arranged within each volume in alphabetical order. The third account was produced between 1951 and 1992.

The accounts can help in many ways. The most obvious is to compare the same parish across a gap of roughly fifty years, essentially at the start of the Industrial and Agricultural Revolutions, and then again in the midst of them. In many cases the change within parish life can be dramatic, with the descriptions of key occupations and local traditions changing radically as time progressed. If your ancestor was a handloom weaver in Perth, for example, the first account describes the rapid development of the weaving industry within the burgh from the 1770s onwards. However, when you consult the second account, it then describes the hardship endured by handloom weavers, with their calling all but wiped out by mechanisation and a drop in demand – a classic case of boom and bust. Such records may explain why many families flocked to a particular area at a set point, and perhaps migrated away again a couple of generations later.

More specifically, if you cannot find the baptism of a child before 1855 in the Church of Scotland parish records, an examination of the accounts will describe which other denominations were present at the time, helping you to target additional record sets that you can then try to locate. If your ancestor leased land in a parish, consulting the accounts will also help you to identify the names of the principal landowners, which can help to target the appropriate estate papers, possibly containing rental rolls, tacks and other useful materials.

As well as being available in most major libraries, the first two statistical accounts have also been digitised and made freely available online or, less usefully, at Google Books.[34]

Notes

1   *Illustrated London News*, 19 March 1864. Both articles on the flood in this issue are quoted at http://freepages.genealogy.rootsweb.ancestry.com/~mossvalley/mv2/sheffield-flood. html#ARTICLE2. Details of the compensation paid out to the victims' families and the survivors are at http://www2.shu.ac.uk/sfca (it has not been possible to identify either Thomas Wilkinson or Dean here) with links to several other websites on the flood.

2   Foreword by Asa Briggs to James Munson (ed.), *Echoes of the Great War: the Diary of the Reverend Andrew Clark 1914–1919* (Oxford University Press, 1988). If you don't believe me about the tedium of such biographies, try to struggle through the autobiographies of the great Scottish music hall star Harry Lauder and the writer Jerome K. Jerome. Both contain more than their fair share of unfunny anecdotes, but neither provide insights into the worlds of which they were key members. Modern political memoirs generally obey the same rule. The Pepys diaries are online at www.pepysdiary.com and the Paston letters can be read at http://ota.oucs.ox.ac.uk/headers/1685.xml. There are many print editions of the Pepys diaries, although fewer for the Paston letters. *Alan Clark Diaries* (Weidenfeld & Nicolson, 1993); Chris Mullin, *View from the foothills: the diaries of Chris Mullin* (Prospect, 2009).

3   Mark Bostridge, 'Life on the Wing', *The Guardian*, 19 January 2008, http://www. guardian.co.uk/books/2008/jan/19/fiction6. See also the introduction to the Lutterworth Press edition of the diaries at www.lutterworth.com/product_info. php?cPath=22_32&products_id=1407.

4   William Plomer (ed.), *Kilvert's Diaries* (Jonathan Cape, 1964), pp. 108–9. David Price appears in the 1871 census aged 40, 'a farmer of 128 acres'. His wife Margaret is aged 22. They have two young daughters (TNA RG 9/5510, f31). Two other memorable diaries by clergymen are James Woodforde, *The Diary of a Country Parson* (Oxford University Press, 1978). (Woodforde was rector of a small Norfolk parish in the late eighteenth century.) Andrew Clarke's diaries (publication details given above) reveal how a parish near Chelmsford coped with the strains of the First World War.

5   Figures at www.bl.uk. The British Library was founded in 1753 and was part of the British Museum until 1973. The original reading room, where once Marx, Lenin and many lesser men and women studied, is now part of the Great Court at the museum. The British Library building next to St Pancras was opened in 1998. Family historians may know it as the home of the India Office collections, which is a major resource if your ancestor lived or worked in the Indian sub-continent.

6 Admission details at www.bodley.ox.ac.uk. The oath has had to be taken by every new
    reader since the seventeenth century, although these days you can just sign a declaration
    rather than declaim it aloud. It was originally in Latin but now can be taken in over fifty
    different languages. The phrase about smoking was added fairly recently. The text of the
    oath can be found in the Bodleian Library entry on Wikipedia.

7 www.bl.uk; www.amazon.co.uk.

8 www.abebooks.co.uk; www.connectedhistories.org.

9 Google Books can be found at http://books.google.co.uk.

10 www.archive.org.

11 It can now be downloaded at www.archive.org/details/palmersindextot38unkngoog.

12 By comparison circulation departments today calculate that each newspaper is read
    by three to four people. See the National Readership Survey at www.mediauk.com/
    article/32742/newspaper-circulation-figures.

13 A flavour of the sort of stories and advertisments which appeared in a provincial
    newspaper can be found in extracts from the *Cumberland Chronicle* from the 1770s at
    www.pastpresented.info/cumbria/chronicle1776.htm.

14 Found on Rictor Norton, 'Remarkable Unions', *Early Eighteenth-Century Newspaper
    Reports: a Sourcebook*, http://grubstreet.rictornorton.co.uk/unions.htm. FamilySearch
    suggests that it might be the marriage of John Feltwell and Ann Blake on 4 September
    1726.

15 Found at Rictor Norton, 'Crime and Punishment, 1700–1703', *Early Eighteenth-Century
    Newspaper Reports: a Sourcebook*, http://grubstreet.rictornorton.co.uk/17001703.htm.
    Hodgsdon probably refers to the small Hertfordshire town of Hoddesdon.

16 The Proceedings of the Old Bailey 1673–1913, www.oldbaileyonline.org. On the other
    hand, FamilySearch has details of the baptism of a Laurence Corbet in St Dunstans in the
    East in June 1653. We would also need to check the records of the Fleet prison at TNA.

17 Address to catalogue: http://catalogue.bl.uk/F/?func=file&file_name=find-b&local_
    base=NPL.

18 The previous paragraphs were based on a press release issued by BrightSolid and the
    British Library to be found at www.brightsolid.com/news/recent-news/british-library-
    and-brightsolid-partnership-to-digitise-up-to-40-million-pages-of-historic-newspapers.

19 *Gentleman's Magazine*, August 1776, p. 78. Unfortunately, this volume has yet to appear online.

20 TNA have extensive collections of these magazines and some are online at Ancestry.
    North Eastern Railway Magazine, December 1915 (ZPER 63/5). The March 1916
    edition said the jumble sale had raised £19: 'If you had been present you might have
    mistaken Pilmoor for York station by the crowds of people gathered together' (ZPER
    63/6). Hartlepool had been shelled by three German cruisers on 15 December
    1914, which caused extensive damage. More at www.thisishartlepool.co.uk/history/
    bombardmentofhartlepool.asp.

21 *The Snapper*, April 1911. There are also ships' magazines for the Royal Navy. Look out for
    commissioning books, which were prized memoirs of voyages. Even prisoner-of-war camps
    produced magazines, of which the most famous is *In Ruhleben Camp*, produced in the
    German camp for internees during the First World War: see http://ruhleben.tripod.com.

22 This section is based on my article in *Ancestors Magazine* (66), February 2008. *Richmond
    Parish Magazine*, March 1861, p. 3.

23 Selections of old parish magazines have been published on CD by Yesterday's Names,
    www.yesterdaysnames.co.uk. A few parishes have put old magazines online, including

www.applebymagna.org.uk/appleby_history/in_focus15_victorian_1.htm (extracts from parish magazines from the Leicestershire parish of Appleby Magna, 1882–93); www.bereregis.org/ParishMagazine.htm (Bere Regis, Dorset, 1887–1935); www.sungreen.co.uk/_Bream/StJamesParishMags.htm (Bream St James, Gloucestershire, 1867–2000).

24 http://books.google.com; www.bodley.ox.ac.uk/ilej; www.ncse.ac.uk/index.html.

25 *London Gazette*, 16 November 1671, p. 2. The royal household seems to have had difficulties controlling its pets, for on the same page there is another small advertisement for another dog lost in St James' Park, 'full of blew Spots, with a white Cross on his forehead, and about the bigness of a Tumbler'.

26 *London Gazette*, 18 October 1901, p. 2. He died in 1922 and is buried in Richmond cemetery. The medal is in the King's Liverpool Regimental Museum. I have been unable to find a service record for him.

27 *London Gazette*, 22 June 1815, p. 3 (No 17028). The Earl of Uxbridge lost his leg during the battle. According to his entry in the *Oxford Dictionary of National Biography*: 'As the battle was ending, a grapeshot passed over the neck of Wellington's horse and smashed into Uxbridge's right knee as he rode beside the duke. "By God, sir, I've lost my leg!" he is supposed to have exclaimed. The duke momentarily removes the telescope from his eye, considers the mangled limb, says "By God, sir, so you have!", and resumes his scrutiny of the victorious field. The leg had to be amputated that night and was buried in a Waterloo garden under an elaborately inscribed "tombstone".' The saw which hacked off Uxbridge's leg is on display at the National Army Museum.

28 www.london-gazette.co.uk.

29 www.historicaldirectories.org.

30 www.sog.org.uk.

31 Hurriers carried baskets (corves) of coal from the face of the working to the bottom of the shaft, where they were winched to the surface. It was back-breaking work.

32 Royal Commission on Children's Employment in Mines and Manufactories. First Report (Mines and Collieries), Appendix (1842.XVII.1), p. 71, which is quoted on the Victorian Web: www.victorianweb.org/history/ashley.html. Incidentally, Patience Kershaw is listed in the 1841 census as living at home with her family at Northrowam near Wakefield (TNA HO 107/1303/4, f27).

33 Report from the Select Committee on Andover Union; together with the minutes of evidence, appendix and index (1846.663.II), p. 373.

34 www.edina.ac.uk/stat-acc-scot.

Chapter 4

LEAPING BRICK WALLS

It can happen with even the most well-organised research: suddenly the trail for one of our ancestors goes cold. Irritatingly, the records do not appear to survive; or clearly the clerk has made a mistake; or there are two people with the same name in the same place at about the same time; or the ancestor just disappears into thin air. I hope this chapter may give you some clues about what to do, where to go and some background about why you have encountered your problem at all.

Follow the Clues

Family history has often been likened to a detective story. Like Miss Marple we follow clues, but to find our ancestors not the murderer. Each piece of information, or clue, we find in a document could provide a new lead. The clue may be obvious, such as a place of birth in a census return, or it may be well hidden, such a scribbled note in the margins of a service document. Things to look out for are names, dates and places, as these are the key to building up a picture of our ancestor: who were the witnesses at her wedding (they were probably either family members or friends) and where did it take place; what dates was she at school; when was he discharged? They may not always seem important now, but they may prove to be vital clues at a later stage. On occasion the clue might only become clear when you think about it or when you become a greater expert on the subject. On a soldier's document, for example, there may be a mention of a MiD, but you might only discover that it means Mentioned in Despatches a year or two later.[1]

Clues are vital for three reasons:

- They provide **additional information** about your ancestor, or, almost as important, perhaps confirm what you already knew. For example: that he was in

2nd Battalion Coldstream Guards during the First World War. The information you now have allows you to look at other sources that either you had not come across before or did not seem to be of any use. Now that you are certain he was in the Coldstream Guards, and you know the battalion, you can use the war diaries, which will tell you roughly what he did day by day. It may also allow you to find a service record for him, trace in which war cemetery he lies, or read about what the battalion did in the regimental history.[2]

- They may **disapprove a theory**. You may have been told that your guardsman ancestor was at Salonika during the First World War. In fact, the Orders of Battle will tell you that the battalion was part of the Guards Division which saw extensive service in France and Flanders.[3]

- Conversely, a **missing piece of information** and the reasons for this can also be a clue. In the Sherlock Holmes' short story *The Silver Blaze*, Inspector Gregory and the great consulting detective discuss the case: 'To the curious incident of the dog in the night-time.' 'The dog did nothing in the night-time.' 'That was the curious incident,' remarked Sherlock Holmes.[4] So we need to keep a weather eye open. There's usually a reason why such information is omitted or only hinted at. Why was the eldest son, whom you know to have been alive at his father's death, omitted from the father's will? Often this means that he has already received his inheritance rather than because any falling out in the family. More commonly, why is there no father mentioned on the birth certificate? Here the father of the child is not known to the mother or because, for whatever reason, she will not divulge the name. In this case there may be bastardy orders imposed on the father in quarter or petty sessions records to make him contribute towards the upkeep of his ill-begotten child.[5]

A halfway house is what might be called the tangential clue, where you trace somebody else in the expectation that it will lead you to the person you are really interested in. On occasion, for example, it might be easier to search for a member of the same family with a more unusual name rather than the individual themselves. Clearly there are going to be far fewer entries in the census for Josephine Smith than for her sister Jane Smith. If the indexing is poor you could look for a sibling or a parent in the hope that the person you want is also at the family home on census night.

Clues, of course, can be fickle. In particular, it is all too easy to end up following a false trail if we misinterpret the clue or make assumptions which turn out to be wrong. Two John Jeffords were baptised at the parish church in 1751, which one is our ancestor? Pick the wrong one, based on insufficient information or a hunch, and you could waste hours and money tracing somebody else's ancestor. So before you gallop off on a wild goose chase you need to be certain of your facts. As Sherlock Holmes remarked in *The Study in Scarlet*, 'It is a capital mistake to theorise before you have all the evidence. It biases the judgement.'

Getting Copies

It is a very good idea to get copies of all documents that mention your ancestor, partly because they are nice to have, but more importantly they may contain clues that were originally missed. You can usually download low-resolution copies of documents from the online databases. Most record offices will supply photocopies or digital copies for you, although the charge is often high and it may take weeks to process your order.

However, digital cameras will generally take very good images even in poor light. Most record offices, but certainly not all, permit their use, sometimes for a charge. There may be guidance on the website, but you may have to ask when you arrive. Some, like The National Archives, encourage their use, providing special stands and other equipment. At the time of writing the London Metropolitan Archives charge £3 for a day permit and the Essex Record Office a steep £10. You will probably have to sign a declaration indicating that the pictures you take are for your own use. Additionally, of course, you have to treat original records with even greater care than normal. In particular, do not use flash as the intense light produced is very damaging to documents.

It is also important to treat the evidence before you with some caution. The records can be wrong. The clerks of previous generations were every bit as prone to making mistakes as we are. In my family we are not certain when my great-uncle, Stanley Crozier, was killed during the last weeks of the First World War. There are various dates of death given on the Commonwealth War Graves Commission Debt of Honour Register, Soldiers Died in the Great War database and on various war memorials.[6]

Other more common examples of misinformation are the ages given in entries in the census. You would have thought everybody should have known how old they were, but in a surprisingly large number of cases people gave the wrong ages, mostly because they weren't sure as they did not have to write it down very often. A study of Preston

My Great-Uncle Henry Percy Stanley Crozier, Royal Fusiliers. He served throughout the First World War, but was killed in action a few weeks before the Armistice. (*Adrian Lead*)

in the 1851 and 1861 censuses suggested that nearly half of the people changed their ages between the two censuses, indicating that they were unsure exactly when they were born. In almost all cases there was a discrepancy of just one or two years; in fewer than 4 per cent of cases was the gap wider.[7]

Names too may be wrongly spelt, as is still common today. Indeed, changes in how surnames are spelt is probably the most the most common cause of brick walls. The answer lies largely in checking all the variants you can think of and then some more. Also people did not always use their forenames as their parents intended; for instance, I use my middle name. Or the names could be reversed in the document for some reason (Harold James Wilson not James Harold Wilson) or the person could always have been known as something else. In the Oxfordshire hamlet of Lark Rise, for example, all the labourers had nicknames:

> and answered more readily to 'Bishie' or 'Pumpkin' or 'Boamer'. The origins of many of these names were forgotten, even by the bearers, but a few were traceable to personal peculiarities. 'Cockie' or 'Cockeye' had a slight cast: 'Old Stut' stuttered, while 'Bavour' was so called because when he fancied a snack between meals he would say 'I must just have my mouthful of bavour' using the old name for a snack.[8]

You should also doubt what you've been told. Family stories are notoriously suspect, even if there is often a grain of truth there. More importantly, do not assume. Assumptions can be fatal. Just because the eldest son was always named Paul, it does not mean that your Paul was the eldest son: perhaps the mother-in-law kicked up a fuss and insisted the boy was called Joseph. Alternatively, you may have long believed that they were leading lights in the chapel; but they may not always have been. It is clear that many families changed faith as they prospered or because the chapel was just down the road or because they liked (or disagreed with) the minister.

Another Pair of Sparkling Eyes

If you are stuck it can definitely help to discuss your problem with a friend or family member. They may well spot something glaringly obvious that you have missed, because you were too close to the subject. It happens to me all the time. I was looking for the exact date that a woman called Jane Cakebread was buried in 1898, but I had missed the fact that press reports of her death on Saturday the 2nd said that she was to be buried on the following Thursday, that is the 7th, until a friend read though the newspaper and pointed this out to me.

Eventually the trail will grow cold. Either there are no more records to go through or the effort required is not worth it. Inevitably the further back you go the greater chances this will happen: either the records no longer survive, weren't kept in the first place or the record-keeping was so poor that there is no clue you can follow up. However, for eighteenth- and nineteenth-century ancestors it may be worth tracing another branch and then coming back after a few months. You may have learnt more or, because you are no longer so close to the problem, the solution could be staring you in the face.

Ghosts on the Family Tree

Strange though it may seem, you might well come across an ancestor who apparently doesn't want to be found. There are some men and women who seemingly disappear from history and resolutely fail to appear in the records. These are the people who are always away on census night; their births, marriages and deaths unregistered; and when they die their grave lies unmarked. However, like the fossil remains of dinosaurs or trilobites, you know they must have existed. The eminent family historian Jane Cox says, 'some ancestors just do not want to be found', and she may be right. So in the end you may have to respect their privacy. It is not as if you do not have other people to research.

One such person who clearly meets this is criteria is the Zionist activist and artist Isidore Sydney Donn (1860–98), who is known to history, if he is known at all, for designing what became the Israeli flag. We know he exists from a very detailed death certificate issued at Villefranche in France, where he died, from naturalisation papers at The National Archives and from the occasional news items in the *Jewish Chronicle*, such as:

Mr Isidore S Donn, whose name must now be added to the list of Jewish artists in England, has only been settled in his studio at St. John's Wood during the last nine months; he is, however, represented by several portraits and two nude studies … including one of a little boy in a velvet tunic … whilst a small brownish red chalk head is instinct with life and feeling, and particularly pleasing.

He does not appear in the British censuses and there are no birth or marriage certificates, let alone a will or record of passport being issued. His works of arts have long disappeared. He seems to have been born in Vilna (now Vilnius), possibly of British parents, but no local birth records survive. You see what I mean …?[9]

Often the brick wall can be overcome by learning more about the period and the records which are available. As with most things, the more you learn and the more that you do the easier it becomes. There are lots of ways of finding out more. Books and websites are excellent resources, of course, but there are more sociable ways where you can meet fellow enthusiasts and learn from their experiences.

Most towns and cities have a family history society or perhaps a branch of a county or state one. They all organise monthly meetings with experts in the field, publish journals and often organise indexing or research projects. There are also a number of more specialist societies and groups, such as the Families in British India Society (FIBIS), but there are also societies for ancestors who worked on the railways or had Gypsy heritage or came from Germany or Italy. Most are members of the Federation of Family History Societies and contact details are on the federation's website. In addition, there is the Guild of One-Name Studies (GOONS), which brings together people with an interest in one-name studies and other forms of surname study (such as DNA projects). A one-name study is a project researching facts about a particular surname and all the people who have held it, as opposed to a particular pedigree (the ancestors of one person) or descendancy (the descendants of one person or couple). The guild runs several excellent seminars on aspects of family history and one-name studies each year in various places across England and publishes a useful journal every few months. [10]

In addition, there are two national bodies as well. First is the Society of Genealogists (SoG), which is Britain's most important family history society. At its heart is the library, which is the largest specialist genealogical library outside North America with an unrivalled collection of material relating to family history. In particular, it has the largest collection of copies and transcripts of parish registers to be found anywhere. There are particular strengths in runs of genealogical and local history magazines, publications of local record societies and the histories of schools and colleges. There are also considerable archives mainly consisting of papers deposited by genealogists as a result of their researches. The catalogue is online. Education has long been an important part of the society's work and there are two or three lectures or workshops a week, open to members and non-members alike. This can be on all aspects of family history, including courses for beginners, more specialist training sessions and guidance about using genealogical software. The library is open to non-members for a fee.

Secondly, housed in an exquisite sixteenth-century building in Canterbury can be found the Institute of Heraldic and Genealogical Studies (IHGS). The institute has a small and rather quirky library which is particularly strong in heraldry, with many unique collections of material. However, it is probably better known for the range of well-regarded courses and one-day seminars it runs. Some of the courses are now validated by the University of Strathclyde. The courses are essential for anybody thinking about becoming a professional researcher.

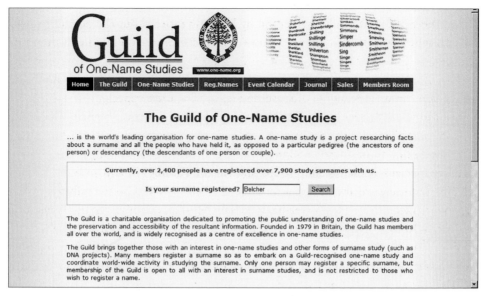

The homepage for the Guild of One-Name Studies. You should join if you are interested in seeing who shared your surname.

In Scotland there is the Scottish Genealogy Society, which has a small library in Edinburgh's Old Town and, in Northern Ireland, the Ulster Historical Foundation, which has premises in central Belfast.[11]

Also of interest may be several quasi-academic societies, which are worth investigating if you are thinking about moving on from family history to related studies like demography and local history. They all run annual conferences and produce both newsletters and journals. These bodies include the British Association for Local History and the Local Population Studies Society, which is for researchers into historical demography. It organises excellent conferences and publishes a quirky newsletter, as well as *Local Population Studies*. Growing out of an Open University course, the Family and Community Historical Research Society involves members engaged in joint-research exercises, for example into allotments and Chartist activities, as well as producing a fearsomely academic journal.[12]

Once upon a time, many adult-education centres provided family history courses. Indeed, I taught a number myself, but fewer and fewer classes now seem to take place. However, it may be worth enquiring whether your local centre still runs them. If they do not there are many alternatives. There are two nationwide self-help associations which organise courses for members: the Workers' Educational Association (WEA) and the University of the Third Age (U3A). They both have hundreds of local groups who organise their own classes using the skills and talents of their members. More formally, a number of universities offer part- or full-time diplomas in family and local history. One of the best courses is run by the University of Strathclyde in Glasgow, but it is worth enquiring whether your local university runs them. There may also be shorter, less formal courses and day schools. Both Oxford and Cambridge University, for example, have departments for continuing education which organise a range of such events.[13]

You can also learn online. One of the most popular ways to do is via podcasts: lectures that you can download and listen to on your MP3 player, smartphone or computer. All of the lectures given at The National Archives are available in this way. Other archives and family history societies may provide a similar service, but if you want something more structured then you should consider an online course. There are several providers but the best is probably Pharos Tutors.[14]

Paying for Research

There are a surprising number of professional researchers who will undertake research for you. Even though I am among their number I am not sure I would always recommend their services, unless you need some records checked at an archive that you cannot visit or you want to use their expertise to overcome a brick wall. If you decide that you need to use a professional researcher, then you must be clear about what you want them to do, in the same way that you would with a plumber or decorator. If you ask for everything about Admiral Lord Nelson, then you would expect to receive a huge amount of information and a correspondingly large bill. However, if you are looking for his lieutenant's passing certificate or a despatch from the Battle of the Nile then the researcher will know exactly what they have to do and will bill you accordingly. If you are not quite sure about what you want, by all means discuss it with the researcher you commission, as it is in both your interests to get this right.

One problem that clients have is knowing how good or thorough the researcher is. Certainly over the years I have heard many complaints from people who have hired researchers whom they subsequently found useless. In some cases I suspect they were not certain about what they really wanted, but sometimes they had clearly been ripped off. I have always believed that professional researchers should be licensed and demonstrate their knowledge of the records and their research skills, with a proper complaints procedure if required. Sadly, in Britain at least, this doesn't exist. As a result anybody can set themselves up as a researcher, often only charging pin money because they enjoy research and not because they actually know anything. If you are looking for a researcher you should employ somebody who is a member of the Association of Genealogists and Researchers in Archives (AGRA). These members are generally the best in their field and have passed a rigorous examination before joining. In Scotland the equivalent is the Association of Scottish Genealogists and Researchers in Archives. Membership requirements are less rigorous in the Association of Professional Genealogists, but it does have members worldwide, with particular strength in North America.[15]

AGRA provides lists of very reliable and experienced professional researchers.

Pitfalls to Avoid

There are several lines of enquiry which if you are wise you should avoid. In particular, many family historians assume that DNA may provide the answers. True, DNA can help with surname research identifying linked branches, but you cannot use it to find exactly where your ancestors came from or the identities of the fathers of bastard children. There are lots of other pitfalls which can trap the unwary and gullible. You especially want to avoid the basic tests, sometimes called 'heritage DNA tests'. All they will tell you is the vaguest of clues about your origins in Africa or the Middle East many thousands of years ago or that you are descended from the original Celtic inhabitants of the British Isles. According to Professor Bryan Sykes at Oxford University, 70 per cent of people in the British Isles are descended in this way. In general the more markers you have checked the more useful the test will be.[16]

The DNA test that most genealogists will end up buying is the Y-chromosome test. The DNA here is passed on from father to son and, as such, can only be taken by men. It mimics the other feature that a father passes to his son: his surname. As a result they are sometimes used by people engaged in one-name studies. Indeed, you will get more out of the science and help others by joining surname studies for your name, if they exist. The message hidden in their DNA reveals that they share a genetic ancestor; the message implied by their shared surname is that that common ancestor lived since the adoption of surnames 700 or so years ago. Put another way, there might be 50,000 men in Britain with the same Y-chromosome DNA result as mine, but the only ones of interest to me when I'm building my family tree are the tiny fraction of that number who share my surname. GENUKI includes an excellent introduction to the whole complex subject by Ian Kennedy, which also profiles a number of British companies that offer tests. Another useful introduction is provided by the International Society of Genetic Genealogy.[17]

If you do decide that this is something you want to follow up there are several American companies which are worth investigating: GeneTree combines a family tree-sharing site with the chance to have your DNA tested. Or as the blurb puts it: 'GeneTree creates opportunities for unlocking human genetic heritage, discovering ancestors, connecting and collaborating with living relatives, and sharing rich media to help discover, document and preserve family histories.' When I tried the site a few years ago I found that I was closely connected genetically to another subscriber in Kansas, who unfortunately did not respond to a request for more information. Probably the most highly regarded of all is Family Tree DNA, in part because it is responsible for over 6,000 surname projects, which is the main reason for doing a Y-chromosome test.[18]

Another method to avoid is past life or historic regression, whereby a therapist is supposed to conjure deeply suppressed memories of people who inherited your body in a past life. Superficially it sounds attractive that as well as your ancestors' DNA coursing round your veins you have some at least of their memories as well. It is all hokum. Years ago I was approached by one of these practitioners who offered to write an article for *Ancestors Magazine*. Being open-minded, I was intrigued. He supplied several case studies of clients' forebears who had been revealed in this way, one of whom was a Lieutenant Robinson who served in the Royal Engineers during the First World War. It was but the work of minutes to check the *Army Lists* to discover that no officer called Robinson was an RE officer at the time. When I pointed this out, the author became strangely silent.[19]

Another genealogical scam, which fortunately seems to have died out, is the book of names. A company, the best known of which was Halberts from Ohio, offered to sell you a book all about your surname. The promotional literature looked very professional and, judging by the copies which were deposited in the Society of Genealogists' archives, a fair number of people were taken in. However, all purchasers received were extracts from the telephone book together with a few paragraphs of boilerplate about the surname in a very cheap binder.[20]

Lastly, and this is more controversial, I have always been suspicious of surname dictionaries and the information they impart. In most cases the definitions are proof that a little knowledge can be a dangerous thing, that they might suggest things which are either untrue, irrelevant or misleading. Michael Wharton satirised these dictionaries in his 'Way of the World' column in the *Daily Telegraph* in 1958: 'The name Musicseller, common in parts of Worcestershire has no connection with music. It is probably of Celtic origin and means "one who removes the eyes of partially gnawed potatoes."'[21]

Undoubtedly it is possible with a few surnames to trace them to a particular district, but in most cases the definition of the surname is meaningless. What good is it to me to know that Fowlers were once catchers of fowl? The name has almost certainly changed a great deal since the first Fowler caught his first fowl. Also, as Fowlers are fairly well spread across the country this logically suggests that when surnames began to be assigned in the early medieval period a fair number of peasants must have been involved in the raising and hunting of ducks, geese and the like.[22]

I am afraid, as with financial products, that the rule is 'if it is too good to be true, then it is too good to be true'. There are few, if any, shortcuts and, like my map reading, you may find that these shortcuts end up taking you the long way around.

Research Concepts

In thinking about problem solving there are also two concepts that you should consider. The first comes from medieval philosophy: the principle of parsimony, which is sometimes known as Occam's Razor after William of Occam, an English-born philosopher of the early fourteenth century. He said that, in essence, the simplest explanation is normally the correct one. In other words, that one should not make more assumptions than are needed. There is also a not dissimilar principle of management: 'Keep it Simple Stupid' – basically, the simpler the structure or the operation the more likely it is to work. It is also a tenet that family historians should follow. Most families lived fairly simple lives, so why make it complicated? So, if you are looking for a solution to a problem, the simplest (and generally most boring) answer is almost always the correct one. Why was he missing from the census? Almost certainly he was not engaged on Her Majesty's Secret Service, but most likely was on contract work making widgets 200 miles away in Wigan or visiting relations and so he is recorded where he was staying.[23]

There's another management principle that you might also want to think about: Pareto's Rule or, more prosaically, the 20:80 rule. This states that a small number of causes are responsible for a large percentage of the effect, in a ratio of about 20:80. So 20 per cent of a person's effort generates 80 per cent of the results. The corollary to this is that 20 per cent of one's results absorb 80 per cent of one's resources or efforts. In family history terms, this means that you shouldn't waste huge amounts of time futilely researching just one ancestor because it becomes increasingly hard to find anything new about them. To an extent, this advice has been superseded by the myriad of online resources where it is easy to do speculative searches. If your ancestor was not present in the 1881 census and you think he might have been a soldier (and his records are not online), you could search the regimental musters. That's nearly 200,000 names in several hundred handwritten registers. It could take you weeks and cost you your eyesight and sanity. You could find him, but then you might not. It probably isn't worth your time or trouble, although I have met plenty of researchers who would relish a challenge of this kind![24]

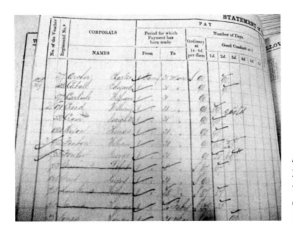

A page from the muster roll for the 2nd Battalion, 2nd Regiment of Foot for 1865. There are usually twenty-five entries for soldiers on each page. (*TNA WO 12/2092*)

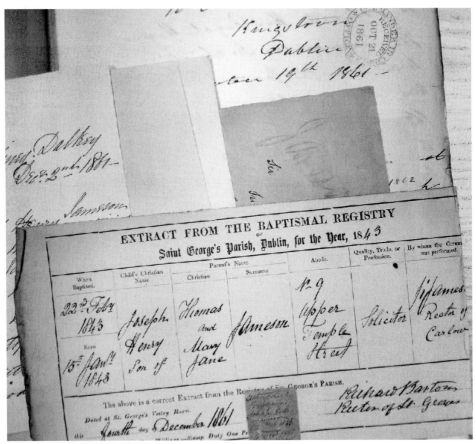

Papers confirm the identity and age of Joseph Henry Jameson, who was buying an ensignry in the British army in 1863. (*TNA WO 31/1320*)

Researching Sideways

One of Britain's best-known family historians, Michael Gandy, talks about the need to trace the family sideways. This may well produce lots of links that might not immediately be clear if you are strictly tracing the blood or direct line. Family members would meet at weddings or at Christmas, or just as likely bump into each other on market day. These kinship networks (to use the technical term) can provide useful clues when seeking our more elusive forebears' origins and perhaps explain otherwise inexplicable acts. A child, for example, might be brought up by an aunt after its parents' death rather than sent to the workhouse or apprenticed to an uncle who was a master fishmonger. Family members crop up in the records as neighbours in the census, witnesses on marriage certificates or on occasion as beneficiaries in wills. This is clearly a more difficult approach but could well solve a number of problems. Even if you don't do this in depth, you need to note down details of your direct ancestor's brothers and sisters when you come across them, as well as their spouses and eventually their children as well.

However, conducting such a study can be hard and time-consuming work, and if your ancestors moved about a lot or had common names then your work might be doubled. Even so, it is important to be aware that your family's history is not just the immediate names on a family tree, but consists of groups of people who are linked by relationships that may go back generations. In some cases there are no immediate family ties, just long-standing friendships.

Sideways research is really a simple form of family reconstruction and its cousin, prosopography. Both techniques can be powerful tools in the hands of demographers and historians, who want to find out how people relate to each either in family groups or, in the case of prosopography, at work or in some other body, such as the residents of a particular street. In the words of W. Newman Brown's 1973 study of Aldenham, Hertfordshire, during the seventeenth and eighteenth centuries, such studies 'present us with the opportunity of considering questions about a world we may recover in part by the use of methodical reconstruction on sufficient scale of materials which for so long have lain unrelated to each other'. A major study using records for Earls Colne in Essex is perhaps an extreme example. It began in the late 1960s when Alan Macfarlane, who later became the project's leader, came across the diary of Ralph Josselin, vicar of Earls Colne from 1640 to 1683, in the Essex Record Office. The many references to fellow villagers made him wonder how much he could find out about them from other records. So he decided to try to gather together everything about the village that might refer to Josselin and his contemporaries. He and his research team were amazed by just how much there was and decided to use this village as an experiment to see whether it was possible to reconstruct a historical community. Much of this information is now online and is well worth exploring.[25]

Wrong Questions

Alternatively, you may be asking the wrong questions of the records. Documents are very impersonal. They are very good at telling you about who owned what and the individual's involvement with the state, local and national, but rarely will they tell you much about family life, personal relationships or why people made the decisions they did. So there may be no way of finding out why Great-Great-Aunt Agatha suddenly upped sticks and left her family. Was it because of a family row, did she become pregnant out of wedlock or was she offered a job 200 miles away? We may never know. Any family letters are likely to have long been destroyed and the incident long forgotten, or still so scandalous that nobody wants to talk about it so there is no oral testament, and the chances of there being other records which might shed light is remote. Remember, though, ultimately there may be nothing you can do: despite looking through a dozen haystacks there may simply be no records of him or her.

Records can perhaps be divided into two types: active and passive. We might say that they are active when they provide evidence that a particular action took place and was recorded, whether it was for legal, business or personal purposes. Many families treasure bibles which record the births, baptisms, marriages and deaths of family members as a link with the past. From July 1837, for example, births, marriages and deaths have had to be registered by law in England and Wales as evidence that the event took place. Plus, it is basic business practice to note down when invoices are issued and paid. Photographs, letters and memoirs are also records of evidence as they confirm a particular event. A family holiday may be recorded in postcards, photographs or even in an autobiography written years after the event. Active records, because they record actions or decisions, are more likely to survive than passive records. Passive records are those used for planning and analysis, where the evidence of a particular action is not required or assumed. Any notes you make while deciding where ancestors should sit on the family tree fall into this category. More seriously, The National Archives have thousands of files planning the D-Day landings in 1944, in which almost every eventuality was accounted for. Afterwards it is often sensible to analyse what went well and what didn't, so that lessons can be learnt for the future. War diaries are kept, for example, so that official historians can examine what each unit did under fire.[26] Also included are working papers, such as drafts of novels or scientific workings.

Occasionally there are overlaps when sets of records fulfil both functions. Account books not only record payments made and received but can be analysed to reveal a company's or a family's financial state of health. RAF squadron records books note each operational flight made by individual aircraft and show which aircrew flew in which plane. Indeed, they are divided into the daily 'Summary of Events' forms (Form 540) and the more analytical 'Detail of Work Carried Out' forms (Form 541). Any research might well involve both types of records. A study of the

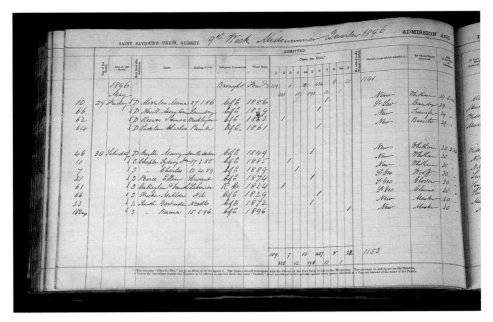

The admission register for Southwark workhouse in 1889, recording the admission of Charles Chaplin and his brother Sidney. The Chaplin brothers would later be sent to the workhouse school at Hanwell in west London. (*London Metropolitan Archives/Ancestry*)

loss of the *Titanic*, for example, could use the blueprints of the ship's construction and the voluminous inquiries into the disaster conducted by the Board of Trade and the US Senate, which are both examples of passive records of planning and analysis. Also under consideration might be the passenger and crew lists and copies of wireless messages, which are active records, showing who was on board, the survivors and those who drowned, and that messages had successfully been sent.[27]

Of course records were created for different reasons than we use them today. Birth, marriage and death registers and certificates are really legal proofs of who we are, to be produced when required; for example, when acquiring a passport. Occasionally one finds examples in nineteenth-century officers' papers at The National Archives as proof that the applicant was over 18. These days, of course, there are lots of alternatives of proving our identities – national insurance numbers, driving licences and utility bills – so certificates have rather fallen out of fashion for the purpose for which they were designed. However, they can still be used to create fraudulent identities, as readers of Frederick Forsyth's novel *Day of the Jackal* will remember.[28]

So we adapt records for our own purposes as best we can. Letters and diaries in particular can offer a valuable insight into the society of the time and how people thought and felt. One of the earliest examples are the Vindolanda Tablets, which shed light on the lives of Roman legionnaires and their families on Hadrian's Wall. Dating from the end of the first century, they were uncovered in 1973 during a dig at the fort. They record official military matters together with personal messages to and from soldiers, their families and slaves. The highlight is probably an invitation to a birthday party. It is the oldest surviving document written in Latin by a woman. Most of the invitation is written by a household slave who clearly was used to writing, with a personal message from Claudia Severa scribbled at the end.[29]

Family historians' interpretations of the records are generally more humdrum. For us, birth and marriage certificates are less about legal proofs and more about proving the most important events in our ancestors' lives, providing other clues in particular about their parents which cannot reliably be obtained elsewhere. If you are researching naval ancestors' Continuous Service Engagement Books, which run between 1853 and the 1920s, provide fairly detailed information about individual naval ratings, showing where they were born with other personal details, ships served, conduct, promotions, medals awarded and when discharged. However, they were created to prove that a man had served long enough to be awarded a pension or had died while in the service so was not awarded a pension, or the rating could be written to show an enhanced or reduced pension on account of their conduct.[30]

Surrogates

If the original records have been lost the chances are that there are other documents that can provide similar, if generally less informative, data. For this reason they are often little known and can be hard to use. Perhaps the best-known surrogate is the Bishop's Transcript, duplicates of parish registers that went to the diocesan authorities annually. They don't always survive, but where they do they can be very useful.[31]

There are a number of alternatives if you can't find a birth, marriage or death certificate, although you do have to know where the event took place and ideally roughly when. There is a network of local registrars whose indexes are generally more accurate than the central ones. They are usually very helpful to enquirers and, as an extra small bonus, buying certificates from them is slightly cheaper than from the central GRO. A number of registrars have deposited older registers at local record offices. Others are putting indexes but not the certificates themselves online, generally through the excellent UKBMD website.[32]

For deaths after about 1840 it might be worth checking Deceased Online, who are slowly putting records of local authority cemeteries and crematoria on to the internet. Coverage is still patchy, but the site is particular strong in London and Scotland. A number of local authorities have published online lists of grave locations in cemeteries under their care. There should be links on the council's website or perhaps through UKBMD.[33]

Parish registers, of course, continue to be kept after the introduction of civil registration, and can be a useful and free alternative. Indeed, they are still kept today. Only registers in current use are likely to be kept by the church, otherwise they should be at the local record office. From the 1860s onwards baptisms, marriages and funerals were listed in parish magazines and more affluent families would publicise such events in newspapers. As such, there is likely to be coverage of weddings and funerals, with guests or mourners and other details such as the messages on memorial wreaths and tributes. Newspapers may also include obituaries, although the custom in Britain is not as prevalent as it is in North America, where most citizens appear to have one, often supplied by the family, attesting to the deceased's saintliness.[34]

It is more difficult to find replacements for the census as so much of what appears is unique. Fortunately very little is missing and there is a good index. If your person wasn't where they should have been, it is worth checking surname variants or seeing whether you can find anybody else who has the same details, such as age or place of birth. Unless they have a common name the chances are that they are the same person, although of course you need to double check. If necessary it might be worth checking further afield: surviving Scottish and Irish censuses are all online and are very similar in format to those for England and Wales.[35]

If your ancestor seems to have disappeared they may have emigrated, so it is worth checking in census records. Even if there is no evidence that they ever left their home town it may be worth a quick look, because at least a third of men, women and children who emigrated eventually returned home – most because of homesickness or because things did not work out. Surprisingly, a reasonable number of people criss-crossed the Atlantic regularly in search of work. The poet W.H. Davies made at least eight such trips on cattle boats in the 1890s, but you could not know this from his entries in the 1891 and 1901 censuses. He also spent time as a migrant worker, before realising (probably in 1897) that:

> I had now been in … America something like five years, working here and there as the inclination seized me, which I must confess was not often. I was certainly getting some enjoyment out of life, but now and then the waste of time appalled me, for I still had a conviction that I was born to a better life … These thoughts haunted all day and that night a great joy came over me; for after my thoughts had tugged and pulled at my heart, all pointing in the one direction, which I saw was towards England … I was up early next morning, had breakfast, and in as happy a mood as I first landed in America, left Chicago for the last time.[36]

The US census has been thoroughly indexed and, except for the parts that are missing, it is all available online at Ancestry or you can order reels at your local family history centre. The first census was in 1790 and the most recent one available is for 1930. The first nationwide Canadian census is for 1851 and then from 1881 to 1911. Both North American censuses are generally more informative than those in the British Isles, including such items as religion and, in the United States, race. An alternative is to look at passenger lists and records of people arriving and departing ports. British passenger lists really only begin in 1890, but a number of other countries insisted that they be kept earlier in the century. The problem is that you have to know roughly where they went and when they went. A very large proportion of emigrants to the US arrived at Ellis Island, off New York City, and records of arrivals between 1892 and 1924 are online, so this is an obvious place to start. If you know the name of the ship then, if you are lucky, Google may come up with a passenger list. An alternative might be Australian and New Zealand newspapers of the period, many of which include lists of passengers newly arrived in the port, and which are increasingly online. The *Otago Witness* for 15 May 1858 records the names of passengers who had arrived in Dunedin on the *Nourmahal* and added that: 'The arrival of the "Strathfieldsaye" and the "Nourmahal" has made a very considerable addition to our population. There are: ploughmen 29, shepherds 6, blacksmiths 4, labourers 72, carpenters 15, butcher 1, saddler 1, domestic servants 64.'[37]

There is also a small chance that for some reason your ancestor was not enumerated or the enumeration does not survive. The Registrar General's reports admitted that a small proportion of people (perhaps 2 per cent) were omitted for some reason or another. Sometimes the householders completing the schedules got the information wrong, omitting a servant or adding a child who wasn't actually there on census night. It took a determined enumerator to go into barns and hedgerows to find tramps who were sleeping rough. For not dissimilar reasons, Gypsies and canal barges also tended to be omitted, and I wonder what response even the most burley and dedicated of enumerators received in the slums and lodging houses of the East End and other rough areas. Of Seven Dials in London in the 1840s and 1850s, one former policeman remembered: 'the half-dozen constables within view would no more have thought of entering it than they would the cage of a cobra.' Immigrant groups, nervous of the state, also avoided the census. In 1911 there was a campaign by the General Register Office among immigrants to persuade them to complete the forms, which were produced in Yiddish, including getting children to encourage their parents to participate through special lessons. In addition, small numbers of enumerators' books have been lost. For 1841, parts of west London are missing, as are small parts of Kent, Essex and Denbighshire. The 1851 returns for Salford and parts of Manchester were severely damaged by water, although painstaking work by the Manchester and Lancashire Family History Society has reconstituted much of the information they contained. The 1861 records for the districts of Belgravia and Woolwich, and 1901 for Deal, no longer survive. No doubt there are other smaller gaps. The commercial data providers should be able to tell you what is missing.[38]

If, by mischance, nothing survives, here are a few last-resort alternatives. The head of household should appear in street and trade directories, but remember they are often a year or two out of date. For the early 1870s it might be worth checking out the Return of Landowners of 1872, which gives owners and occupiers of land more than 1 acre in size. It contains hundreds of thousands of names with both landlords and tenants arranged by county and parish. The Victorians referred to it as being the new Domesday Book, because of the comprehensiveness and the fact that the return was designed to work out who owned the land and how wealthy they were, but it is surprisingly little known about.[39]

More important are the Valuation Office records, although these are only for the 1910s. The 1910 budget introduced several land taxes, including one on the increase in the value of land between its initial valuation and its subsequent sale or transfer, or on the death of the owner. In order to obtain the 'datum line' (the basic valuation from which any increase in value would be calculated), a valuation of land as it was on 30 April 1909 was made. The survey cost more than £2 million, of which barely a fraction was recovered before the act was repealed in 1920. However, these records provide a wealth of information about homes and workplaces in the years immediately before the First World War. The survey's purpose was to value each unit of property – the assessable site value is given at the end of each entry. To provide this, the surveyor needed to inspect the premises and take into account the difference in value between the land alone and the use currently being made of the land – whether built on, cultivated or used for some other purpose such as a recreation ground or a grouse-shooting moor. Although information varies, there is a wealth of detail to be found here, particularly about homes, living conditions and the local environment.

The National Archives has the record maps and field books. The latter recorded the information on each hereditament (property that can be inherited) obtained from the landowners together with visits by the surveyor. The maps provide a visual index to the field book entries. These records are a rich source of information about buildings, land use and patterns of landownership. Information is given about tenure and rents, who paid the rates, land tax, tithes and insurance, and who was responsible for meeting the cost of repairs. Many entries contain a detailed description of the property. This may include when it was built, the construction materials, state of repair, number and use of rooms, whether there was electricity or running water, and sometimes a detailed plan. Gardens, yards, outbuildings, coal sheds, chicken pens, fish ponds and other external features are often described, too. Also worth looking out for are the Valuation Books – at local record offices – which were the first major record of the hereditaments created by the Valuation Office at the start of the survey. They have much of the same information as the field books, but without data from the survey in the field (that, is the descriptions and plans of land and property), and often without the assessable site-value figures. Sometimes the Valuation Books for urban areas contain detailed indexes of street and house names. If you cannot find the record map you require at The National Archives, it may be worth seeing whether the archives has working plans.[40]

In general, if you are looking for service and other records, it is worth remembering that the Georgians and Victorians were inordinately bureaucratic, creating much unnecessary duplication which can be a godsend if the original record no longer survives or your ancestor does not appear in it. The Poor Law authorities in Whitehall, for example, required that already overworked workhouse masters dealt with additional mountains of paperwork, believing that 'clear and accurate accounts must be kept, as well for the protection of the ratepayers and the poor, as of officers themselves'. A committee which investigated the system of workhouse accounts in 1903 found that all the witnesses they interviewed 'expressed the forms of accounts were needlessly elaborate and entailed much useless labour upon workhouse masters'. However, for people researching paupers this means that there are many different sources, so if the workhouse admission and discharge registers are missing, a more than satisfactory alternative are creed registers, which give the religion of the pauper, although do not provide as much information about why an individual was admitted.[41]

The position was much worse with the War Office and the Admiralty, which was not helped by the bizarre way in which the armed forces were administered until well into the nineteenth century. The military historian Richard Holmes called the War Office a 'labyrinth with dark corridors of boards and officials', involving long-forgotten institutions, such as the Board of General Officers, the Clothing Board and the Judge Advocate General. A separate organisation, the Board of Ordnance, supplied armaments for both the army and navy. The organisational shambles was finally and cruelly exposed during the Crimean War.[42]

For genealogists this means there are lots of alternative records for soldiers and sailors. Brief records of officers' services can be gleaned from the published *Army* and *Navy Lists*, which is perhaps just as well, as service records are somewhat patchy, although with army officers it is always worth contacting the regimental museum and archives to see whether they can help. There are also voluminous registers recording the payment of pensions and in the navy, seniority, because here promotion was largely by seniority rather than by merit. For other ranks there are muster rolls, which record payments and deductions to individual soldiers and ratings, together with promotions and demotions. In the army look out for description books which, as the name says, provide physical descriptions and other information about individual privates. They were kept in case privates decided to desert, in which case the physical description would be circulated to the authorities through hue and cry or the *Police Gazette*. In the navy, before service records began to be kept in 1853, there may be pension records and allotment books that record the payments made by sailors to their families at home. For men who served in the army during the First World War, medal index cards provide some information to fill the gaps where the service record is missing. If men died while serving, the Debt of Honour Register and Soldiers Died in the Great War database may provide information about the next of kin and where and when the man enlisted.[43]

Confusion in Indexes

Often indexes in old registers are arranged by initial letter of surname only (or less often by the first two initials), so Fowlers will be mixed up with Fields, Fellowes, Farmers and so on. Your Fowler may be the sixth, tenth or even sixtieth person with that surname, perhaps slotted in between a Fuller and a Fletcher. It is important to go right to the end, because as sure as eggs are eggs, your forebear will be the penultimate entry, and possibly check the index two or three times before you can satisfy yourself that your ancestor is not there.

Notes

1 Not that it would necessarily help very much. Mentions in Despatches are the lowest form of award for gallantry. As the name suggests, individuals deserving of special recognition were traditionally mentioned by name in the despatches prepared by the commander-in-chief after the conclusion of a campaign or war and published in the *London Gazette*. There is no specific medal, although since 1960 those who were so mentioned were entitled to put a silver oak leaf on the row of medal ribbons worn on their uniform. For more see the *Medals Yearbook*, published annually by Token Publishing or Peter Duckers, *British Military Medals: a Guide for Collectors and Family Historians* (Pen & Sword, 2009).

2 In fact, service records of men from the various guards regiments are not with the other First World War service records, but are still with the regimental record office at Wellington Barracks, Birdcage Walk, London, SW1E 6HQ.

3 The Orders of Battle list the whereabouts of each unit on a day-by-day basis. Summaries can sometimes be found online. For the First World War try the excellent Long, Long Trail website at www.1914-1918.net/gdiv.htm.

4 For this and other Holmes extracts quoted in this section see www.bestofsherlock.com/top-10-sherlock-quotes.htm#incident.

5 About 7 per cent of babies were born out of wedlock in the 1840s, declining to 4 per cent by the 1890s at the height of Victorian morality, although there are no figures for shotgun weddings or births suspiciously close to the wedding day. For more about this subject, consult Ruth Paley's wonderfully named booklet, *My Ancestor was a Bastard* (Society of Genealogists, 2008). Also of use is W.E. Tate, *The Parish Chest: a Study of the Records of Parochial Administration in England* (2nd edn, Phillimore, 1983), pp. 214–21 and the entry on illegitimacy in Hey, *Oxford Companion*.

6 No service record or personal papers survive and the date is not given on the Medal Index Card. Plus, there are several actions described in the battalion war diary which could have resulted in his death.

7   Edward Higgs, *Making Sense Revisited*, pp. 84–5.

8   Thompson, *Lark Rise*, p. 54. Most of these nicknames, of course, were never written down and certainly never appeared in any official document.

9   For more about Donn see Melody Arieli-Amsel, *Jewish Lives* (Pen & Sword, 2013). (Thanks to Melody Arieli-Amsel for the tip-off.) The naturalisation papers are in TNA HO 144/339/B12503, *Jewish Chronicle*, 4 April 1894. You can view the death certificate at www.jewishgen.org/viewmate/responselist.asp?key=19413.

10 www.ffhs.org.uk; www.one-name.org. For Scotland see www.safhs.org.uk; Ireland www.censusfinder.com/irish-family-history-society.htm; and the United States www.fgs.org.

11 www.sog.org.uk; www.ihgs.ac.uk; www.scotsgenealogy.com; www.ancestryireland.com. Full details are given in Appendix 2.

12 www.balh.co.uk; www.localpopulationstudies.org; www.fachrs.org.uk.

13 www.wea.org.uk; www.u3a.org.uk; www.strath.ac.uk/genealogy; www.ice.cam.ac.uk/courses; www.conted.ox.ac.uk/courses/dayweekend/index.php.

14 www.nationalarchives.gov.uk/podcasts/default.htm; www.pharostutors.com.

15 www.agra.org.uk; www.asgra.co.uk. In Ireland there is the Association of Professional Genealogists whose website has quite a useful guide to hiring researchers: www.apgi.ie/research.html. www.apgen.org. The UK National Archives also has a list of researchers at www.nationalarchives.gov.uk/records/paid_research.htm.

16 See the Wikipedia article for introduction to Bryan Sykes, http://en.wikipedia.org/wiki/Bryan_Sykes.

17 www.genuki.org.uk/big/bigmisc/DNA.html; www.isogg.org. The best and clearest book is Chris Pomery's *Family History in the Genes* (TNA, 2007) and his website at www.dnaandfamilyhistory.com.

18 www.genetree.com; www.familytreedna.com.

19 The subject is well summed up in a Wikipedia article at http://en.wikipedia.org/wiki/Past_life_regression and a webpage from a practitioner is at www.mikepettigrew.com/afterlife/html/hypnotic_regression.html.

20 Dick Eastman wrote a number of articles about Halberts at http://blog.eogn.com/eastmans_online_genealogy/search.html. See also pages on Cyndi's List about myths and scams, www.cyndislist.com/myths.

21 Reprinted in Michael Wharton, *The Stretchford Chronicles* (Papermac, 1981), p. 28. If you are interested in the subject look out for books by George Redmonds, which are both authoritative and well written. His latest, co-written with David Hey & Turi Hunt, is *Surnames, DNA, and Family History* (Oxford University Press, 2011).

22 One of the pioneers of modern family history, George Pelling, did trace his family back to the village of Pelling in Sussex; see George Pelling, *Beginning your Family History* (7th edn, Federation of Family History Societies, 1998). David Hey cites a number of examples of how surnames can be linked to various places in the Peak District and around Sheffield in his *Family History and Local History in England* (Longman, 1987), pp. 26–45. Surname distribution maps based on the 1881 census and the 1998 phone book are at http://gbnames.publicprofiler.org. The site is fun to play with, although it isn't much use because it is arranged by historically meaningless postal districts rather than by county. However, Philip Dance's Surname Studies website offers a serious approach to the topic at www.surnamestudies.org.uk.

23 Wikipedia has good articles on both Occam's Razor and the KISS principle. Sherlock Holmes, however, would have disagreed. In *The Sign of Four*, Arthur Conan Doyle wrote:

"'You will not apply my precept," [Holmes] said, shaking his head. "How often have I said to you that when you have eliminated the impossible, whatever remains, however improbable, must be the truth?'" If you, in fact, discover that your ancestor was engaged in cloak-and-dagger activities then you should consult Phil Tomaselli, *Tracing Your Secret Service Ancestors* (Pen & Sword, 2009).

24 Vifredo Pareto (1848–1923) was an Italian economist. See the article by Arthur Hafner at www.bsu.edu/libraries/ahafner/awh-th-math-pareto.html. In the case of the muster roll even minor clues, such as discovering where he was at a certain time (perhaps from the birth certificate of one of his children), can really narrow down the search and thus make it realistic.

25 For more about prosopography see the entry in Wikipedia and if you want to take it further there is an introduction from Oxford's Modern History Research Unit at http://prosopography.modhist.ox.ac.uk. W. Newman Brown, 'Wider Reconstruction', *Local Population Studies* (10), 1973, pp. 55–6. *Local Population Studies* contains many articles based on family reconstruction, some of which can be read at www.localpopulationstudies.org.uk. The Earls Colne study is at http://linux02.lib.cam.ac.uk/earlscolne/intro/index.htm.

26 Even to the extent of preparing a resignation letter had the invasion failed. According to the US National Archives, late on the afternoon of 5 June 1944, the Allied Supreme Commander Dwight D. Eisenhower scribbled a note intended for release accepting responsibility for the decision to launch the invasion and taking full blame in the event that the effort to create a beachhead on the Normandy coast failed, www.archives.gov/education/lessons/d-day-message/images/failure-message.gif.

27 The records are at TNA in series AIR 27 and may be added to DocumentsOnline in due course.

28 Mainly series ADM 45 for the navy and WO 31 for the army. In recent years the General Register Office have tightened up procedures, particularly for obtaining death certificates that are less than fifty years old. This was the loophole identified by Frederick Forsyth back in 1971.

29 Wikipedia has a good introduction to the Vindolanda Tablets. Examples from the tablets, with a lot of background information, are online at http://vindolanda.csad.ox.ac.uk.

30 The engagement books are at TNA and online through DocumentsOnline in series ADM 139 and ADM 188.

31 For more about Bishop's Transcripts see Chapter 5.

32 http://ukbmd.org.

33 www.deceasedonline.com.

34 There are various websites, mainly American, with obituaries, most of which are listed at www.cyndislist.com/obituaries.

35 Scottish ones between 1841 and 1911 are at www.scotlandspeople.gov.uk. There is a fee to use them. Only the 1901 and 1911 Irish censuses survive (the others were largely pulped for waste paper or otherwise destroyed during the First World War). They can be consulted, free of charge, at www.census.nationalarchives.ie. Censuses for the Channel Islands and the Isle of Man are included with the English and Welsh censuses, as are some returns of men on naval ships and, in 1911, men serving in the British army overseas together with their families.

36 W.H. Davies, *Autobiography of a Super-Tramp* (Oxford University Press, 1992), pp. 120–1. See also Davies' entry in the *Oxford Dictionary of National Biography*. He seems to have left

for America in 1892 and finally returned to Wales after losing a foot in an accident on his way to the Klondike gold rush in 1899.

37 Canadian censuses can be searched at www.collectionscanada.gc.ca free of charge. No Australian and New Zealand censuses survive. British outward-bound passenger lists are with Findmypast, while Ancestry has those for ships arriving. These records stop in 1960 and are only for ships going to and from ports outside Europe and North Africa. The Ellis Island website is www.ellisisland.org. Irritatingly, you have to register and as a result you may receive endless begging letters. There are lots of other records online that provide lists of passenger manifests and equivalent records, including the Immigrant Ship Transcribers Guild at www.immigrantships.org and especially www.cyndislist.com/ships. My great-great-grandfather John Fowler was the master of the *Nourmahal* immigrant ship which made a number of voyages to Australia and New Zealand in the 1850s and 1860s. Ancestry has a large collection of immigration records to Australia at www. ancestry.com.au. *Otago Witness* quote at http://freepages.genealogy.rootsweb.ancestry. com/~nzbound/nourmahal.htm.

38 The accuracy of the census is discussed by Higgs, *Making Sense*, pp. 117–19. It could be my poor research skills, but personally I have found that in over nearly thirty years of using census records I have been unable to trace about one in ten people of all ages and backgrounds. It would be interesting to hear readers' experiences. Michael Paterson, *Voices from Dickens' London* (David & Charles, 2006), p. 219.

39 For more about directories see Chapter 3. The Return of Landowners was published as a Parliamentary Paper in three parts for England and Wales, Scotland, and Ireland. Both FamilyRelatives and TheGenealogist have put the records online.

40 Valuation Books for the City of London and Westminster (Paddington), however, are in series IR 91 and online at Ancestry. The very complicated system for using these records is described in several TNA in-depth research guides available on the TNA website. See also Geraldine Beech, 'The 20th century Domesday book', *Ancestors Magazine* (30), February 2005.

41 'Report of the Departmental Committee appointed by the President of the Local Government Board to inquire into Workhouse accounts (cd. 1440) 1903.XXVI.567', p. vi. See also Simon Fowler, *Workhouse: the People, the Places, Life Behind Closed Doors* (TNA, 2007), p. 69. Most Poor Law material is at local record offices, although Poor Law records for London are increasingly available online through Ancestry. Findmypast will be putting up records for Manchester by the end of 2012.

42 Richard Holmes, *Redcoat: the British soldier in the age of the horse and musket* (HarperCollins, 2001), pp. 101–3.

43 The records described here are at TNA. They are described in the research guides, which can be downloaded from TNA's website. The best books are probably my *Tracing Your Army Ancestors* (Pen & Sword, 2008) and *Tracing Your Naval Ancestors* (Pen & Sword, 2011). None of the pre-First World War records are yet online, although some indexes to naval pensions and allotment books are available through TNA catalogue. Both Ancestry and DocumentsOnline have the medal index cards. DocumentsOnline also offers all naval service records. Surviving First World War service records for soldiers are with Ancestry (although the indexing is difficult to navigate). The Debt of Honour Register is at www. cwgc.org and both Ancestry and Findmypast have Soldiers Died in the Great War.

Chapter 5

DISTANT ANCESTORS

It is fairly simple to trace most of your lines back 170 years or so, to the beginning of the census and civil registration in the 1830s and 1840s. Without too much effort, it should also be possible to go back a generation or two, certainly to the beginning of the nineteenth century and perhaps even to 1780. However, every year you venture back beyond 1837, the more difficult it becomes. If your ancestors came from the property-owning classes, things will be easier because they are likely to have created records that survive. It is much harder for the majority of us whose forebears were labourers and servants, because less remains in the records about these people. Even so, it should be possible to trace one or two of your lines to the early eighteenth century and perhaps even as far back as the 1660s. The really persistent or lucky could get back to the beginnings of parish records in 1538. It is much, much harder to research medieval records and realistically you can forget the old adage that the family appears in Domesday Book. It is said that, with the exception of the royal family, only two families can with certainty trace their lineage back to an Anglo-Saxon forebear. One of these is the Arden family of Warwickshire, who are traceable back to Aelfwine, the pre-Conquest sheriff of Warwickshire, and his son Turchill. The other is the Berkeley family of Berkeley Castle in Gloucestershire.

The main problem lies in bridging the seventy-year gap between the compilation of Domesday Book in 1085 to the mid-twelfth century, when the main series of public records start with the Pipe Rolls, which include details of the king's income. Dugdale, the seventeenth-century herald who traced the Arden family, was able to take them back to 1086 because he found the records of a lawsuit of 1208 which contained a pedigree.[1]

There are some particular problems in researching your Tudor, Stuart and Georgian ancestors:

1 It can be much harder to identify your ancestors because far fewer forenames were in common use. Most men were called John, Thomas, William, Samuel or, after 1714, George, and women were Ann, Elizabeth, Mary, Sarah or Jane. This means that it is likely that at some stage you will be stumped by two Elizabeth Croziers or John Fowlers being christened at the same time and not knowing which one is your ancestor.

2 Old documents can be difficult to read, particularly if you go back much before 1700. More of a problem is that documents can be written in Latin. This is almost universal before the Reformation, but many documents remained in Latin until 1733, when English finally became the language of the courts. Fortunately, most clerks had little grasp of Latin themselves so the language in documents bears little resemblance to that spoken by Cicero and Julius Caesar, but often follows more familiar English grammatical conventions. Archive staff should be able to help you puzzle your way through simple documents but if you want to know more there are several guides to get you started. There is also a simple guide to reading old handwriting by Ruth Davies in Appendix 1. Even so, you will need perseverance and to build up your skills in reading handwriting.

3 Inevitably records have been lost over the generations. Most parish records have gaps where the registers have long been destroyed, and the survival of other records may also be patchy. Parts of Devon, the whole of Sussex and four Welsh counties, for example, are missing from the returns of hearth tax collected between 1662 and 1666. Occasionally there are ways around the missing records. Duplicate copies of parish registers, known as the bishop's transcripts, were sent to the diocesan record office (see below). The later hearth tax returns, between 1669 and 1674, contain lists of taxpayers who originally appeared in the earlier returns that have long been lost.

4 The recordkeeping varies greatly. In some places immaculate and detailed records were kept, while in others just the bare minimum of information was recorded. If the clerk was lazy or incompetent there is rarely anything that can be done now to rectify the position. In the preface to his transcription of the parish registers for Richmond in Surrey, J. Challenor Smith grumbled about the town's parish clerks, 'who passed on, each generation to the next, a tradition of slovenliness and neglect in regard to their duty. The "method" adopted … would seem to have been to compile the Registers at intervals of many years, from some memoranda and notes as had not been mislaid or lost.' This seems to have been repeated in many parishes.[2]

Record Societies

One of the problems in going back beyond the 1830s is gaining an understanding of what the documents are trying to tell you. If you are lucky some of the work may have been done for you as many records, particularly those before about 1700, have been published by record societies and similar bodies. These societies were formed in the decades before the First World War to publish transcripts of old documents. Most counties have one or more such societies, and despite the arrival of online resources they still continue much as they always did. Most operate from local record offices and publish an annual volume consisting of a transcript of a document or series of documents prefaced by a detailed introductory essay that places the transcribed document in context. The record might be the minutes of a local vestry, a set of overseer's accounts, or early court and taxation records. There are also several national societies, such as the British Record Society, which concentrate on publishing indexes to probate records and hearth tax returns, and the Harleian Society publishes material relating to heraldry, including heraldic visitations (an important genealogical source). A number of family history societies, such as Wiltshire's, have also published a number of indexes to local records. There were also a number of short-lived record societies in the nineteenth century which published mainly medieval and Tudor material thought to be of interest to genealogists. The Royal Historical Society has a list of all such publications on its website, based on information taken from the various volumes of E.L.C. Mullin's *Texts and Calendars*.[3]

A contemporary woodcut of a hearth. Charles II's hearth tax is an important source for family and local historians, although not all of it survives. (*Author's collection*)

Until the 1990s, the Public Record Office published many transcripts and calendars of public records. They include the *Calendars of State Papers*, which summarise official papers produced by the government from the reign of Henry VIII to 1782. The *State Papers* contain information on every facet of early modern government, including social and economic affairs, law and order, religious policy, crown possessions and intelligence gathering, as well as some references to foreign policy. They can also include private and official letters, musters, reports, commissions and instructions, council orders and correspondence, memoranda and draft parliamentary bills. Not all the records included in these calendars are at Kew: the editors hunted far and wide for material. They are a surprisingly good source for genealogy as they include many lists of names, including such things as petitions from merchants or lists of men called to serve in the militia, as well as letters and other material about individuals.[4]

The National Archives has an almost complete set of these publications, and the Society of Genealogists has a pretty good run as well. Most local record offices should have sets for their counties as well as some volumes of the *Calendar of State Papers*. University libraries can also have runs. Some publications are now available online, such as British History Online in particular, which has many volumes. This site is generally free, but there are some volumes for which you have to pay to get access. Many books, chiefly those published before the Second World War, may well have been digitised and should be available through Google Books and the Internet Archive (see Chapter 3).[5]

Snobbery in the Indexes

Although the scholarship of many of these volumes is generally impressive, users of the Victorian and Edwardian editions need to be aware that the texts may well be heavily edited. In particular, lists of names may only include those thought to be from the aristocracy and gentry, or petitions or tax returns may be omitted from calendars as they were thought at the time to be extraneous material.

Births, Marriages and Deaths

Parish Registers

Parish registers are the oldest continuously kept records of genealogical content and are of course still maintained today. Originally they were ordered to be maintained in 1538 by the Lord Chancellor Thomas Cromwell, who thought that they would be a useful means 'for the avoiding of sundry strifes, processes and contentions rising from age, lineal descent, titles of inheritance, legitimation of bastardy, and for knowledge whether any one person is our subject or no'. Fewer than one church in ten has registers going back this far, as in many cases they were lost, while in others the order was ignored. However, most have registers that go back to the early seventeenth century, although there are often gaps, particularly during the Commonwealth period (1649–60), when records were supposed to be kept by a secular official.[6]

Apart from the gaps, entries in seventeenth- and eighteenth-century registers often leave much to be desired. They will give the name of the child baptised (sometimes with its father's name); the names of the bride and bridegroom; and the name of the person being buried. In general, the older the register, the terser the entries. Depending on

A page from the parish register for Richmond, Surrey, which was transcribed and published by the Surrey Parish Register Society. (J. Challenor Smith, The Parish Registers of Richmond, Surrey, p. 73)

the thoroughness or interest of the clergyman or his clerk, additional information may be given, perhaps a note that the individual came from outside the parish, their occupation or whether they were 'base born' (illegitimate). In the registers for Richmond, Surrey, for example, in the baptisms for 28 October 1708 there is an entry for 'Thomas, son of Ino [Jonathan] Griffis of p. St Martins, saddler' next to 'Jane Stevens, dau of Ino'; in marriages for 19 October 1708 'Joseph Greenway of the par of Walton and Mary Hind of the par of Walton'; and on 5 December 1708 'Tho, Eager, baker and Mary Gardiner, both of this parish'. In the burial register for 25 August 1708 there are entries for 'May Buck, dau of Mr Henry Buck' and 'Anne Gravenor a maid from Mrs Jane Wicks'. Very occasionally a waspish comment, generally on a person's morals or religious beliefs, may be found. At Cantley, Yorkshire, the incumbent noted after a baptism on 12 October 1754: 'Mary Daughr of Martha Hazlewood … born above a year after her husband left her.'[7]

The lax way in which marriage registers in particular were kept long caused concern. By the 1730s and 1740s increasing numbers of couples were choosing to marry outside their home parishes, generally because it was easier or more fashionable. There were a number of high-profile cases of under-age heiresses marrying unscrupulous suitors, much to the distress of their parents and high society in general. The position was complicated by the fact that a number of areas claimed to be outside the authority of the Church. The most famous such area was around the Fleet Prison on the western edge of the City of London, known as the Liberty of the Fleet. It claimed exemption from Church authority because the wardenship of the prison was in private hands and only the Crown had visitation rights.

Marriages conducted here were cheap and no questions were asked. Unfrocked clergy and prison chaplains conducted a roaring trade in and around the prison in 'marriage shops'. Joshua Lilley, for instance, advertised that at the Hand and Pen, by the Fleet Ditch, marriages were performed 'by a Gentleman regularly bred at one of our Universities and lawfully ordained'. By the 1740s about 15 per cent of all marriages in England were celebrated in the Fleet and it has been estimated that about a third of marriages in the first half of the eighteenth century were clandestine. Such marriages, conducted secretly without banns or licences, were valid in the eyes of the Church provided the couple were of legal age, gave their consent and there were no impediments. Such marriages need not be performed in a church, provided it was conducted by a clergyman following the service laid down in the *Book of Common Prayer*. At the end of the seventeenth century, the vicar of Tetbury, Gloucestershire, recorded that almost half of his parishioners were married clandestinely or cohabiting and he was having little success in having them marry in his church.[8]

This was stopped by Hardwicke's marriage act of 1753, which introduced official printed registers on 25 March 1754, where each page and entry was numbered to make it obvious if they had been tampered with. As well as the names of the parties being married, the registers included details of witnesses and the clergyman who married them and by what means, that is by banns or by licence. By banns means that the wedding was announced in the church three weeks before the event was due to take place, to give parishioners an opportunity to object if either partner was under age or already married. The diarist James Woodforde often recorded banns in his diaries. On 27 February 1791 he wrote that he had:

> published the Banns for the first time between my Maid Nanny Kaye and William Spragge of Attlebridge … on my return from Church … I told her that I hoped that she might repent not of what she was about to do. She is about 34 and he about 20, with an indifferent character.[9]

In the eighteenth century probably one-third of marriages were conducted by licence, although numbers fell off after the introduction of civil registration and it is now no longer possible to marry in this way. You could choose where to get married and it allowed some degree of privacy because banns were not called. 'Very few,' reported a French visitor in 1697, 'are willing to have their affairs declar'd to all the world in a publick place, when for a guinea they may do it snug.' They are worth pursuing because the paperwork may provide more information than a parish register entry. The records give the name of bride and groom, the name of the church for which the licence was issued and a note of consent by parent or guardian if either party was under age. However, it was not unknown for this to be falsified. Licences were granted by a variety of church authorities: if the bride and groom lived in separate dioceses they had to apply to the Archbishop of Canterbury's vicar general; if they lived in different

A page from a post-1754 marriage register showing the layout and information to be found in these records. (*Author's collection*)

provinces (e.g. York and Canterbury) they had to obtain a faculty office licence. The rules were often ignored, however. Archbishops' licences from 1534 are held at Lambeth Palace Library, with indexes between 1694 and 1850 online at Findmypast. Otherwise, records are likely to be found in diocesan records, which are normally at local record offices, although those for the archdiocese of York are at the Borthwick Institute in York. For example, licences issued by the bishop of London from 1521 are at the London Metropolitan Archives. Access online is patchy, although those for London between 1597 and 1700 are on Ancestry and Findmypast. Later ones will be added to Ancestry in due course. The National Library of Wales holds about 90,000 bonds and affidavits relating to marriages held in Wales between 1616 and 1837 with indexes. Otherwise there may be published indexes. The Society of Genealogists has the best collection.[10]

Hardwicke's Act did not affect births and deaths, which continued to be recorded much as the incumbent or the churchwardens thought appropriate. This changed in 1812 with Rose's Act, named after the MP George Rose who saw it through Parliament. Officially prescribed printed registers now had to be kept, in which details of the parents of those baptised were recorded, together with the father's occupation and often their address. Burial registers also contained more details about the deceased, including their age and residence at time of death. The registers have little changed since then. In addition, they were to be kept in a 'dry well painted iron chest, in some dry and secure place, either at the parsonage or in the church'. This may explain, in part at least, why most registers survive from this period onwards.[11]

If you are very lucky, the parish in which your ancestors lived might have used the much more detailed Dade registers, between the late eighteenth century and 1812. They were named after William Dade, a Yorkshire clergyman. A baptismal entry in these registers included the dates of birth and baptism, the position of a child in the family, the occupation and place or origin of the father and mother, and often details of the child's grandparents. A typical entry might be:

> Rebecca, 1st daughter of Robert Westwood of Saxton, Taylor, son of Thomas Westwood of Kelfield, Husbandman, by Rebecca his wife, son of John Pallister of Stillingfleet, farmer [and] Frances, dau of Isaac Cawthorne of Miclefield, Lab[oure]r, by Elizabeth his wife, daughter of Samuel Goodall of Milford, collier [born] May 30 [bapt] June 5.[12]

Burial entries recorded the age of the deceased, his or her parentage (no matter how old the person was), occupation, cause of death and the name of the husband in the case of a married woman. They were used mainly in parishes in County Durham, Northumberland, parts of Yorkshire and Lancashire, but they can occasionally be found elsewhere.[13]

Perhaps the biggest problem with the parish registers is that they are not complete, even though it was compulsory to get married and be buried in an Anglican church and have your children baptised there. There are various reasons for this. The very poor, particularly in the teeming industrial towns which sprang up towards the end of the eighteenth century, may not have seen the necessity of it. Non-conformists sometimes refused to do so for doctrinal reasons, although most went through an Anglican wedding ceremony because it was the only legal ceremony (from 1752 only Jews and Quakers were exempt). In addition, the clergy had to be paid to conduct ceremonies. In September 1714, the excise officer John Cannon noted in his diary that at his marriage to Susannah Deanne at St Katherine Coleman he had to pay 10s to the minister, 5s to the clerk and 2s 6d to the sexton. This was well over a week's wages for an agricultural labourer. Also, at various times, notably between 1782 and 1794, a stamp duty of 3d was levied on all entries, all of which proved a deterrent to the impoverished.[14]

Parish registers are almost always held by local record offices. The National Library of Wales has most Welsh registers, with copies at the appropriate local record office in the principality. However, The National Archives at Kew has a few registers from chapels at garrisons and naval bases, together with those non-conformist registers which were deposited after the introduction of civil registration in 1837 and in 1857. Matters are somewhat complicated by the existence of numerous parishes, known as peculiars, which were outside the jurisdiction of the local diocese, so their records may not necessarily be where you expect them to be. The best-known examples are Westminster Abbey, which as a royal peculiar is not responsible to the bishop of London, and the parish of Masham in North Yorkshire, which was outside the diocese of York. Full details of peculiars, and the whereabouts of records, are given in Phillimore's *Atlas* and record office staff should be able to tell you about ones locally.[15]

The largest collection of transcripts, indexes and facsimiles is held by the Society of Genealogists. In addition, many years ago they published a multi-volume *National Index to Parish Registers*, which describes each register in some detail. Most volumes of the index are long out of print, but reference libraries and archives should at least have copies for their counties.[16]

With registers from 15,000 or so English and Welsh parishes it can be difficult to find exactly where your ancestors lived. It is a problem which once concerned genealogists, so there are many indexes and other finding aids. However, they are swiftly being superseded by transcripts, indexes and images online. In particular, Ancestry and Findmypast are busy indexing and digitising many large collections of parish records. Ancestry has taken on the massive task of dealing with London, in partnership with the London Metropolitan Archives. In Lancashire, Findmypast are tackling the parish registers of Greater Manchester. Across the Pennines, Ancestry again is putting up west Yorkshire registers. You will need to check their websites to see what is available. In addition, Findmypast has a large collection of indexes compiled by societies and individuals to parish registers.[17]

The biggest index is FamilySearch, provided by the LDS Church, whose members have over the years indexed thousands of parish registers. However, it is no means complete. Certain counties are covered better than others. Also, the quality of the indexing varies, so you should try to see the originals if possible. Lastly, and most importantly, the index only covers baptisms and, to a lesser extent, marriages. For doctrinal reasons very few deaths are recorded here as the LDS Church believes that when your body physically dies your soul survives. For burials, you need to consult the *National Burial Index*. Compiled by the Federation of Family History Societies, the most recent edition has some 14 million entries submitted by member societies. It is particularly good for deaths from 1812, although again coverage is patchy. Many reference libraries and local family history societies have copies on CD. Some entries are also available on Findmypast.

There are also several other indexes which can also be useful on occasion. The largest is *Boyd's Marriage Index*, which was compiled by the eminent genealogist Percival Boyd and a team of volunteers at the Society of Genealogists before the Second World War. It contains over 7 million names, covering about 15 per cent of marriages which were conducted between 1538 and 1837, though coverage varies. Boyd himself admitted: 'Those who use this index are warned that it must be treated as a "lucky dip", if you find what you want, well and good; if you don't, you have searched nothing.' Almost all of East Anglia is complete and London and Yorkshire are also well represented. Boyd used his own system to categorise surnames into similar groups, so entries are not always as they appear in the register itself. He also worked on a smaller burial index, which contains just over 500,000 entries of deaths of men in London. Both indexes are available at Findmypast.[18]

Ancestry has a couple of marriage indexes, including *Crisp's Marriage Licences Indexes (1713–1892)*, which consists of abstracts of marriage licenses for Londoners. The indexes may include information on the places of origin and family members in addition to the marriage date, location and spouse's name. There is also *Pallot's Marriage Index (1780–1837)*, which covers almost every parish in the City of London, with 1.5 million marriage entries. There are also entries from 2,500 parishes outside London. Several registers transcribed in the index no longer survive having subsequently been destroyed or lost.

Bishop's Transcripts

If the parish register is missing it is definitely worth checking to see whether there is a bishop's transcript. In 1598 parishes were required to send to their bishop an annual list of baptisms, marriages and burials. It was an onerous task, and as the parish clerks were not paid for the work, not all did it. In the 1880s Chester Waters commented that this system was a 'lamentable picture of episcopal negligence, parochial parsimony and official rapacity'. Where they survive they are usually at local record offices. Phillimore's *Atlas* will tell you what survives where. Some are indexed on FamilySearch, but otherwise very few are yet online. However, Ancestry and Findmypast generally include them when they put sets of parish registers online.[19]

Related Records

Parish registers are the starting point for research before 1837. However, there are other not dissimilar records. Here are some suggestions of other sources you might consider:

Non-Conformist Registers: Not everybody was a member of the Anglican Church or agreed with what it preached. A few pockets of Catholicism remained, particularly

An example of a bishop's transcript. In general these records were not well kept, but can occasionally be useful if the parish register, of which they are a copy, is missing. (*London Metropolitan Archives/ Ancestry*) in Lancashire, after the Reformation. Known as recusants, they were subjected to considerable persecution, often in the form of particularly heavy taxation, and they were not allowed to hold elected positions or become army or naval officers. Although conditions improved during the eighteenth century, Catholics were not fully emancipated until 1829. Lists of recusants can sometimes be found in quarter sessions records at local record offices and in tax records at The National Archives. Of particular interest here are the recusant rolls in series E 376 and E 377: annual returns of Catholics, arranged by county, who had property forfeited or fined for their beliefs. These rolls record convictions, fines, rentals for forfeited lands and details of chattels seized. Unfortunately, these records are difficult to use and are in Latin, although a number of volumes have been transcribed and published by the Catholic Record Society.[20]

A larger and increasing proportion of the population did not believe that the Church of England had gone far enough in breaking with the Church of Rome and Roman practices. The English Civil War led to a short-lived triumph of the Puritan tendency. After the Restoration there was a growth of sects which broke totally from the Church. One of the first was the Quakers. The most important denomination, and certainly the most influential, was the Methodists, under John Wesley, which split from the Anglican Church in the late eighteenth century. By the time of the religious census of 1851 there were over a hundred different denominations, ranging from Methodists to Muggletonians via the Countess of Huntingdon's Connexion. The new industrial towns and Wales became centres of non-conformity (as these beliefs were often described). Increasingly they wished to baptise, marry and be buried in their own chapels, and kept registers accordingly. Technically everybody had to use the Anglican Church for these ceremonies, and many did, particularly for marriages, although increasingly they did not. Occasionally there are comments in parish registers about the baptism, marriage and burial of non-conformists or the numbers of dissenters locally. After recording the burial of Ann Parrot, on 18 June 1736, in Beeston, Nottinghamshire, the vicar added the comment, 'a dissembling canting hollow presbitarian', and in Betley, Staffordshire, the incumbent regularly noted non-conformist baptisms, for example, '1705 Aug 28, Lydia, d. of Mark Tomkin Anabaptist was born'.[21]

The prime resources are the non-conformist registers, which were surrendered to the Registrar General on the introduction of civil registration in 1837, with a second batch being deposited in 1857. Although the earliest ones date from the late sixteenth century, the majority begin after 1750. In addition, the collection includes records of several informal registers established by the Methodists and other beliefs, notably the one at Dr William's Library. The originals of these registers are at The National Archives. However, they are all online at TheGenealogist with detailed indexes on FamilySearch.

Registers in use in 1837 or 1857 were not surrendered and may well now be at local record offices. Many of the denominations also have their own archives and historical societies, which may be able to help. Their archives are unlikely to have many registers, but will have material if your ancestor was a minister or an important lay figure. The largest and perhaps best known of these is Friends Library in London, which has large collections of material relating to Quakers, including copies of many registers.[22]

Miscellaneous Lists: These were occasionally demanded by central government, generally demanding an oath of loyalty to the Crown or the established religion. They are rarely complete, either because men declined to sign or, more often, because the records no longer survive. Generally they only contain names or signatures. The most important of these was the protestation return of 1641 and 1642, which was an oath of loyalty to the king. Initially it was just taken by MPs and peers, but was extended to all men over the age of 18. Failure to sign would mean that they were not able to hold office. A letter was sent by the Speaker of the House of Commons to the county sheriffs, instructing them to take the

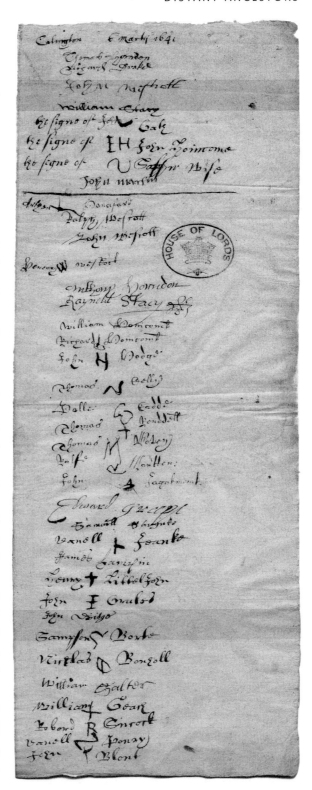

A page from the protestation returns for Callington, Cornwall, dated 6 March 1641, listing all the male inhabitants of the village who swore an oath to Parliament. (*Parliamentary Archives*)

protestation with the justices of the peace in their county, and then the incumbent of each parish was to read the protestation to his parishioners and they were all to sign. This took place in February and March 1641–42. The protestation returns were then sent back to Parliament. The returns are now with the Parliamentary Archive, but not everything survives. They are complete for Devon and Dorset, for example, but missing for London and Norfolk. A number have been transcribed and published.[23]

Also of use are militia lists. The tradition of calling up able-bodied men to defend the locality in case of invasion dates back to Saxon times. Indeed, there may be patchy records at local record offices for the medieval, Tudor and Stuart militias. However, the system was reformed during the Seven Years War in 1757. The militia became particularly important during the Napoleonic wars, when invasion was expected several times. Men between the ages of 18 and 45 could be called up for service by ballot, although it was possible to get out of service by finding a substitute to fill your place. Each parish was required to provide lists of men who could serve in the militia. There were some exceptions, including clergymen, apprentices, articled clerks and former soldiers and sailors; even so, David Hey says that the returns 'provide the best occupational census returns that is available before … the nineteenth century'.[24]

The lists give the occupation, but may also note other circumstances, such as whether he was a poor man, whether he had children and whether he was able-bodied (sometimes a clue might be given if he was not, such as 'lame' or 'broken-bodied'). The lists are largely found at local record offices, but a few are at The National Archives. As well as lists (sometimes called musters), there is likely to be a host of other correspondence relating to the organisation and administration of the militia, including material about the finding and payment of substitutes. Surprisingly often there are certificates of service awarded to individual volunteers. The local unit or regiment was officered by local landowners who fancied playing at soldiers, together with former army officers. Again there may well be papers about their appointment and lists of officers together with the units they commanded. Findmypast includes The National Archives' militia records from series WO 96, although these are mainly from the 1870s onwards and in any case are certainly not complete.[25]

Women Before 1837

It is much harder to find information about mothers, wives and daughters because women, irrespective of social class, rarely appear in the records; on occasion they are even missed out of indexes. Percival Boyd's index to London burials between 1538 and 1872, for example, contains no women:

Only males are included (children being omitted when so designated in the registers), because for genealogical purposes the date of a man's death is more important than that of a woman who, unless she were sole [a spinster] or a widow, could not make a will except with the consent of her husband.[26]

This is not to say that they were not important members of society. Indeed, in 1651, Robert Burton claimed that England was 'a Paradise for women and hell for horses', but they had separate and generally supporting roles to the men folk. Writing of the middle classes in the eighteenth century, Amanda Vickery argues that:

> The married housewife was a pillar of wisdom and worth, with a prominent position in the hierarchical institution that society recognised as both normal and fundamental to social order, the male-headed conjugal unit ... Women did not see themselves as passing guests in the houses of men, but as householders in their own right. Wives were subject to their husband's authority, yet they were equal souls in the marriage, often fond bedfellows and domestic allies.[27]

This was perhaps as true among the working classes, where women had to contribute financially to the family income and where it was not unknown for widows to take over their husband's shop or trade on his death. Additionally, well into the nineteenth century wives worked on the land alongside the men or at home in cottage industry. Most women who sought employment before marriage became servants on farms or in the households of the middle and upper classes.

There are several other factors that help to explain why women are less frequently found in the records, the most important of which is that a woman's property became legally her husband's on marriage; this remained the case until the Married Women's Property Rights Act of 1882. For most couples who had little or no property this was, of course, rather irrelevant, but to the middling sort and aristocracy such matters were of great concern. Though a wife retained any freehold lands (unless they were formally transferred), her husband acquired a life interest in the rents and profits of her lands. In addition, all her moveable goods and chattels became his. She was unable to enter contracts on her own behalf, but her husband was held liable for her debts. However, the developing law of equity provided for the creation of trusts by which married women were able to keep control of property. The couple and their families tried to take care of this through marriage settlements, creating trusts, assigning dowries and sorting out other legal and financial matters. Despite their repetitious nature and arcane terminology, they are worth struggling through as it is possible to gain some idea of the financial position of the bride's family and what both parties considered important.[28]

It was almost impossible to divorce, except through an Act of Parliament, although ecclesiastical courts could grant limited separation. The London Consistory Court was the main court dealing with matrimonial disputes. It covered London, Middlesex and parts of Hertfordshire and Essex. These cases may involve matrimonial matters

A recipe for 'Doughnutts' found in Margaretta Acworth's recipe book. Such documents are rare and offer a direct link to our ancestor's stomachs. (*TNA C 107/108*)

such as divorce and separation, breech of promise, arguments over estates and probate, defamation, and 'criminous conversation'.[29]

There were certain roles which women were not expected to occupy, although the rules governing this were not as hard and fast as they would become in the Victorian era. Women ratepayers could become churchwardens, although this was rare, and small numbers of women became camp followers in the army or supernumeraries on board naval ships, providing rudimentary nursing and laundry services.[30]

This means that there are far fewer records naming individual women before 1837 than there are for men. The few women who left wills, for example, had to be either spinsters or widows. Daughters, brides and the deceased will, of course, appear in the appropriate parish register. A number will appear as supplicants in Poor Law records, either seeking support for themselves and their families, or as elderly and infirm paupers (or possibly as nurses employed to care for them). Alternatively they may appear in court cases, either directly as the accused or indirectly through giving evidence.

However, there are some records that specifically reflect on women's life in this period. A few recipe books survive and provide a direct link back to our ancestors' stomachs 200 or more years ago. They are commonplace books of favourite culinary recipes, but sometimes also include medicines, kept by the mistress of the house to help her and her cook prepare favourite dishes. If they survive they may be in family or, occasionally, financial papers. The recipes themselves are rather different to those found in modern cookbooks. In particular, only a general guidance to oven temperatures is provided, because the heat source in each kitchen (mostly at this time an open fire) was different and cooks would have been expected to know what worked best in their kitchens. A typical recipe might be like this one for sugar cakes, which was found in a recipe book of 1720 within a collection of financial and tithe papers at the East Riding Archives and Local Studies Service in Beverley:

> To make sugar cakes. Take 3 pounds of finest flower, a pound of fine sugar, clowes & mace each an ounc finely searced, 2 pound of butter, a little rose water, knead & mould this well together, melt your butter as you put it in then mould it with your hand forth upon A bord, cut them round, lay them on papers & put them in an oven, be sure it be not too hot so let them stand til they be colourd.[31]

Of particular concern to women was childbirth, which was difficult and dangerous, not helped by inadequate or non-existent midwifery. The first specialist maternity or lying-in hospitals were established in London during the 1740s. Provincial cities quickly followed suit and by the end of eighteenth century most large towns had one.[32] They were generally run by boards of (male) governors appointed by the charities which funded them. Patients could only be admitted by a letter from a subscriber or after their case was brought before the governors. Women about to give birth to bastards were rarely admitted. One of the first was the British Lying-in Hospital, which was set up in Brownlow Street in Soho in 1749 to care for the distressed poor with special attention to the wives of soldiers and sailors. An account of 1787 said of the hospital that 'Here are 6 wards and in each 6 beds. The wards are clean and quiet: provision good: kitchen and pantry clean. This is a good institution, and proper attention is paid to the patients who continue here 3 weeks after they are delivered.'[33] One such patient was Mary Woonton, the wife of a guardsman, who the governor's minute book indicates was admitted on 5 May 1775. She gave birth to a son – Giles – on 26 May. Unfortunately they both died shortly afterwards. The annual report for 1775 notes that she was one of twenty-one patients and thirteen newborns who died during the year, out of 570 births.[34] Even so, mortality was considerably better here than at home. About 2 per cent of babies died at the Lying-in Hospital in 1775, compared with about one death in six for babies under 1 amongst the general public.[35]

A fortunate few widows and elderly spinsters could spend their declining years in almshouses, provided for in bequests made by rich benefactors. The oldest almshouses are nearly a thousand years old. Most towns will have one or two at least and are an unusual link to the past. Indeed, some 1,800 continue to operate today as a form of sheltered accommodation. Who was admitted depended very much on the whim of the original benefactor. Most almshouses were for men or for small numbers of men and women, while others were specifically for women. In Yorkshire, for example, Margaret, Countess of Cumberland, founded Beamsley Hospital in 1593 for thirteen poor widows, after she found 'many old women in and around Skipton decrepit and broken down by old age, who were in the habit of begging for their daily bread'.[36]

Taxation

Taxation records are a very important source for researching ancestry pre-1837, more so than they are afterwards, largely because they are contain lots of names. Indeed, after parish registers they may well be the most important source. Of these records the most useful single source is one of the least used: rate books. Rates were a tax on the notional value of houses levied by local government and were payable by all but the very poorest inhabitants. Originally they had been a levy to help churches, but by the Reformation they were beginning to be used for non-ecclesiastical purposes. Rates for bridges were authorised by an act of 1530/31 and those to pay for gaols shortly thereafter. A wide range of different rates could be levied to pay for the poor, highways, removal of vagrants or even the eradication of vermin. Each parish vestry (the basic unit of local government) or borough was responsible for both setting rates as it saw fit and collecting the amount assessed. This was normally done by appointing collectors to physically call on ratepayers. He recorded payments in rate books which, where they survive, are at local record offices. Few records, however, seem to survive before 1744, when ratepayers were given the right to inspect the books, but they can go up to the 1960s.

As well providing information about the value of a property (and its size and location), they can act as surrogates to directories and even as a replacement for early censuses. I once did research for a client about his ancestor, Edwin Ridley, a wine merchant who lived near Clerkenwell Green in London for nearly twenty years before his death in 1838. Some of the most useful information came from rate books at Islington Local History Centre, where he appears every year until 1839, when the ratepayer was noted as being R. Ridley (presumably a son). In 1840 the house was empty, so the family had moved away. The house had a rateable value of £32 and total value of £40, about average for the street. The rates were 2s 10d in the pound and he paid about £4 10s 8d per annum. It was described as being a house rather than a 'house and shop' as other premises in the street were. The landlord was a Mr Fisher. The fact that even a respectable and presumably well-to-do figure like Edward Ridley rented his property is not unsurprising as very few householders in the nineteenth century, perhaps no more than one in ten, owned their own houses. Rate books are held by local record offices, but due to their voluminous nature they ⟩ often been heavily weeded. Only ones for every fifth year survive at Richmond ⟩ Studies Library, for example.[37]

The hearth tax assessment for Pudding Lane in the City of London compiled in August 1666 a few weeks before the Great Fire broke out in a baker's shop in the street. (*TNA E 179/255/32 pt4 p6*)

Central government was always short of money and came up with a wide range of ways to extract money from citizens. Taxes were generally raised to pay for a military campaign or war and ceased when the national emergency came to an end. Some taxes are well known, such as the hearth tax of the 1660s and 1670s, but others have almost been forgotten, like the eighteenth-century taxes on silverware, dogs, hair powder and so on. Most taxes were short-lived and badly administered, so were fairly easy to evade. With the proposal for the introduction of a poll tax to help pay for a war against the Dutch, Samuel Pepys confided to his diary of January 1665–66:

> I do fear I shall be very deeply concerned, being to be taxed for all my offices, and then for my money that I have, and my title, as well as my head. It is a very great tax; but yet I do think it is so perplexed, it will hardly ever be collected duly.[38]

The impositions of the eighteenth-century window tax, for example, could be mitigated by bricking up a window or two. Even for the rich the tax burden was not onerous, as Liza Picard points out, 'there was no inheritance tax, no income tax [before the Napoleonic wars], only 5s in the pound on income from land and multitudinous taxes on status symbols such as footmen and carriages, which could be borne without strain'.[39]

Most surviving records are at The National Archives in series E 179, which, according to the archives, 'provide the overwhelming bulk of the information now available about taxes and taxpayers in England during five centuries of English history'. The series contains detailed records of taxation levied in England and Wales from about 1190 to 1690. Most, but by no means all, rolls contain the names of individual taxpayers and the amount of tax paid. The series has been exhaustively indexed and a database can be searched online by place or by type of tax, although not by name of individual taxpayer. In addition, a reasonable proportion of the records have been transcribed and published by local record societies with detailed name indexes where appropriate.[40]

The earliest records relate to the Carucages, a tax on land which was levied on several occasions between 1194 and 1224. Of more interest are records of the taxes imposed on the income and moveable property of more prosperous individuals, known as lay subsidies, which survive between 1225 and 1334. Lay in this context means anybody who was not in a holy order, as the clergy were exempt. The most important of these lay subsidies was levied a number of times between 1290 and 1334. It is sometimes referred to as the 'tenth and fifteenth' because it was levied on one-tenth of moveable property in towns and one-fifteenth of such property in the poorer countryside (although the proportions taxed at each levy varied). The rolls, or lists of taxpayers, are a major source for both family and local historians as they offer a rare insight into England before the Black Death. In addition, these rds also show the use of surnames for the first time in any great number. Indeed, arold Flood described lay subsidies as being 'an alphabetical roll-call of the wealthier inhabitants … in the early fourteenth century …' The records are easy to use, being essentially lists of names of the people who paid the tax (almost always the male head of the household) with how much they paid. The records are arranged by parish within hundreds and then counties. Lay subsidies ceased to be assessed directly on individuals in 1334 and were replaced by fixed quotas paid by parishes or towns, charged at a fifteenth on most of the country, but at a tenth on the royal lands or demesne and boroughs. These records rarely include names.[41]

The next tax to contain many names were the poll taxes, which were levied in 1377, 1379 and 1381. The tax was abandoned after the Peasants' Revolt of 1381. The 1377 returns are the most complete, for there is evidence of widespread evasion in other years. In 1377 the tax was levied at 4d per head for everybody over the age of 14 with the clergy paying a shilling. Rich and poor paid the same amount. Only beggars and the hopelessly impoverished were exempt. As with the lay subsidies, the records just give the individual and how much they paid. Individuals in a particular household are listed together. In 1379 and 1381 richer individuals paid more. In addition, an indication of their marital status, occupation or rank is given in the returns. The poll tax was revived at least eight times after 1641. The survival of records is patchy, but where they do survive they are likely to be at local record offices.[42]

Further lay subsidies were revived by Henry VIII and again records survive in TNA series E 179. Those for 1523–24 offer best coverage for southern England and the Midlands, while in the north the best coverage is in 1543. Again you can get some idea of the wealth of individuals from the amount they paid. In the Leicestershire village of Kibsworth, John Polle was assessed at £23 in goods in the lay subsidy of 1524, as against some of his middling neighbours who were rated at a mere £3 or £4, and ten more who were taxed on wages of 20s per annum. As the lay subsidies of the early fourteenth century and the 1520s were not dissimilar, it is possible to compare how villages had prospered over the years and see which families had remained. John Polle's family, for example, had been in the village since at least the 1280s.[43]

FROM THE EXPERTS …

Dr Nick Barratt gives his top three tips for medieval genealogy:

1. Mind your language

The further back in time you work, the harder it becomes to figure out what people were saying, because many official records were handwritten rather than printed. Not only that, the language of the law courts, manorial administration and central government was Latin until as late as 1732 – and many of the words or phrases were abbreviated to save space. You may also encounter Anglo-Norman French in the high middle ages, from the fourteenth century onwards, as well. The science of deciphering old handwriting and shortened words is known as palaeography, and you will need to tackle the techniques fairly quickly.

Luckily, most archives now provide access to Latin or Anglo-Norman dictionaries and other works to help you make sense of the documents you are working on – and there are a few neat tricks to help as well. You can always look at a document after 1732, when the equivalent text will be written in English, to help you translate key words or phrases from Latin, or at documents during the Interregnum, following the execution of Charles I in 1649, when all official records were also English by decree of the Parliamentarians who governed.

Furthermore, the advent of digitisation has made it possible to view original images of key sources that are not only transcribed – or extended – but also translated as well; one such example is the Fine Rolls project for the reign of Henry III.

2. Check your diary

Alongside problems with language, you will also need to keep an eye out for the peculiarities in the way documents were 'dated', because there were various systems in use to assign a date which changed over time. The most important ones to look out for include the reference to saints' days as fixed markers in the year – the day after Michaelmas, for example, is always 30 September. Dates in official documents were usually described according to the regnal year, such as VI Henry VII – the sixth year of the reign of Henry VII, or 1491 – with the start of the year determined by the day on which the monarch ascended the throne. You will also have to contend with legal terms (Michaelmas, Hilary, Easter and Trinity), moveable feast days (Easter), the fact that the year started on 25 March not 1 January until 1752 (giving rise to dates such as 10 January 1705/06) and finally the adoption of the Gregorian calendar in 1752 which resulted in 2 September being followed by 14 September that year, and a disparity in the official date before 1752 with other parts of Europe that had adopted the reforms as early as 1582.

3. Going local

One of the biggest changes you will encounter will be a different style of research, focusing more on local history as much as that of your own ancestors. Basically, precise geography matters. This is because records that specifically mention your ancestors are going to be very hard to track down; unless they became embroiled with officialdom or held land or were on the margins of society most people simply don't appear at all, aside from entries in parish registers (and then there's the problem of making sure you've got the right person in the absence of corroborating evidence).

Consequently, a great deal of medieval genealogy takes places at a conceptual level, when you know where your ancestor lived and you spend your time trying to work out what society was like at that time. This means looking at the two main tenets of local life – the Church and the manorial system – to see how their dual influence affected your ancestors' lives. Then it will be necessary to sift through parish material and private estate records to build up a picture of the area, after which you can make reasonable assumptions about occupation, standard of living, type of dwelling, social mobility and wealth.

Dr Nick Barratt is perhaps Britain's best-known genealogist and a prolific reviewer and commentator on all aspects of history, notably family history. He has worked with a variety of companies, celebrities and television presenters, often compiling their family history. He is CEO of Sticks Research Agency.

The restoration of Charles II in May 1660 led to a return to the old problems of a pressing shortage of funds. One answer lay in taxing the hearths found in houses, 'it being easy to tell the number of hearths which remove not as heads or polls'. The resulting hearth tax was levied several times between 1662 and 1689, initially at 2s per hearth. Householders who possessed fewer than two hearths were exempt – very roughly a third of the population. The returns give a rough idea of a person's wealth – the more hearths they had, such as the Earl of Dorset's house at Knole near Sevenoaks with eighty-five fireplaces, the richer they were likely to be. Sometimes the returns also include other information, such as status or rank, e.g. the addition of titles such as Sir, Widow, and Esquire. Records survive for two distinct periods, between 1662–66 and 1669–74, most of which are in TNA series E 179, although a few lists are at local record offices. The tax was payable on Lady Day and Michaelmas, with two lists being drawn up each year. Approximately eight different lists for each county were returned to the Exchequer, although the survival rate for each county is patchy. While Warwickshire is well covered, other places like Berkshire only have one list, which is incomplete. In addition, there are some subsidiary lists which may provide some information, including certificates of exemption listing householders too poor to be assessed. The records are arranged by county, hundred and then parish. You may not need to use the originals as an increasing number of lists are being edited and published by the British Records Society.[44]

In the late seventeenth century and during the eighteenth century an increasing number of taxes were imposed on consumer goods. There are few records at Kew, although registers and other records can often be found at local record offices. Details should be available through the Access to Archives database. A fascinating example is the marriage duty tax, which would have meant, had it worked and had more than a handful of records survived, that we would have had a registration system

140 years before one was actually introduced. Despite its name, the tax was imposed upon burials, births and marriages as well as on bachelors over 25 years of age and childless widowers. It came into force in May 1695, initially for a five-year period, but was later extended until August 1706. To make the legislation work it really required a complete enumeration of the people in order to identify all bachelors and widowers, together with detailed records on people's wealth (as the rich were to pay more): a levy of 4s was levied on the burials of ordinary people, rising to £50 4s for archbishops and dukes. All this was beyond the administrative capabilities of the period, so it was widely ignored and few records survive. Remarkably they include returns from eighty of the ninety-four parishes of the City of London, so we have a list of the majority of Londoners over the age of 14, including servants and apprentices.[45]

One tax for which there are no records about individuals is income tax. The tax was first introduced in 1798 at a rate of 10 per cent on the total income of the taxpayer from all sources above £60, with reductions on income up to £200. As this was a considerable sum, it was paid by relatively few people and it brought in rather less than anticipated. The tax was abolished in 1815 and Parliament decided that all documents connected with it should be collected, cut into pieces and pulped. It was reintroduced in 1841 as a temporary measure, levied on incomes over £150, so again at least initially it was only paid by a fairly small proportion of the population.[46]

More records survive for another tax initiative introduced during the French wars: death duties, which were actually three different taxes on legacy, succession and estate duty, and were payable from 1796 on large estates. The scope of estate duty was extended throughout the nineteenth century. Before 1805 the death duty registers cover about a quarter of all estates. By 1857, there should be an entry for all estates except for those worth less than £20, although unless the assets were valued at £1,500 or more, the taxes were rarely collected. Registers survive up to 1903. For researchers with middle-class ancestors they are an important resource, as entries can show what happened to someone's personal estate after death, the estate's worth, details of the deceased and executors, as well as details of estates, legacies, trustees, legatees, annuities and the duty paid. They can also give the date of death and information about the people who received bequests or who were the next of kin. The records are in series IR 26 and IR 27 at Kew, with records before 1811 available through DocumentsOnline. Findmypast has copies of the registers, but not the records themselves.[47]

Related Records

Often entries in taxation rolls can be used with other sources to build up more about individuals. Here are a few suggestions of other records where you might well find additional information:

Probate Records: Any person with any amount of land or possessions should have made a will. They survive from the fifteenth century. The problem, however, is finding them, because they were proved by a wide range of ecclesiastical courts. The most important of these courts was the Prerogative Court of Canterbury, whose records are at The National Archives and copies of wills can be downloaded from DocumentsOnline. There is a pretty good index which you can search by place and trade as well as by name. In England, north of the Trent the most important court was the Prerogative Court of York, whose records are at the Borthwick Institute at the University of York. Many of its probate records are online at Origins. There were also many smaller ecclesiastical courts, where smaller landowners had their wills proved, with records at local record

A copy of the will for my ancestor, the Rev. Paul Belcher of Heather, Leicestershire. Much of it is to do with settling the affairs of his daughters to ensure that they were well provided for. (*TNA PROB 11/1632*)

offices. Indexes to wills proved at these courts may have been published by local family history and record societies; Origins are working on a national wills index, in which they intend to index all wills at local record offices. Ancestry has many wills proved in ecclesiastical courts within the diocese of London.[48]

Probate Inventories: These accompanied wills and were used to value the deceased's estate and help creditors claim unpaid debts. They are perhaps the most intimate way to get an impression of the lives of men and women who otherwise remain little more than eccentrically spelled entries in parish registers. They were compiled between the end of the fifteenth and the middle of the eighteenth century. Inventories are a record of the physical possessions owned by the deceased, so they do not include land. They were usually compiled a few days after the testator's death by two appraisers appointed by the executors, who went from room to room noting down every item they came across and assigning a monetary value. As inventories could be presented as evidence in court, the appraisers seem to have valued items fairly, although a neatly rounded valuation may be evidence that they were not taking their task as rigorously as they might. They can be very revealing about the lifestyle of the deceased. Take, for example, the Hertford maltster Nathaniel Hale. The inventory, taken in November 1671, valued his household at £355 10s, showed that he had one of the few clocks in the district, a separate parlour furnished with carpeted tables and leather chairs, and five upstairs rooms all equipped with bedsteads and feather bedding. In addition, there were a number of small items, such as twenty-seven 'paire of sheets [worth £15], five dozen of napkins, three longe tabellcloaths, 15 short ons [worth £7 10s]'. Goods held by shopkeepers might also be appraised and recorded in inventories. Thomas Oliver, who was a mercer in Much Wenlock, Shropshire, left behind 'cloaths, stuffs and all other mercery in ye shopp' worth £149 1s 2¼d, as well as 'grocery of all sorts' valued at £27 18s 8d. In addition, the eagle-eyed appraisers came across 'Ould lumber as boxes etc and things otherwise forgotten or out of sight'.[49]

Small collections of inventories are at local record offices. Sometimes they physically accompany wills, but often enough they are found separately. The National Archives also has several series of inventories for wills proved at the Prerogative Court of Canterbury between 1417 and 1858, although inventories after 1710 generally only survive when the will was contested. They have been indexed so they are easy to search by name through the online catalogue.[50]

Manorial Courts: Of medieval and early modern times, these dealt with a wide range of administrative concerns of the manor as well lesser criminal offences. There were two courts, the court baron and the court leet, each creating its own set of records, commonly referred to as the court rolls. Both were presided over by the lord of the manor or his steward. The court baron enforced the customs of the manor and was a private perquisite of the lord. It dealt with matters to do with land and inheritance. Many financial transactions, such as debt payments, came before the courts: disputes between neighbours or the regulation of farming in the common fields. The court appointed the reeve and beadle or bailiff, who looked after the lord's interests in the manor, the hayward and some other posts, such as the swineherd and woodward. There were personal matters brought to the court, such as marriages, births out of wedlock among bondwomen, the departure from the village by a villein without prior permission. The court leet dealt with public affairs of the manor: petty crime and the infringement of bylaws, and other matters such as the assize of ale and bread. The historian Zvi Razi, who studied these courts, concluded that it is 'hard to conceive how a villager could have avoided appearing before the court from time to time'. The richer villagers – those who might have more property to contest – were more frequently in attendance than the poor. However, a remarkable amount of information about village society can be gained from these records, making them invaluable for tracing rural ancestors before about 1700. From the eighteenth century onwards the business of the manorial courts declined.[51]

Records of manors owned by the Crown are at The National Archives, and other records may be found at local record offices. The best place to find which records survive is through the Manorial Documents Register, which is maintained by The National Archives. There is a database, arranged by county, at www.nationalarchives. gov.uk/mdr, it is by no means complete but is being added to regularly. A small number of manorial rolls have been published.[52]

Title Deeds and Land Records: One of the largest collections of records at local record offices are those relating to the purchase and sale of land. There are tens of thousands of deeds and related papers for properties in town and country dating from the thirteenth century, if not before. They may seem difficult to use because they tend to use incomprehensible technical jargon and, before 1733, were often written in Latin. However, this verbiage conceals some basic facts: they are largely about who bought and sold a piece of land, what it consisted off and how much it sold for. Taken together, these deeds can show an individual or family rise to prosperity by buying land and building a considerable estate or, conversely, a family having to sell land to pay off debts. These records are largely to be found at local record offices, often in collections of papers deposited by solicitors or in estate papers. However, be aware that on occasion they may have ended up in archives hundreds of miles from where the land is, so you may need to use the National Register of Archives or Access to Archives in order to identify where the deeds you are looking for are to be found. In addition, there were registries of deeds for Middlesex and Yorkshire, which were precursors of the National Land Registry, where deeds were deposited. These registries begin about 1708 and were still in business as late as 1970. Where there is an online catalogue, deeds are usually described in some detail and so you may feel there is no need to order up the original.[53]

A typical example of a title deed and land holding record is for the Essex parish of Arkesden for 1606/07:

> Admission of Thomas Morris on surrender on Andrew Laws. A piece of land (containg 7 rods), in Shrubbs field in Arkesden, between land of Henry Tayler south and John Morris north one head abutting on Minchens balke west and on land of the vicarage of Arkesden east, copyhold of the Manor of Menchens in Arkesden with the Rectory. Court of Richard Coutts, esquire Steward: William Nightingale, gentleman.[54]

Scotland Before 1855

Before the Act of Union in 1707, Scotland was a separate nation despite the Union of Crowns which took place on the death of Queen Elizabeth in 1602. This sense of separateness continued well after. This is reflected in the very different legal system, which is still used today: the established Church was Presbyterian (not Anglican as in England and Ireland) and many different records were created by Scottish authorities.

Scotland was also a much poorer country than England and most people had a much lower standard of living, so there is much less about ordinary people who had few possessions to leave behind. This was widely noted by contemporary visitors: Dr Johnson, for example, was observed by James Boswell in his *Journal of a Tour to the Hebrides*, saying: 'Your country consists of two things, stone and water. There is, indeed, a little earth above the stone in some places, but a very little; and the stone is always appearing. It is like a man in rags; the naked skin is still peeping out.' As a result, Scottish genealogy is very different to that elsewhere in the British Isles. To English eyes the records can sometimes be very strange.[55]

Despite their name, the Old Parish Registers (OPRs) bear little resemblance to their English equivalents and they can be even less informative. The ScotlandsPeople website, where indexes and images of these records can be found, warns: 'Do not expect too much from OPR birth & baptism records. The amount of information recorded can be variable and most entries contain very little detail.' In particular, many parishes do not have a burial register because of the belief that one's soul lives forever. Most registers begin only in the eighteenth century; indeed some only start in the 1820s, although a few go back to the mid-sixteenth century. Also, as in England, a proportion of Scottish families did not register for one reason or another. Baptisms will normally give you the date and name of child, but the names of the parents are less likely to be found. Some babies were baptised twice, in both its parents' home parishes. Marriage records are more often a confirmation of the banns being proclaimed rather than the marriage itself. Again there may be several entries as banns may have been read in both of the couple's home parishes. However, despite all these caveats they are the major source for going back beyond the beginning of Statutory Registration in 1855, and you should be able to find many of your Scottish ancestors back into at least the eighteenth century here.[56]

Not everybody, by any means, was a member of the Church of Scotland. There was always a sizable Catholic minority, particularly in the Highlands and Islands. Catholic Registers are also available on ScotlandsPeople: records here go back to the early eighteenth century. Records of other denominations are generally with the National Records of Scotland. The Scottish Archive Network (SCAN) provides an online catalogue to the holdings of fifty archives across the country, so this may be the best place to start.[57]

Another very different set of records to their English equivalents are testaments. Until 1868 only movable property could be included in a testament, while immovable property passed to the eldest son or daughter. Before 1824, wills were proved in Commissary Courts; thereafter responsibility passed to Sheriff Courts. There were twenty-two such courts, but Edinburgh's was the most important as it had jurisdiction over all of Scotland and it was also where Scots who died overseas had their wills proved. The records are now all available through ScotlandsPeople. Other sources that have no real English equivalents are the records relating to sale of land (or rather its transfer because all land technically belonged to the Crown). There are several series of records that can help, notably the registers of sasines and retours, which are held by the National Records of Scotland who also have a number of useful registers and guides. They should be able to tell you about the land that your ancestors bought and sold.[58]

Of course, a unique feature of Scottish life was the clan system, which was particularly strong in the Highlands. Much too much misty-eyed tosh has been written about clans from Sir Walter Scott to modern tourism board brochures, but occasionally it can be useful to know more about them. The term *clan* comes from the Gaelic and means 'children' or, more loosely but more appropriately, 'family'. Branches of a clan that owe allegiance to the clan chief are known as septs. The Highland clan was really a family; a family in which everybody believed they were all, from chief to blacksmith, descended from one founder or progenitor. They regarded themselves as very close kinsmen. At its heart was the patriarchal chief who provided protection and handed out justice. Each clan had its own customs and laws as well as its own methods of justice. It offered protection not only to its people but also to those of its associated septs and sometimes to members of smaller clans, against the oppression of stronger and more warlike clans. The clan system was largely destroyed after the failed Jacobite rising in 1746, which resulted in the Highland Clearances. They have left few written records behind. Instead they have bequeathed many unique surnames, as well as the tartan.[59]

FROM THE EXPERTS …

Forfeited Lands

Emma Jolly explores the records of the Forfeited Estates Commission for England and Ireland:

Following the Jacobite Rising of 1715, which saw Catholics and other supporters of the House of Stuart rise up in support of the 'Old Pretender' James III, in June 1716 Parliament took action against the rebels by establishing the Forfeited Estates Commission (FEC). The commission was created 'to inquire of the estates of certain traitors, etc.'. In most cases the result was that the rebels' lands were seized and then sold. Surviving records for England and Ireland are at The National Archives under letter code FEC, while those for Scotland are at the National Records of Scotland (NRS).

In September 1716, the English commissioners moved to Preston (and from here some travelled to Ireland). Here, they received discoveries of superstitious estates – those 'of which the revenues were to be devoted to periodical prayers, etc., for the dead'. They also collected a list of sworn deponents, which includes original information on persons actively involved in the battle in the town, which saw the defeat of the rebels in November 1715. Whilst this work was taking place, roving commissioners travelled to other parts of the country to investigate the rebels. In November 1716, the commission left Preston for Newcastle, where they stayed for less than three weeks. The records they collected here, many relating to property in Northumberland, are useful in reflecting the final phase of the rebellion.

FEC records are particularly useful for genealogists who have traced their ancestors back to the early eighteenth century. As the papers are name indexed, it is straightforward to check if your ancestor appears in them. You can do this using The National Archives' online catalogue or consulting the PRO handbook. The handbook also includes lists of places mentioned, a separate county index of rentals and surveys, an alphabetical list of wills and the full list of documents with their reference numbers. For example, A3 is 'A receipt of payment of money owed to the Commissioners by Aldcliffe Estate (late Albert Hodgson) in Lancaster, co. Lancaster'.

A broad cross-section of early Georgian society is named in these records, including Jacobites, commission employees, the new owners of the estates and witnesses. Above all, they are an essential resource for anyone with Roman Catholic ancestry. They are particularly strong for people and places in Lancashire, but there are also records relating to estates in other counties, including those of Northumberland, Westmorland, Cumberland, Durham and Yorkshire in the north of England; and a smaller number of references to Oxfordshire, Essex, Middlesex, Nottinghamshire, Gloucestershire, Lincolnshire and Berkshire. In Ireland, Tipperary and Kilkenny feature heavily, alongside Wicklow, Waterford, Carlow, Wexford, County Dublin, Kerry and Meath.

Among them may be found wills and detailed land records, and you may find reference to state or confirm familial relationships – such as widows of the rebels who were executed. They may then lead to other records at local archives.[60]

Emma Jolly is a genealogist and writer who specialises in researching families and society through her genealogic service. Her latest book, *Tracing your British Indian Ancestors*, was published by Pen & Sword in February 2012.

Notes

1 Details of some 200 landowners who appear in Domesday Book are at www.domesdaybook.co.uk/landindex.html, with more sources listed at www.medievalgenealogy.org.uk/guide/dom.shtml. The Ardens and Berkeleys are discussed in Neil Kirk et al., *Domesday Exhibition Guide* (Millbank, 1986), pp. 5–9. A few pre-Conquest thanes are given at www.roffe.co.uk/thegns.htm (the whole site offers a very interesting insight into England at the time of the Norman Conquest). See also Anthony Camp, *My Ancestors came with the Conqueror* (Society of Genealogists, 1990).

2 J. Challenor Smith, *The Parish Registers of Richmond, Surrey* (Surrey Parish Register Society, 1905), p. v. Also at www.archive.org.

3 For more about these societies see Carter & Thompson, *Sources*, pp. 7–8. Details of BRS publications are at www.britishrecordsociety.org. The Harleian Society has a website at http://harleian.org.uk. www.royalhistoricalsociety.org/textandcalendars.htm.

4 A *Calendar* contains a summary of the contents of individual records. It is unlikely entries will contain names, but they should indicate that the item is a list of names and whether it is a petition or whatever. In this work the Public Record Office took over from the Record Commission, which published a number of volumes between 1800 and 1837. The domestic series of *Calendars of State Papers* are described by Carter & Thompson, *Sources*, pp. 193–4. TNA describe the various runs of state papers in a set of in-depth research guides at www.nationalarchives.gov.uk/records/researchguides. They are now online available at university libraries.

5 Generally university libraries, outside London, are happy to let the general public use their facilities. You may have to pay a fee or indicate what you want to use before you are allowed in. You will also not be able to borrow books. Details are normally given on the appropriate page on the university website. www.british-history.ac.uk.

6 Quoted in Edward Higgs, *The Information State in England* (Palgrave, 2004), p. 39. Details of each parish register, showing gaps and where they are to be found, is given in Cecil Humphery-Smith, *The Phillimore Atlas and Index of Parish Registers* (3rd edn, Phillimore, 2002). The change in the 1650s is sometimes called the Commonwealth Gap. See also Tate, *Parish Chest*, pp. 47–8.

7 J. Challenor Smith, *Parish Registers*, pp. 118, 158, 274; Hey, *Family History and Local History in England*, pp. 50–1. Tate also includes a number of examples.

8 More is given in Jane Cox, *Tracing Your East End Ancestor* (Pen & Sword, 2011); Maureen Waller, *The English Marriage: Tales of Love, Money and Adultery* (John Murray, 2009), pp. 133–5. The Fleet Prison registers are now at TNA in series RG 7 and available online through TheGenealogist. They contain details of some 200,000 marriages. The registers have been transcribed by Mark Herber, *Clandestine Marriages in the Chapel and Rules of the Fleet Prison* (3 vols, Francis Boutle, 1998–2001).

9 Wikipedia has an entry about the act at http://en.wikipedia.org/wiki/Marriage_Act_1753. See also Waller, *English Marriage*, pp. 145–6. Banns books are at local record offices, which record the reading of the banns. They are often ignored by researchers but can occasionally be useful if the original register has been lost. *Diary of a Country Parson*, p. 395. The happy couple married on 6 April 1791. FamilySearch records the marriage of William Spraggs to Anne Kaye on that day.

10 Quoted in Cox, *East End*, p. 79. An excellent leaflet describing the records and their uses is at www.york.ac.uk/inst/bihr/guideleaflets/marriagebondguidance.pdf. See also Melanie Barber, 'Records of Marriage and Divorce in Lambeth Palace Library', *Genealogists' Magazine* (20), 2000.

11 Tate, *Parish Chest*, pp. 50–1.

12 Quoted in Roger Bellingham, 'Dade parish registers', *Local Population Studies* (73), 2004, p. 51. The parish is Saxton in Elmet. Bellingham notes that even for Dade registers this was particularly comprehensive. See also R.A. Bellingham, 'Dade Registers', *Archives* (27), 2002.

13 For more information see the article on the Pontefract FHS website www.pontefractfhs.org.uk/Dade_registers.htm and the discussion at www.rootschat.com/forum/index.

php/topic,39818.0.html. There were also Barrington registers, used in a few parishes in the West Country, which were basically simplified Dade registers.

14 See Tate, *Parish Chest*, p. 50. Cannon diary quote from Tim Hitchcock, *Down and Out in Eighteenth Century London* (Hambledon and London, 2004), p. 205. *Boyd's Marriage Index* suggests that Cannon married a Susan Collins. The kind-hearted James Woodforde generally did not charge his poorer parishioners for reading the banns, baptising, marrying or burying them. At 4*d*, the stamp duty was roughly a third of a day's pay for a labourer.

15 In series ADM 338 and WO 156 for navy and army respectively. Beer drinkers may be familiar with Theakston's Old Peculier, which is named in honour of the Masham's ecclesiastical status.

16 www.sog.org.uk/prc/intro.shtml.

17 The Manchester project should be complete by the end of 2012. At the time of writing west Yorkshire is mainly post-1812 and includes some examples of Dade's registers.

18 Described at www.findmypast.co.uk/content/sog/london-burials. Boyd's surname classification system is similar in concept to the American Soundex system, which classifies surnames by how they sound. This was first adopted in the 1930s when the early US censuses were indexed.

19 Usually abbreviated as BTs. The records are sometimes called parish register transcripts. Quoted by Tate, *Parish Chest*, p. 52. See also Jeremy Gibson, *Bishop's Transcripts and Marriage Licences, Bonds and Allegations* (2nd edn, FFHS, 2001).

20 A detailed introduction to recusant history is at www.catholic-history.org.uk/nwchs/recushandbook.htm#Primary_next. Also of use are the pages on the Elizabethan Era website, www.elizabethan-era.org.uk/elizabethan-recusants-recusancy-laws.htm. A summary of TNA's holdings is at www.nationalarchives.gov.uk/records/research-guides/catholics.htm. The Catholic National Library in Farnborough also has many resources (www.catholic-library.org.uk/) and the Catholic FHS has published many records and provided other indexes (www.catholic-history.org.uk/cfhs).

21 Tate, *Parish Chest*, pp. 58, 65.

22 Quaker registers are particularly detailed. More about Friends Library is at www.quaker.org.uk/about-library. For Methodists, the Wesley Historical Society has significant holdings, see www.wesleyhistoricalsociety.org.uk. Over the years the Society of Genealogists and the Family History Partnership have published many guides to researching particular denominations, which are worth looking out for.

23 Details of the returns are on the Parliamentary Archives' online catalogue portcullis at www.portcullis.parliament.uk. Incidentally, the returns for Derbyshire are with the Derbyshire Record Office. What survives is listed in Jeremy Gibson & Alan Dell, *The Protestation Returns 1641–42 and Other Contemporary Listings* (FFHS, 1995). Examples for Kidderminster from the 1820s are at www.worcestershire.gov.uk/cms/community-and-living/records/search-our-records/online-indexes.aspx#kidderminster.

24 Entry about the militia in Hey, *Oxford Companion*, pp. 495–6. See also Chambers, *Early Modern*, pp. 147–8.

25 Tudor and Stuart militia records are described in Jeremy Gibson & Alan Dell, *Tudor and Stuart Militia Rolls* (FFHS, 1991). They are listed and their whereabouts given in Jeremy Gibson & Mervyn Medlycott, *Militia Lists and Musters 1767–1876* (4th edn, Family History Partnership, 2004). Access to Archives should also be able to tell about collections of militia records at local record offices. A few lists have been published by local record and family history societies.

26 From *Genealogists' Magazine*, March 1935, quoted at www.findmypast.co.uk/content/
    sog/london-burials.

27 Burton quotation at www.units.muohio.edu/miamimoo/images/thompsj9/wmn.html.
    Amanda Vickery, *Behind Closed Doors: At Home in Georgian England* (Yale University Press,
    2009), p. 9. Peter Laslett suggests the position was much the same a century earlier, see his
    The World We Have Lost, p. 2.

28 In legal terminology married women were sometimes referred to as 'femme covert'.
    See Keith Wrightson, *Earthly Necessities: Economic Lives in Early Modern Britain* (Yale
    University Press, 2000), p. 43. Many such accounts are given in Waller, *English Marriage*.

29 The records of the court are at the London Metropolitan Archives with indexes between
    1703 and 1714 only on Origins. The Origins website has a useful guide to the records:
    www.origins.net/help/aboutbo-lccd.aspx. 'Criminous conversation' is better known as
    criminal conversation or crimcon. It was a legal action taken by a cuckolded husband
    against his wife's lover. The idea was to receive damages from the lover. More at http://
    virtuallinguist.typepad.com/the_virtual_linguist/2010/03/criminal-conversation.html
    and Wikipedia. This is explored in more detail in Hallie Rubenhold, *Lady Worsley's Whim:
    An Eighteenth-Century Tale of Sex, Scandal and Divorce* (Vintage, 2009).

30 For churchwardens, see Tate, *Parish Chest*, p. 33. Camp followers and their naval
    equivalents are rarely mentioned in muster rolls or other records. Just one woman, for
    example, Jane Townshend, appears on TNA's Trafalgar database.

31 East Riding Archives and Local Studies Service reference DDJA/72. A facsimile of the
    recipe is at www.eastriding.gov.uk/cs/culture-and-information/archives/document-of-
    the-month/?assetdet803983=85079. The compiler of this recipe book is not known, but
    I have tried the recipe and it is delicious! TNA has a recipe book compiled by Margaretta
    Acworth, the wife of a prominent merchant, which was transcribed and updated by Alice
    & Frank Prochaska in *Margaretta Acworth's Georgian Cookery Book* (Pavilion, 1987).

32 Surviving records are generally to be found at local record offices. They are listed on
    the Hospital Records Database at www.nationalarchives.gov,uk/hospitalrecords. Patient
    records less than a hundred years old may still be closed to public access.

33 Jon C. Lewis, *London the Autobiography* (Constable, 2008), p. 187.

34 More about the hospital can be found on Wikipedia and Your Archives, http://
    yourarchives.nationalarchives.gov.uk/index.php?title=The_British_Lying_in_
    Hospital%2C_Holborn. Unusually, patient registers before 1868 are at TNA in series
    RG 8 and online at www.thegenealogist.co.uk. Other records are at London
    Metropolitan Archives. The reference for the 1775 minute book is H14/BLI/A/01/03
    and the statistics is in an 1805 history of the hospital (H14/BLI/AG//2).

35 The mortality rate is given in Laslett, *The World We Have Lost*, p. 112. Most deaths in
    hospital were from puerperal fever.

36 Quoted by Robert Burlison, *Tracing Your Pauper Ancestors* (Pen & Sword, 2009), p. 62.
    Again records are largely at local record offices. Three boxes of records relating to
    Beamsley Hospital are with the Yorkshire Archaeological Society in Leeds.

37 Very little as been written about rate books and certainly there are no examples yet
    online. This section is based on Tate, *Parish Chest*, pp. 25–9. See also Ida Darlington, 'Rate
    Books', in Munby & Thomson (ed.), *Short Guides* (Vol. 1). For Edwin Ridley I used the
    rate books of St James Clerkenwell for the years between 1822 and 1840 at Islington
    Local History Centre. For the proportion of homeowners see Vickery, *Behind Closed
    Doors*, pp. 7–8 and footnote 13.

38 Entry taken from www.pepysdiary.com. Pepys eventually paid £50.

39 Picard, *Dr Johnson's London*, p. 278. In 1762, window tax was 1s per window up to twelve, or 1s 6d for households with more than twelve windows; see Picard, *Dr Johnson's*, p. 338. The tax had to be paid weekly.

40 Introductory note to series available through TNA catalogue. The database is at www. nationalarchives.gov.uk/e179. The records are explained in detail in M. Jurkowski et al., *Lay Taxes in England and Wales, 1188–1688* (Public Record Office, 1998). See also Richard Hoyle, *Tudor Taxation Records* (Public Record Office, 1995).

41 See the entry for lay subsidies in Hey, *Oxford Companion*, p. 466; and Chambers, *Medieval Genealogy*, pp. 90–4. A number of rolls have been transcribed and published by county record societies. Those for parts of Cumberland, London, Sussex and Yorkshire are online at http://british-history.ac.uk/catalogue.aspx?type=2&gid=53. Janice Brooker & Susan Flood, *Hertfordshire Lay Subsidy Rolls 1307 and 1334* (Hertfordshire Record Society, 1998), p. vii.

42 See Chambers, *Medieval Genealogy*, pp. 95–8. The surviving returns of the 1377 poll tax have been published by the British Academy in three volumes, edited by Carolyn Fenwick. (In the late 1980s, the imposition of a new poll tax and the resulting unrest contributed to the downfall of Mrs Thatcher in 1990.) Most are listed in Jeremy Gibson, *Protestation Returns 1641–42 and Other Contemporary Listings* (FFHS, 1995).

43 Michael Wood, *The Story of England* (Viking, 2009), p. 281. Again a number of returns have been published by local record societies.

44 Quoted in Hey, *Oxford Companion*, p. 423. The entry offers a useful introduction to the tax, its records and the use that can be made of them. The records are summarised in Elizabeth Parkinson, 'The Hearth Tax', *Ancestors Magazine* (82), 2009. A few lists can be downloaded from www.hearthtax.org.uk. More about the tax can be found on Roehampton University's Centre for Hearth Tax Studies website at www.roehampton. ac.uk/hearthtax.

45 Some records of silver and carriage taxes, for example, are in series T 47 at Kew; see Derek Morris, 'Silver and Carriage Duties', *Genealogists' Magazine* (30:5), 2011, pp. 147–51. The returns were published by the London Record Society in 1966 as *London Inhabitants with the Walls*, and they are now online at http://british-history.ac.uk. The records are at the London Metropolitan Archives. Small collections may occasionally be found at other record offices. More about the duty is at www.londonlives.org/ static/LSDSMDA.jsp. See also Jeremy Boulton, 'The Marriage Duty Act and Parochial Registration in London, 1695–1706', in Kevin Schürer & Tom Arkell (eds), *Surveying the People: The Interpretation and Use of Document Sources for the Study of Population in the Later Seventeenth Century* (Cambridge University Press, 1992).

46 However, another set of returns were supposedly saved by the king's remembrancer and are now in series E 182 at Kew. The series comprises summaries of money collected with details of defaulters, as well as some records of window and other late Georgian taxes, but unfortunately is virtually impossible to use. A brief but thorough history of income tax can be found on the HM Revenue and Customs website, www.hmrc.gov.uk/history/ taxhis1.htm.

47 For more see the research guide on death duties at www.nationalarchives.gov.uk/ records/research-guides/death-duty-records-1796-to-1903.htm.

48 Details at www.nationalwillsindex.com. For more about probate records see Karen Grannum & Nigel Taylor, *Wills and Probate Records* (TNA, 2009).

49 Beverley Adams, *Lifestyle and Culture in Hertford: Wills and Inventories for the Parishes of All Saints and St Andrew, 1660–1725* (Hertfordshire Record Society, 1997), p. 75; Barrie Trinder & Nancy Cox (eds), *Mariners & Mariners of the Severn Gorge: Probate Inventories for Benthall, Broseley, Little Wenlock and Madeley, 1660–1764* (Phillimore, 2000), p. 92.

50 Selections of inventories have been published by local record societies. See also Karen Grannum & Nigel Taylor, *Wills and Probate Records* (TNA, 2009); and Simon Fowler, 'A price on everything', *Family History Monthly*, August 2011, p. 192.

51 Zvi Razi, *Life, Marriage, and Death in a Medieval Parish: Economy, Society, and Demography in Halesowen, 1270–1400* (Cambridge University Press, 1980), p. 2.

52 For more about the courts see Jonathan Brown, *Tracing Rural Ancestors* (Pen & Sword, 2011).

53 The best book on the subject is N. W. Alcock, *Old Title Deeds* (Phillimore, 2001). Also useful is Nick Barratt's *Guide to Your Ancestors Lives* (Pen & Sword, 2010). The Scottish system is very different. A good introduction can be found in Bruce Durie, *Scottish Genealogy* (The History Press, 2009). The Middlesex deeds registery is at the London Metropolitan Archives (www.cityoflondon.gov.uk/NR/rdonlyres/E69300BA-9550-4705-8534-01896C87A54E/0/LH_LMA_middlesexdeeds.PDF); the one for the West Riding of Yorkshire is in Wakefield (www.archives.wyjs.org.uk/wyjs-archives-w-r-registry-d.asp#intro); the East Riding Record Office has the registry for east Yorkshire and the North Yorkshire Record Office has the office for the North Riding. In addition, there was a small registry for the Bedford Levels in the Fens, whose records are now at the Cambridgeshire Record Office.

54 Essex Record Office reference D/DC 23/20, dated 17 March 1606/07. The deed was entered in the manorial court for the parish.

55 Quoted, along with many other less than complimentary quotations about Scotland, at www.samueljohnson.com/scotland.html#355. This poverty was one reason for the mass voluntary and involuntary emigration from the country. If you are researching Scottish genealogy you really do need to buy a guide. One of the best is Durie, *Scottish Genealogy*. The ScotlandsPeople website has some useful pages describing the records on its site and how to use them. The National Records of Scotland also has a number of guides to records at www.nas.gov.uk/guides/default.asp.

56 www.scotlandspeople.gov.uk/content/help/index.aspx?r=554&405. OPRs can also be ordered from the local LDS Church family history centres and entries appear on FamilySearch as well. In many cases the entries here are as informative as the records themselves. Indeed, my Aberdonian godparents managed to trace several of their Farquhar lines back to the sixteenth century using these records.

57 www.scan.org.uk. There is also a useful knowledge base to Scottish research in general.

58 The records are complicated to use and understand. For more information, see Durie, *Scottish Genealogy*, pp. 119–26 or the online guide to sasines provided by the National Records of Scotland, www.nas.gov.uk/guides/sasines.asp.

59 A brief introduction is at www.fife.50megs.com/clan-system.htm with more at www.scotland.org.uk/guide/clan-system. Tartans, however, are largely an invention of the nineteenth century. The Scottish Register of Tartans is the official 'repository of tartan designs' at www.tartanregister.gov.uk.

60 Further reading: Derek Barlow, *Records of the Forfeited Estates Commission* (HMSO, 1968); Emma Jolly, 'Jacobite Material: the records of the Forfeited Estates Commission for England', *Genealogists' Magazine*, 2006, p. 28.

Chapter 6

DEEP ROOTS: GENEALOGY AND THE WIDER WORLD

G enealogy can be more than just tracing the history of your family. It has been used to:

- Offer an explanation as to how a people came to exist
- Provide evidence of a tribe or nation's superiority over others
- Reinforce social structure

There are also clear links between genealogy and oral history. Many cultures prepare and recite genealogies going back many generations, as in the case of the Griot praise singers of West Africa. We are probably more familiar with the various genealogies in the Bible which reinforce the feeling that the Jews were special and, in particular, stress the descent of Jesus from the Prophets as occurs in the first chapter of the Gospel according to Matthew: 'So all the generations from Abraham to David *are* fourteen generations; and from David until the carrying away into Babylon *are* fourteen generations; and from the carrying away into Babylon unto Christ *are* fourteen generations.'[1] Before the Bible was written down these genealogies would have been memorised by succeeding generations. Even today they are surprisingly easy to remember and have a powerful resonance, especially when proclaimed in Hebrew.

Most ancient cultures had similar traditions, although they have faded with increased Westernisation and with the arrival of writing. One place where this survives is in West Africa, where Griot praise singers can recite the pedigrees of the rich families who employ them back twenty generations or more. According to the Fulani proverb, 'a tree with deep roots is not easily blown over'. Tribes, clans and individuals find their sense of identity in the history and achievements of their ancestors.[2]

The Griots are the 'artisans of the spoken word'. They appear every time the spoken word needs to be repeated, given heightened value, remembered, presented in a special manner as in music or praise, or used as a social lubricant. Above all, they are performers and indeed a number have recently carved out successful musical careers in Paris and New York. Griots were traditionally a caste, the attendants of kings, warlords, nobles and later of Islamic scholars as keepers of history and genealogies, of sayings, songs and music. In a world where writing was practically unknown they had to guarantee not only the survival of their people as a culturally and historically defined group, but also the social status of the nobles they were attached to.[3]

The first person to write about Griots was the Moroccan traveller Ibn Battuta. In 1352 he was received at the court of Mansa Suleyman, King of the Empire of Mali, where he encountered a host of Griots playing on their lutes and singing the king's praises. It is certain, however, that there were Griots in Mali many centuries before Ibn Battuta arrived there.

Different people in West Africa tell different stories about the origin of Griots, but here is a current Griot, Hassan Tamboura's, version. Once upon a time in Mali there lived a beggar called Sura Gato. Gato was accustomed to beg from the prophets of God and one day he went to beg from a prophet called Ali Badara. When Badara refused to give him anything, Sura Gato ran to the marketplace and began to list in a loud voice all the prophets in Mali, conspicuously omitting Badara's name. The prophet flew into a rage and threatened to cut out Sura Gato's tongue, so the frightened beggar revised his list to include Ali Badara, who was so relieved that he showered Gato with gifts. So it was that Sura Gato became the first Griot.

The story of Sura Gato illustrates the different powers of Griot and patron, and their uneasy, co-dependant relationship. Even today, a fascinating symbiosis exists between the Griots and the families they serve. The ancestors of Hassan Tamboura in Burkina Faso praised the ancestors of the current chief, and his sons will praise their sons. A Griot bestows history and honour on his patron, and in return the patron bestows cattle and grain on his Griot.

The Griot tradition came to prominence in Alex Haley's *Roots*, which was published in 1976. The author was a black American writer who travelled to Gambia to research his family tree. There he found Fofana, an old Griot who knew the genealogy of his Gambian ancestors and performed it to musical backing:

> Spilling from the griot's head came an incredibly complex Kinte clan lineage that reached back across many generations: who married whom; who had what children; what children then married whom; then their offspring. It was all just unbelievable. I was struck not only by the profusion of details, but also by the narrative's biblical style.

Unfortunately, this was largely made up. Researchers have found that Alex Haley had manipulated the man. The historian Donald R. Wright interviewed Fofana and thought that as an informant he was 'neither Griot not too highly respected an elder – [he] was clearly second rate' and concluded that Fofana had told Haley what he wanted to hear.[4]

Clearly, the passing down of the family tree orally may have been universal in all societies, only fading with the arrival of writing. Even in Britain, where literacy was almost universal by the mid-nineteenth century (and common two centuries before), the oral tradition continued, particularly in areas where there was little movement of population. When the former MP Hervey Rhodes came to see Sir Anthony Wagner at the College of Arms after his elevation to the peerage in 1964, Rhodes was asked about his ancestry. He 'gave a wonderful answer. He told me that as a child he had been taught to say: "I'm Hervey of Jack's of Bill's of Jack's of Joe's of John's of Thomas's of Dean Head".' This took the pedigree back to the early eighteenth century. Indeed:

> When [Rhodes] stood for his constituency after the War he took a meeting in a corner of it where he was not known and introduced himself by reciting this pedigree. An old man with a white beard audience stood up and said 'He was not Thomas of Dean Head. He was Thomas of Dean Head Clough', Dean Head Clough being the less important of two adjacent weavers' houses.

Rhodes had been born at Saddleworth, high up in the Pennines, in 1895.[5]

In Wessex too a tradition of remembering pedigrees survived until the late nineteenth century at least, but here, according to Thomas Hardy, the peasantry was keener to remember the antecedents of their social betters than their own. He wrote in a letter to Lord Lytton that: '[The] traditions of the local families … are remembered by the yeomen and the peasantry long after they are forgotten by the families concerned.'[6]

In Iceland, and to a lesser extent parts in Polynesia, these pedigrees are part of nation building. The spirit of the modern Icelandic nation is still intimately bound up with an extraordinary series of stories – the sagas – which tell the tale of the island's settlement and the early settlers from the late ninth century to the thirteenth, when the sagas were first written down. The sagas tell of hardy and independent men who left Norway rather than be subservient to the king, together with their generally bloody adventures in their new home.

During the long, dark winter months there can have been little else to do for amusement but tell stories. You can get a flavour of what life must have been like at the recreation of a ninth-century farmhouse near Buðardalur. I still remember that when I visited one day in late August a few years ago a chill wind and sharp showers buffeted the farm, which lay low on a south-facing hillside covered with earth. Inside, however, it was remarkably homely and one can imagine the family at ease around the fire telling and retelling the heroic deeds of ancestors which had taken place

200 or 300 years previously. *Laxdæla Saga*, for instance, describes Ketill Flatnose, a powerful and well-born lord who found he could not prosper in Norway under the rule of Harald Finehair. When he learnt the king was intending to make him a vassal, Ketill called his kinsmen together and said they were either going to have to flee Norway or stay and be hounded off their lands and perhaps be put to death. Two of his sons announced that they would got to Iceland, where there was rumoured to be excellent land for the taking, an abundance of stranded whales, plenty of salmon and good fishing grounds all the year round. Although Ketill did not make the journey, two of his sons and a daughter and their kinsmen settled in southern Iceland.[7]

The tales gave succour to Icelanders during the long centuries of Norwegian and Danish colonial neglect, from the time Iceland lost its independence in 1265 until it achieved it once again in 1944. Now, in times of renewed uncertainty following the collapse of the Icelandic banking system in 2008, there is again an emphasis on the sagas and their messages of resilience and fortitude. In recent years a network of museums and visitor centres have been established across the western half of the island, retelling stories from the sagas.[8]

Of particular interest is the *Landnámabók* – the *Book of Settlement* – which describes in considerable detail the descendants of the original settlers and traces important events and family history into the twelfth century. More than 3,000 people and 1,400 settlements are mentioned; 435 men are listed as the initial settlers, the majority of them settling in the northern and south-western parts of the island. It remains an invaluable source for both the history and genealogy of the Icelandic people. Its author, Ari the Learned, said that he wrote the book and its companion the *Íslendingsbók* – the *Book of Icelanders* – so that Icelanders could 'all the better meet the criticisms of foreigners when they accuse us of being descended from slaves or scoundrels, if we know for certain the truth about our ancestry'.[9]

It is not surprising, therefore, that family history is immensely popular in Iceland. According to Sally Magnusson:

> The Icelanders do like to talk ancestry. It is a more common subject than the weather – and believe you me in a country where you can be served up a light dusting of snowflakes, followed by sunshine, ran and then a feet-lifting blizzard all in the course of a day, that is saying something. You can hardly last two minutes among strangers without someone asking '*Af hvað ætt ertu?*' ('What line are you from?') and there is at least a page a week devoted to genealogy in one national newspaper.[10]

However, there is a paradox, why 'such passionate republicans ... should be so keen to prove their descent from kings'.[11]

The ancestry of about 80 per cent of Icelanders since medieval times has been plotted on family trees, the majority of whom are descended in some way from two sixteenth-century bishops. A recent DNA sampling indicated that ultimately 85 per cent of the population are descended from either Norsemen or Celtic women. The sagas said that the women were originally slaves, but historians now believe that many of the early settlers came from mixed communities in Ireland and northern Scotland. One Icelander told me that he felt immediately at home on the streets of Dublin, because so many Dubliners looked like his neighbours. The city had been a major Viking settlement in Ireland.

Superficially, the colonisation of New Zealand by Polynesian settlers crossing the Pacific Ocean using phenomenal navigational skills has many similarities to that of Iceland. Certainly much of what we know of the event is through the survival of oral genealogies. However, New Zealand *whakapapa* cannot be compared to the Icelandic sagas either by their tone or the subjects they cover. Indeed, they are very different to any European concept of genealogy, being as much about explaining the place of the Maori people in their world as about remembering the heroic exploits of the ancestors. The anthropologist Cleve Barlow defined *whakapapa* as being the 'genealogical descent of all living things from the gods to the present time'. They include not just the genealogies but many spiritual, mythological and human stories that flesh out the genealogical backbone. With the introduction of writing, the visualisation is slowly changing to that of European genealogical tradition, with the Maori 'descending' from their ancestors. Another term, '*Te Here Tangata*', literally 'The Rope of Mankind', may also describe genealogy. Here users visualise themselves with their hands on this rope, which stretches into the past for the fifty or so generations, back from there to the instant of creation and on into the future for as long again. We are just one link looking back at our ancestors and forward to our descendents yet to come.[12]

Unfortunately, *whakapapa* only began to be written down in the nineteenth century and then often by European missionaries and researchers who interpreted them through the prism of their own experiences and beliefs. This reduces their value to the historian and has reduced their usefulness to the genealogist. According to Michael King, they 'offer names without remains – that is stories without evidence – while archaeology offers [remains] without names – evidence without stories'.[13]

Oral traditions passed down from generation to generation tell of accounts of an ancient homeland called Hawaiiki and a great migration across the South Pacific, probably from Tahiti to the North Island. Both the oral tradition and archaeological evidence suggest that the first settlement took place between about AD 1250 and 1300. Nevertheless, it is difficult for historians to find out much about how the settlers actually lived from the *whakapapa*, which is more about the ancestors and their descendents rather than a manual of farming. Unlike the sagas, which tell of the bravery of the first Icelanders, *whakapapa* are more about keeping alive the names and deeds of recent ancestors who may have done brave things but were not primarily heroes. Initially they were the men and women who had been left behind in Hawaiiki, but these people inevitably receded into a kind of Arthurian dream world. The Maori, too, lived commonly in tribes known as *hapu*, unlike the original Icelanders who preferred to keep a considerable distance between themselves and their neighbours. Also, many *whakapapa* reinforce the importance of the tribe, telling how the tribe was formed and by whom, and the lines of descent of its members. The Tuhoe people, for example, recite their *whakapapa* back to Huti, the progenitor of the *Hapu Tamakaimoana*. At the same time they would declare the tribally identifying proverb: 'Tuhoe extravagant with food, with precious things and with human life.'[14]

Traditionally, most Maori would be familiar with the *whakapapa* for their direct forebears and as proof of membership of a tribe, and perhaps as evidence that they are *tāngata whenua* (that is, in effect, belonging to a place rather than being a visitor to it). These days *whakapapa* are still recited on ceremonial occasions. For many they have come to be regarded as little more than family trees, but they are much more complicated than this, reflecting a world where the Maori was once at harmony with nature and sought to explain the world around them.

This is quite unlike anything that could be found in the UK. Until the nineteenth century, genealogy within the United Kingdom was really a branch of antiquarianism along with local history and archaeology – but even here there was an element of fantasy. By the standard of later centuries, the genealogical research was inevitably quite poor. The records were hard to find and there was little incentive to be accurate. In any case, history itself was often viewed as often being little more than myth. In 1607, Henry Lyte of Lytes Cary in Somerset compiled 'A table where it is supposed that Lyte of Lytescarie sprange of the race and stock of Leitus (one of the five captaynes of Beotia that went to Troye) and that his ancestors came to England first with Brute'. The family seat was alleged to derive its name from 'Caria in Asia' and the family coat of arms contained 'Three sylver swannes, as from the shield which Leit at Troy did beare'.[15]

It was also intricately bound up with the class system, which so pervaded British life. All the county histories of the seventeenth and eighteenth centuries contain pedigrees or discussions of the antecedents of local families alongside descriptions of local attractions and town histories. By including such pedigrees the authors recognised that the landed gentry were the backbone of local society and had been so for many generations. The greatest of early historians was Sir William Dugdale, whose *The Antiquities of Warwickshire Illustrated* (1656) was dedicated to 'the gentlemen of Warwickshire', with extracts from genealogical records, pedigrees and the like 'as the most proper persons to whom it can be presented, wherein you will see very much of our worthy ancestors, to whose memory I have erected it, as a monumental pillar'.[16]

By the beginning of Queen Victoria's reign in 1837 the production of such histories had largely come to an end. Instead, genealogy had become a study in its own right. There was little or no emphasis on the ancestry of ordinary people, but instead genealogists grappled with the family trees of the nobility and the gentry. This largely remained the case until the 1970s. In Sir Anthony Wagner's well-regarded *English*

Genealogy, which was first published in 1960, for example, there is scant reference to either civil registration or the census. Instead, he argues that 'Through genealogy the transient flat dweller of the cities can join himself to the peasant rooted in ancestral soil or the baron ruling from his castle ... He can by conscious effort recover the support of that sense of membership in a kindred which was once the common birthright'.

Genealogy, it was argued, was a way of communing with a simpler and more romantic past, vividly portrayed in the novels of Sir Walter Scott, which gave generations of middle-class families a romanticised view of their ancestors' lives. Indeed, Scott's house Abbotsford, near Melrose in the Scottish Borders, is really genealogy carved in stone: full of coats of arms and the, at best, semi-fictional genealogies of the Border reivers, whose brutal lives he celebrated in his novels. By researching the pedigree of one's ancestors or, if they were too commonplace, some noble family who took your fancy, you could achieve a whiff of a courtly chivalry. Sir Anthony argued: 'For the imagination of surprisingly many modern Englishmen pre-industrial England has the quality of a lost home.'[17]

The newly rich tried to graft an ancestor or two to add respectability to an otherwise proletarian family tree, by commissioning a pedigree which would 'prove' a link to the nobility or the gentry of the past. As late as the 1930s, the motor manufacturer and philanthropist Lord Nuffield paid to have his family tree traced. The researchers found an ancestry back to a William Morrice, who 'held land in Swarford (of the Manor of Hook Norton) in 1278'. There was then an unexplained gap of 250 years to 'John Morris at south Leigh, who held land there under the Manor of Eynsham to 1524. These are the probable ancestors of the Morris family of Kiddington.' Such actions were, of course, condemned by serious genealogists, such the anonymous writer of *The Right to Bear Arms* in the 1870s, who grumbled:

> Why do people object to having their arms described as 'bogus'? Because in the frantic struggle to get into Society nine men out of ten will tell lie upon lie, to prove that their fathers were not labourers or '*dans cette galère*,' and will therefore use bogus arms to show that they and their people are not of the vulgar crowd. That is what I call snobbery, rank, utter and absolute.[18]

Conversely, you might play down the number of poor people on the tree. Thomas Hardy, whose interest in genealogy underlies a number of his novels, elaborately charted a branch only distantly related to his mother whose members were mainly professional, while entirely omitting closer relatives, such as numerous first cousins who belonged to the labouring and servant classes.[19]

Additionally, where families can rise in society they can of course fall. The Society of Genealogists has two beautifully illustrated albums compiled by Miss Louise Cecilia Bazalgette Lucas. Any doubt about the quality of the research is immediately overwhelmed by page after page of hand-coloured coats of arms or gold-leaf marginalia which take the breath away. The whole point of the album, however, was to commemorate a family that Miss Lucas clearly felt had suffered generations of decline. In the introduction she wrote:

> We used to be big people once, but have gone done in the world. People who a hundred years ago we turned up our noses, now turn up their noses at us … We had married heiresses had gone mounting up to the top of fortune's wheel, and it had been well with us But alack, in these later days we had been too well known at Epsom and Newmarket. We had been very much at home at Crockford's [gambling club] … [and] had generally misbehaved ourselves, and in consequences, our many acres had passed into the hands of Manchester gents, with fat snug faces, who wage war of extermination against the letter h and use big words when little ones would have done better.[20]

There was quite an industry in providing such pedigrees. As the genealogical writer Walter Rye pointed out:

> Of course one can readily understand that the new man, whose successful trading has taught him that he can – and ought to – get anything by paying for it, should expect that on paying a perfect pedigree, Norman for choice, can be turned out for him on demand without the necessity of any research.

Most people approached a professional genealogist to undertake the work for them. There was no professional organisation to ensure standards were met or to weed out the charlatans (which, unfortunately, largely remains true today), so anybody with a modicum of Latin and a passing knowledge of the plea rolls could set themselves up as a genealogist. It is little wonder that professional genealogists often had a bad name, particularly among their fellow researchers. In 1839, the Scottish historian William Turnbull described Thomas Christopher Banks as being 'of the busy, meddling, troublesome and officious individuals, professing themselves "Genealogists", who tend so much to perpetuate blunders and misrepresentations in matters of general and family history, if indeed they do not *wittingly* aid and abet in the fabrications of impostures like the present'. Sixty years later a 'Dr' Herbert Davies, the son of a Birmingham small tradesman, defrauded Colonel William Shipway while supposedly tracing the colonel's family tree. Davies even wrote an article for the *Western Daily Press* on the subject and granted interviews to local reporters in which he figured as the 'Principal Genealogical Specialist'. Through the persistence of England's best-known genealogist, William Phillimore, Davies was eventually prosecuted at the Old Bailey and was sentenced to three years in prison.[21]

By the late 1960s genealogy was beginning to turn into family history. An ageing population with a better educational background than the previous generation and time to devote to such pursuits meant that for the first time non-professionals could devote their time to researching their family trees. They accepted that their families had no pretensions to noble grandeur – real or imagined. They were happy that their ancestors were labourers and servants with the occasional soldier or petty criminal to add spice.

Even in Victorian times not everybody was interested in researching the families of the nobility and gentry. Some families were realistic about where they came from. In 1870 William Derrick sadly acknowledged in his diary:

> As far as I know anything of those who have borne the name [of Derrick] in England, they mostly seem to have been people more or less of mark in their own way, although I am bound to confess that their aspirations never appear to have been of a very exalted kind. I am not certain however that I did not once see the name given as one of the very earliest English poets, but if so I am afraid it was only a misprint for 'Herrick'.[22]

Walter Rye was more encouraging: 'It is more honourable by far to trace your descent sturdily and clearly to some medieaval yeoman or tradesman than by straining coincidences, presuming identities and fudging judiciously to attempt to hook on to some noble or well-descended family of the same name as yours, or something like it …' One family who took Rye's advice was the Chamberlain family of Birmingham. Neville Chamberlain (who became prime minister in 1937), along with his father Joseph, the self-made son of a prosperous shoemaker, and half-brother Austen took a keen interest in their antecedents. Chamberlain's diary for the winter of 1914 records a visit to Bradford-upon-Avon, where the family had originated in the sixteenth century, to look for the ancestral home. They knocked on the door of a cottage which was opened by one Daniel Chamberlain, who Neville notes was a typical 'rustic' wearing a smock. There were a few minutes stiff conversation before the visitors from Birmingham departed. Neville reflected that his ancestor 300 years previously must have looked much the same.[23]

We have an account of how an individual conducted research into his ordinary family before the majority of records we are familiar with today were available. Edwin Lyne was a middle-ranking civil servant in Dublin, although his family had been yeoman farmers in the Midlands for many generations. During the late 1870s, he became aware that a Mary Lyne of Reading had left £500 unclaimed on her death and he set out to see whether they were related. He began by inserting appeals in the personal columns of the newspapers. Naturally, the responses varied. William Line of Banbury wrote: 'my father and grandfather belonged to Littleburn, and other matters seem to answer to it. So hearing from you I hope that it may be that "I am the rightful owner". May I ask sir what it is, money, land or otherwise, and what quantity. Waiting a reply …' However, the appeals did produce a number of long-lost cousins who helped Lyne in his researches, by visiting former servants and other possible relations in the hope of finding useful information. Sometimes potential informants had just died. Richard Philips helpfully wrote in October 1881: 'My cousin Mary David died ... about a year since she could have told us almost everything you want to know.'[24]

Of course, Edwin Lyne could not rely entirely on the memories of his relations. He had to find firm facts. So he turned to two of the key sources still employed today: parish registers and Prerogative Court of Canterbury (PCC) wills. Lyne wrote to clergymen in parishes where there may have been Lynes, asking them to search their registers for him. In many places his enquiries roused a great deal of interest. Thomas Plumb, the sexton at Little Compton, Warwickshire, took his two daughters 'down to the church this evening and cannot find such a headstone as you state'. Elsewhere the enquiries were received with a great deal of grumbling about the work that they would involve. At Fredington, Warwickshire, the Rev. R.E. Williams complained: 'I find upon trial that the task of examining the register is more than I have time for ... the earlier entries are written in a most difficult handwriting and are faded through age.'

Eventually he came across a proper genealogist, in the form of Capt. G.J.M. Glubb, late 38th Bengal Light Infantry. Their correspondence is full of references to medieval and Tudor Lynes scattered throughout the West Country, although the connection to Lyne's line was unclear. Glubb was almost an obsessive. He once wrote to Lyne asking him to 'tell me as soon as it is convenient where I can see the Calendars of Bills of Assizes temp Philip and Mary as I must find out about Lyne and Glubb'.

Like many family historians, Lyne became rather obsessed with his ancestry. His letters are full of minute detail about his ancestors, driving one of his cousins, Augustus Matthews of Stroud, to comment: 'I am become so puzzled with the different branches of the Lyne family that the more I think of it the less I know about it, that it is folly my thinking the subject over.' Unfortunately, the Lyne Collection is incomplete. We don't even know when Edwin died and there are no pedigrees to show his work, let alone a written account of his family history. What is clear, however, is that although he never managed to claim that £500, he derived great pleasure from his research.

A century after Lyne worked on his family tree, the hobby was transformed by two media phenomena. Over the past few years the *Who Do You Think You Are?* television shows, in which the ancestry of a celebrity is traced, have proven hugely successful. The programme first aired in the United Kingdom in 2004 and the format has subsequently been sold to many other countries. In Britain over 6 million people regularly tune in and the first American series was the most viewed show on NBC when it was shown in early 2010. Critics (and many genealogists) have complained about the artificiality of the show and the over-emotional reactions of the stars to the discoveries made, yet the programme clearly has a resonance for viewers, many of whom have been encouraged to take up their family history as a result.

Thirty years ago similar criticisms were levied at Alex Haley's *Roots*, which became a publishing and television sensation. In the book Haley tells how he traced his black American ancestors back to 1767 in the Gambia. Over a million copies of the book were sold after publication in 1976 and when the television mini-series was shown the following year, *Time* reported:

> A California restaurant owner complained of a 40 per cent drop in business. At a Harlem tavern in New York City, patrons insisted that the jukebox be turned off while they discussed the TV program they had just watched; in Los Angeles, the owner of one discotheque closed down operations altogether.

The programme touched Americans of all backgrounds. Karen Bernard, 26, a white Brooklyn teacher, told *Time*: 'I cried all the way through one show. I have a child, and the fact that black women lived in fear of losing their children was devastating.'[25]

Literary critics were less impressed. Dennis Potter of the *Sunday Times* likened the dialogue to 'wet face flannel … redolent of soapy water', and Paul Theroux, reviewing the book for *The Times*, found: 'As genealogy it is tendentious, as history it is probably inaccurate, but at fiction it is shocking, gripping and boring in about equal parts.' However, on both sides of the Atlantic they agreed the book had a real impact because it told an intriguing story of one family's experience. As the *Daily Express* gushed: 'The dialogue in this epic is imagined but the events and characters are real … This is the true story of one man's family.'[26]

Journalists and academics soon revealed the shortcomings in Haley's book. Firstly, Alex Haley had to pay $650,000 to Harold Courlander for plagiarising his book, *The African*. Also, as early as April 1977 the *Sunday Times'* correspondent in West Africa, Mark Ottaway, concluded that 'the Gambian section of the story has little basis in provable facts'. Even the genealogy proved to be flawed: Gary B. Mills and Elizabeth Shown Mills checked Haley's research, finding that the book was 'a work which fails not only the most critical but even the most basic standards of genealogical inquiry'. Nevertheless, none of this much mattered to readers and viewers.[27]

Roots had two major and perhaps related impacts. First, it persuaded ordinary African-Americans, and to a lesser extent black Britons, that they and their ancestors had a fascinating history worth further investigation. It also inspired hundreds of thousands of other people on both sides of the Atlantic to research their family's past. Mike Tepper, of the Genealogical Publishing Company in Baltimore, told *Time*: 'Roots has shown that what seemed remote and mysterious is in fact knowable and within our grasp. It has awakened a smouldering awareness of facts we only thought were unknowable.' Mr Harold Brooks-Baker, the publishing director of Burke's Peerage, told *The Times* in 1984 that 'Haley made it respectable to be interested in your family even if the background wasn't glamorous. And he made people aware that it is important as well as interesting to know who your ancestors were.' Archives and libraries across the United States reported increased numbers of visitors. Even the staid New England Historic Genealogical Society in Boston was besieged. Its historian noted: 'Society members increased, book loan services and researchers tripled ... Additional chairs and tables were placed in the Library to accommodate the overflow of readers.'

In Britain, membership of the Society of Genealogists doubled between 1976 and 1986, and the series had a similar impact countrywide.[28] Although, here, the family history boom was probably encouraged as much by an influential domestic television series in which the newsreader Gordon Honeycombe researched his family history in Ealing. It was first shown in 1979 and repeated several times over the next few years. Even so, John Carey writing in *The Times* in 1984 concluded: '[Haley's] publication was probably the key event in the transformation of family history from an interest confined to a few more or less erudite enthusiasts into a discipline with a mass appeal.' This was acknowledged by Haley in a 1978 interview: 'Roots came out at exactly the right time in the social climate of the United States ... I get letters from people of all kinds telling me the book has stimulated their interest in their personal history and in history in general ...' In Australia, Paul de Serville commented in *Ancestor*, in December 1978:

> There is as we all know a boom in genealogy. Some like to think this is a result of Roots, but the growing interest predates that indifferent program by many years. There are deeper causes, more deserving of attention. In the first place, genealogy has benefited from the general interest in the past and in its preservation.[29]

Although there are superficial similarities, genealogy in the United States is very different to that in the United Kingdom. It is less concerned with class and more with identity and patriotism. In a society, which for the most part prided itself on its egalitarianism and where there was no aristocracy, there was much less interest in researching the nobility or the landed gentry. Instead, genealogists traced the descendents of early settlers or the antecedents of presidents, signers of the Declaration of Independence and other patriotic heroes. In Boston, the New England Historic Genealogical Society was set up in 1845. It is the oldest surviving family history society, pre-dating the British equivalent by six decades. In a circular to potential members its founders argued that:

> The minds of men are naturally moved to know something of their progenitors – those from whom they have derived their being; and there seems to be an increasing interest in this subject; many are trying to trace their genealogy back at least to the first settlers – the early pilgrims of this country ... We wish, by united action, and through the aid of our extensive collections of printed and manuscript works, to furnish the means to every person descended from an early inhabitant of New England, of tracing his genealogy and history.[30]

For the most part, research stopped at the Atlantic because it was difficult to discover where the ancestors originated in the 'Old Country', which for most meant England and Scotland. It was only after the Second World War that interest in genealogy really spread much beyond those of British origin.

Genealogy in America has long been bound up with patriotism in a way that would be inconceivable elsewhere, with researchers keen to confirm the all-American wholesomeness of their ancestry. This was encouraged by the various patriotic societies where applicants had to prove descent from a particular group. The most famous such society is the Daughters of the American Revolution (DAR), which was established in 1890, although it was not the first: the Sons of Revolutionary Wars was set up in San Francisco in 1876. Membership in the DAR was open to anyone:

> who is descended from a man or woman who, with unfailing loyalty to the cause of American Independence, served as a sailor or soldier or civil officer in one of the several colonies or states or in the United Colonies or States, or as a recognised patriot or rendered material aid, thereto; provided the applicant is personally acceptable to the Society.[31]

Another variant, something which was almost unheard of in Britain, was the attempt to trace all the descendents of a particular individual who had arrived in America at some distant point in time. The first published genealogical work in the American colonies was *A Genealogy of the Family of Mr. Samuel Stebbins, and Mrs. Hannah Stebbins, His Wife: From the Year 1707 to the Year 1771, With Their Names, Time of Their Births, Marriages and Deaths of Those That are Deceased*, which was published in 1771, tracing the descendents of Rowland Stebbins, who left England for Roxbury, Massachusetts. Within a century dozens of such studies were being published each year. An interesting spin-off is the family get-together to reunite all the descendents of a particular individual. There's even a commercial magazine for organisers of such events. There have been a few such reunions organised in Britain, but it is something that has never really taken off in the UK.[32]

Genealogy and the Third Reich[33]

On rare occasions family history can be more than just a hobby but, potentially, a matter of life or death, particularly when the government is promoting a racist ideology as happened particularly in Nazi Germany and under Apartheid in South Africa.

Nazi race laws attempted to identify and then eradicate Jews and Jewish presence from German life. It was a policy supported with varying degrees of enthusiasm by the majority of the population. Being a *volksgenosser* (racial comrade) conveyed certain privileges denied Jews, Slavs and those of mixed backgrounds (*mischlinge*).

For example, only pure Aryans could become army officers; *mischlinge* could only hope to rise to the rank of non-commissioned officer. Jews, of course, were excluded altogether. More practically, payments for child support were only given to those who had proved their Aryan credentials.

This meant that millions of Germans had to prove they had 'Aryan blood'. By the end of the Third Reich almost everybody except the very old and the very young had had to do this. Legislation was first introduced within weeks of the Nazis coming to power in January 1933, initially in the civil service, but this was soon extended to other areas. From 1935 proof of Aryan status had to be provided before marriages were permitted and Aryans were forbidden from marrying Jews or those of mixed race.

However, for certain positions, for example as senior civil servants and the higher ranks of the Nazi Party, candidates had to trace their ancestry back to 1800 (known as the 'large documentation'), and, in the case of the SS, back nearly 200 years, to 1750, to prove that they had 'pure' ancestry. Some 8.5 million people joined the Nazi Party between 1919 and 1945. Even non-party members who joined organisations like the Hitler Youth or Women's Federation (and membership was all but compulsory for many of these bodies) had to prove the purity of their 'Aryan descent'. At their peak the Hitler Youth had 8.7 million members and the Women's Federation 2.3 million.

Initially, everybody who was affected by the new laws had to prove that they, their parents and grandparents were of pure German stock, but this proved impossible to enforce rigorously, so eventually individuals were allowed to swear that so far as they knew their immediate ancestors were Aryan. Even so, individuals who did not 'look' Aryan might be subjected to more investigation, as were men and women with supposedly Jewish names, such as Israel and Sarah.

It was also not unknown for research to turn up an unknown Jewish ancestor with all the dangers that this entailed. The greater number of Jewish ancestors, the greater the degree of discrimination. Initially, even people with one Jewish grandparent were to be classified as Jewish, although this was eventually abandoned. About 1 million people were thought to have been proven to have had mixed heritage out of a total population of 60 million.

Even for the 'small documentation' going back three generations, an individual had to provide seven birth records, showing religion, three sets of marriage records and often other evidence as well. Occasionally this information could prove to be humiliating. The mother of Field Marshal Eric Milch, one of Hitler's top generals whose father was Jewish, had to provide evidence that her son was the result of an adulterous liaison with an Aryan. The records consulted often went back decades before the introduction of civil registration in 1875 and involved looking at church books (roughly similar to parish registers), which were usually kept by the local church, all of which had to be certified by the local registration officer or the church or synagogue official. This could be a lucrative sideline, although the state tried to keep the charges low. A sexton in Brandenburg made between 250 and

300 Reichsmarks per month from genealogical researches in his parish's records – a not inconsiderable amount for the period.

Many people carried an *Ahnenpass* containing details of their immediate ancestry. These were passport-sized documents with the names and religion of their ancestors certified by the town hall or minister. Blank ones could be bought from stationers and some companies gave them away to customers. The City Savings Bank at Haynau, in Silesia, for example, provided customers with a swastika-bedecked blank genealogical table containing two quotations: the first from *Mein Kampf* encouraged racial purity; the other encouraged savings. In addition, publishers sold supplements where the holder could add additional genealogical information or present pedigrees in different ways, as well as holders to protect the booklets.

Genealogy in Germany before 1933 was very much a minority interest with an emphasis on the roots and antecedents of nobility. In all fairness, Nazi racial ideology was not something that genealogists had much thought about, although many felt that their subject could help with the study of eugenics (the application of theories of selected breeding to the human race). They were not alone in their interest in eugenics: many people in the United States and in Britain, for instance, shared this belief.

German genealogists, archivists and librarians were naturally quick to comprehend the benefits and opportunities that the Nazi regime offered them. The official Reich Genealogical Authority files contain expressions of gratitude to the regime for finally giving genealogy its place in the sun as well as revelling in that status. An essay by Dr Georg Meyer-Erlach from Wurzburg City Archives in 1936 celebrated the fact that:

> For decades kinship research was science's Cinderella. While other branches of learning were represented by university chairs and encouraged by the state, people dismissed us with a pitying laugh. That has now changed thanks to the regime of Adolf Hitler. Today genealogy has tasks of state-level importance to fulfil.

The 400 or so licensed professional genealogists especially benefited. To hire a professional to research a family tree back a century might cost between 50 and 70 Reichsmarks. It is clear from surviving licence applications that most researchers were motivated by an interest in family history rather than for ideological reasons. However, this was not always the case. A bookseller in Bautzen, Saxony, for example, declared himself knowledgeable about 'genealogy, racial questions and eugenics' and was ready 'to place his abilities at the service of the RSA', and an lawyer from Hamburg noted that his chief interest was researching Jewish blood in local families.

The new system was administered by the Reich Genealogical Authority (*Reichssippenamt*, RSA). All pedigrees had to be approved by the authority and it investigated problematical cases where the Aryan claims of an individual were not clear: 7,692 cases in 1934 alone. By the late 1930s, as most people who needed to had proved their racial origins, they began to organise the microfilming of church records. This was increasingly important as the condition of the registers suffered because of the use that was being made of them. The Authority had to cajole the records from parishes reluctant to send them to Berlin for filming. During the war the RSA was involved in proving the racial background of ethnic Germans from the areas in Eastern Europe that had been conquered by the Nazis, as well as seeking to preserve synagogue and related records which otherwise might have been destroyed.

The Authority maintained its own genealogical databases to help staff and enquirers trace individuals. Gercke brought 400,000 cards with him from the NSIO, which became the basis of a massive card system. In 1937 alone over 100,000 cards were added to it. Typically, cards carried information such as profession and birth, marriage and death dates, and were organised where possible by extended family. Baptisms were especially important as these confirmed an individual's religion at birth. There was also a mass of material on Jewish ancestry, including 7,000 registers and 160,000 files on individual families, which had originally been compiled by the Jewish Genealogical Association but were taken over by the Nazis in 1939 and added to subsequently. There were also local projects. In Berlin, Pastor Karl Themel organised a carding project with 1 million cards showing where Berliners had been baptised in one of the city's many Protestant churches from the eighteenth century.

At its peak, the RSA employed 126 staff, including fifteen Jews under an eminent Jewish genealogist, Dr Jacob Jacobson. The Jewish staff were deported to Theresienstadt concentration camp in 1943; only Jacobson survived. There were also a large number of volunteers who helped maintain the card indexes.

What is surprising is that there seems to have been very little resistance to the system or attempts to circumvent it, which suggests that it was widely accepted by Germans whatever their supposed racial origins. Opposition seems to have been solely on practical or personal grounds, although some parishes resisted letting go of their registers, because they objected to the use that would be made of them – this was part of a wider battle between the Nazis and the Evangelical Lutheran Church. Provided the records existed the system was almost foolproof. There was very little latitude allowed to researchers or officials, particularly as the RSA was largely staffed by Nazi Party zealots. Dr Jacobson did his best to help partial Jews find an Aryan paternal ancestor who might have plausibly conducted an adulterous relationship with a Jewish mother or grandmother. However, he particularly resented helping those who were suspected of being a tiny part Jewish if their only aim in erasing their Jewish blood was to secure a better position in the system.

The collapse of the Third Reich in 1945 brought the system to an end; one American genealogist noted: 'One of the few good results of Hitler's domination of Germany has been the formation of genealogical institutes in nearly every town where the families must show their genealogical antecedents for at least three generations. This should make research much easier there.'[34] The surviving records of the RSA are now with the German Federal Archives in Berlin. Only in recent years has there been a resumption of interest in family history and definitely not genealogy. The hobby is now reasonably popular, but for many Germans today there remains a hint of a past they would rather forget.

Notes

1 The Bible, Matthew 1:7.
2 The section on Griots is largely based on Stephen Davies, 'Chants of Memory', *Ancestors Magazine*, 2006, p. 32. See also his website www.voiceinthedesert.org.uk.
3 Nicholas S, Hopkins, 'Memories of Griots', *Alif: Memories of Contemporary Poetics* (17), 1997, p. 46; Cornelia Panzacchi, 'The Livelihoods of Griots in Modern Senegal', *Africa* (64), 1994.
4 Donald R. Wright, 'Uprooting Kunta Kinte: on the perils of encyclopaedic informants', *History in Africa* (8), 1981.
5 Anthony Wagner, *A Herald's World* (Author, 1988), pp. 93–4.
6 Quoted in Tess O'Toole, *Genealogy and Fiction in Hardy: family lineage and narrative lines* (Macmillan, 1997), p. 8.
7 Sally Magnusson, *Dreaming of Iceland: the Lure of a Family Legend* (Hodder & Stoughton, 2004), p. 108.
8 I visited many of them in August 2009 during a press trip and my impressions were written up in 'Twelve hundred years of family history', *Ancestors Magazine*, 2010, p. 89.
9 Quoted in Magnusson, *Dreaming of Iceland*, p. 83.
10 Magnusson, *Dreaming of Iceland*, p. 81.
11 Magnusson, *Dreaming of Iceland*, p. 108.
12 Definition given on Wikipedia. The concept is explained in more detail at http://maaori. com/whakapapa and in Te Ara/Encyclopedia of New Zealand www.teara.govt.nz.
13 Michael King, *The Penguin History of New Zealand* (Penguin, 2003), p. 67; Joan Metge, *The Maoris of New Zealand* (Routledge & Kegan Paul, 1967), p. 1.
14 King, pp. 73, 77–8.
15 J. Horace Round, *Studies in Peerage and Family History* (Archibald Constable, 1901), pp. x–xi. Taken from 'The Lytes of Lytescary', *Somerset Archealogical Transcriptions*, 1892. The house now belongs to the National Trust. Henry Lyte (1529–1607) was a noted herbalist. The best genealogy of family history is Michael Sharpe, *Family Matters: a history of genealogy* (Pen & Sword, 2011). Also of interest is the centenary history of the Society of Genealogists: *A Centenary of Family History* (Society of Genealogists, 2011). The pretensions of the society and genealogy as a whole is gently mocked in this blog: http://thelocalhistoryandfamilyhistorysocietyleague.wordpress.com (thanks to Penny Law).
16 Quoted in John Beckett, *Writing Local History* (Manchester University Press, 2007).
17 Wagner, *English Genealogy* (Phillimore, 1963), p. 3.
18 The pedigree was published in Vol. 13 of *The Complete Peerage* and is online at www. headington.org.uk/history/famous_people/nuffield_ancestry.htm. Quoted in Round, pp. xxvii–xxviii.
19 Robert Gittings, *Young Thomas Hardy* (Penguin, 2001), p. 44.
20 Lucas Papers Vol. 1, now at the Society of Genealogists.

21 Walter Rye, *Records and Record Searching* (2nd edn, 1897); William Turnbull, *The Stirling Peerage. Trial of Alexander Humphries … styling himself Earl of Stirling before the High Court of Justiciary for Forgery on 29 April 1839 …* (Edinburgh, 1839), p. 2; W.P.W. Phillimore, *The 'Principal Genealogical Specialist' or Regina vs Davies and The Shipway Genealogy 'Being the Story of a remarkable Pedigree Fraud'* (Phillimore, 1899); www.oldbaileyonline.org/browse. jsp?id=def1-3-18981121&div=t18981121-3#highlight.

22 Unpublished diary of William and Louise Derrick. Thanks to their descendent Bruno Derrick for permission to quote from it.

23 Walter Rye, *Records and Record Searching* (2nd edn, 1897). The Chamberlain Papers are found in the University of Birmingham Special Collections. Papers related to the family's genealogy are in pieces AC1/1/8/1-22. The reference for the diary is NC 2/20.

24 This section is based on my article 'Pre-Adamite Ancestry: Adventures in Victorian and Edwardian Genealogy', *Genealogists' Magazine*, 2001. The Lyne Papers are at the Society of Genealogists.

25 'Roots Grows into a Winner', *Time*, 7 February 1977.

26 *Sunday Times*, 17 April 1977; *The Times*, 18 April 1977; *Daily Express*, 7 April 1977.

27 Entry for Alex Haley on Wikipedia; Mark Ottaway, 'Tangled Roots', *Sunday Times*, 10 April 1977; Gary B. Mills & Elizabeth Shown Mills, '"Roots" and the new "Faction": a legitimate tool for Clio', *Virginia Magazine of History and Biography* (89), 1981.

28 Stefan Kanfer, 'White Roots: looking for Great-Grandpa', *Time*, 28 March 1977; John Carey, 'Light from the shade of a family tree', *The Times*, 24 March 1984; John A. Schutz, *A Noble Pursuit: The Sesquicentennial History of the New England Historic Genealogical Society 1845–1995* (Boston: NEHGS, 1995), p. 195; Society of Genealogists Annual Report 1980 (SoG, 1981). See also Jonathan Freedland, 'Through the past darkly', *The Guardian*, 13 October 2004.

29 Cary, *The Times*, 24 March 1984; Trevor Fishlock, 'Proud of his roots', *The Times*, 26 August 1978; Paul de Serville's editorial in *Ancestor*, December 1978.

30 J.M. Bulloch, 'A Hindrance to Genealogy', *Scottish Historical Review 1*, 1903; www.newenglandancestors.org/about/3114.asp.

31 Frederick K. Virkus (ed.), *The Abridged Compendium of American Genealogy: First Families of America* (Chicago: Marquis, 1925), pp. 3, 100. Over 1 million applications between 1889 and 1970 are available on Ancestry. They include ones from Winston Churchill and Harry S. Truman; see also http://blog.eogn.com/eastmans_online_genealogy/2011/06/ ancestrycom-releases-the-sons-of-the-american-revolution-membership-applications-1889-1970-in-honor-.html.

32 The Stebbins book is still in print at www.quintinpublications.com/category/Sq_St; *Reunions Magazine* is at www.reunionsmag.com.

33 This section was written using the following texts: Deborah Hertz, 'The Genealogical Bureaucracy in the Third Reich', *Jewish History* (11), 1997; Eric Ehrenreich, *The Nazi Ancestral Proof: Genealogy, Racial Science, and the Final Solution* (Indiana University Press, 2007); Beate Meyer, Hermann Simon, Chana Schütz, *Jews in Nazi Berlin: From Kristallnacht to Liberation* (University of Chicago Press, 2009); http://www.servinghistory. com/topics/Ahnenpass.

34 Evan L. Reed, *Ways and Means of Identifying Ancestors* (Chicago: Ancestral Publishing, 1947), p. 5.

Appendix 1

READING OLD HANDWRITING

FROM THE EXPERTS ...

Ruth Davies suggests shortcuts to help read old documents.

As a genealogist it is very frustrating to come across an old document that can't be read. Typical documents that can cause difficulties include parish register entries, wills, inventories and deeds. However, the skills to reading old handwriting (or palaeography as it is called) can be acquired by any persistent genealogist. The following are some guidelines to get you started.

Get hold of a large and clear copy of the document. You may have to ask for an original document to be brought out to photograph, rather than trying to work off a scratchy microfilm. Good lighting and a magnifying glass are also extremely useful.

Check the age of the document. Handwriting went through different fashions and different scripts were used for different purposes. If you have an idea of the age and handwriting style, you can match it up with other, clearer and perhaps transcribed examples of the same kind of script. Is it Victorian italic, written by someone with a leaky pen? Or is it secretary hand, which was a popular style in the sixteenth and seventeenth centuries? (http://paleo.anglo-norman.org/palindex.html is an excellent palaeography website, with many examples of handwriting from the thirteenth century to the sixteenth century, together with transcriptions.)

Transcribe what you can. If you have a photocopy of the document then number the lines down the left-hand side of the copy and start to transcribe line by line, numbering your transcribed lines as you go. Underline or use square brackets for anything you are unsure about or have to miss out.

Once you have transcribed some words then you can begin to construct an internal alphabet, where certain letter shapes in known words can be matched up with the same letter shapes in unknown words. Be patient here and take breaks. Coming back fresh to an unknown word or phrase can make you suddenly realise what it is. Be aware that different letters may alter their shape depending on the whim of the scribe and the state of their writing implement. Transcribing tricky words backwards, letter by letter, prevents any assumptions from being made about what it might be.

Watch out for odd spellings and archaic words. You may have transcribed a word perfectly correctly but still not know what it means. Many inventories, for example, are littered with odd-sounding items such as a dobnet, kibbe and bowe pott. There is an excellent little book called A Glossary of Household, Farming and Trade Terms From Probate Inventories by Rosemary Milward that can help with these. There is also an online directory to be found at www.british-history.ac.uk/source.aspx?pubid=739.

There were many forenames in use in past centuries that have now fallen out of favour, such as Cyriack, Effery and Mehitabel, and these may be tricky to recognise. This website gives a comprehensive list: http://homepages.rootsweb.ancestry. com/~oel/givennames.html.

Finally, watch out for phonetic spelling, which was extremely common. Try saying an unknown word out loud. You may even get an idea of the local accent.

Above all, exercise patience. Transcribing a document can feel very much like cracking a code and it requires both persistence and intuition to get results.

If you wish to go further with this intriguing branch of genealogy then take a course. There are a number of online courses available, such as this one from The National Archives: www.nationalarchives.gov.uk/palaeography/default.htm. This covers documents written in English from 1500–1800 and includes exercises and transcriptions. An online course from the Scottish Archive Network (SCAN) is at www. scottishhandwriting.com/index.asp. It contains examples of Scottish secretary-hand documents from 1500–1700s and transcription tests.

Ruth Davies is a qualified archivist who has worked at a number of record offices in England and Wales. She has also designed and taught adult education classes in family history. Recently she has started a research service as an independent researcher and transcriber, mainly at the Flintshire Record Office. She also teaches Pharos' old handwriting course.

Appendix 2

USEFUL ADDRESSES

National Institutions

Bodleian Library
Broad Street, Oxford
OX1 3BG
Tel: 01865 277162
Web: www.bodleian.ox.ac.uk

British Library
96 Euston Road, London
NW1 2DB
Tel: 020 7412 7000
Web: www.bl.uk

British Library Newspapers
Colindale Avenue, London
NW9 5HE
Tel: 020 7412 7353
Web: www.bl.uk

British Postal Museum and Archives
Freeling House, Phoenix Place
London, WC1X 0DL
Web: http://postalheritage.org.uk

BT Archives
Third Floor Holborn Telephone Exchange
268–270 High Holborn, London
WC1V 7EE
Tel: 020 7440 4220
Web: www.btplc.com/thegroup/btshistory/btgrouparchives

Cambridge University Library
West Road, Cambridge
CB3 9DR
Tel: 01223 333000
Web: www.lib.cam.ac.uk

Catholic National Library
St Michael's Abbey
Farnborough Road, Farnborough
GU14 7NQ
Web: www.catholic-library.org.uk

Commonwealth War Graves Commission
2 Marlow Road, Maidenhead
SL6 7DX
Tel: 01628 507200
Web: www.cwgc.org

Library and Museum of Freemasonry
Freemasons' Hall
60 Great Queen Street, London
WC2B 5AZ
Tel: 020 7395 9257
Web: www.freemasonry.london.museum

Friends Library
173–177 Euston Road, London
NW1 2BJ
Tel: 020 7663 1135
Web: www.quakers.org.uk/library

London Metropolitan Archives
40 Northampton Road, London
EC1R 0HB

Tel: 020 7332 3820

Web: www.lma.gov.uk; website of the former Guildhall Library Manuscripts Department (absorbed by LMA in 2010) www.history.ac.uk/gh/livapp.htm

The National Archives
Ruskin Avenue
Kew, Richmond
TW9 4DU
Tel: 020 8876 3444
Web: www.nationalarchives.gov.uk

National Library of Wales
Aberystwyth
SY23 3BU
Tel: 01970 632800
Web: www.llgc.org.uk

Parliamentary Archives
Houses of Parliament, London
SW1A 0PW
Tel: 020 7219 3074
Web: www.parliament.uk/business/publications/parliamentary-archives

Military Museums and Archives

Army Museums Ogilby Trust
Web: www.armymuseums.org.uk has details of all local regimental museums.

Fleet Air Arm Museum
RNAS Yeovilton, Ilchester
BA22 8HT
Tel: 01935 840565
Web: www.fleetairarm.com

Imperial War Museum
Lambeth Road, London
SE1 6HZ
Tel: 020 7334 3922
Web: www.iwm.org.uk; www.iwmcollections.org.uk

National Army Museum
Royal Hospital Road, London
SW34 HT
Tel: 020 7730 0717
Web: www.national-army-museum.org.uk

National Maritime Museum
Romney Road, Greenwich, London
SE10 9NF
Tel: 020 8312 6565
Web: www.nmm.ac.uk

RAF Museum
Graeme Park Way, London
NW9 5LL
Tel: 020 8295 2266
Web: www.rafmuseum.org.uk

Royal Marines Museum
Southsea
PO4 9PX
Tel: 023 9281 9385
Web: www.royalmarinesmuseum.co.uk

Royal Naval Museum
HM Naval Base, Portsmouth
PO1 3NH
Tel: 023 9272 7562
Web: www.royalnavalmuseum.org

Family History Resources

Federation of Family History Societies
PO Box 8857, Lutterworth
LE17 9BJ
Web: www.ffhs.org.uk

General Register Office
PO Box 2, Southport
PR8 2JD

Tel: 0845 603 7788
Web: www.gro.gov.uk/gro/content/certificates

Guild of One-Name Studies

Box G, 14 Charterhouse Buildings
Goswell Road, London
EC1M 7BA
Web: www.one-name.org.uk

Institute of Heraldic and Genealogical Studies

79–81 Northgate, Canterbury
CT1 1BA
Tel: 01227 768664
Web: www.ihgs.ac.uk

London Family History Centre

64–68 Exhibition Road, London
SW7 2PA
Tel: 020 7589 8561
Web: www.londonfhc.org

Society of Genealogists

14 Charterhouse Buildings
Goswell Road, London
EC1M 7BA
Tel: 020 7251 8799
Web: www.sog.org.uk

Scotland

General Register Office for Scotland

HM General Register House
2 Princes Street, Edinburgh,
EH1 3YY
Web: www.gro-scotland.gov.uk

National Archives of Scotland

HM General Register House, Edinburgh
EH1 3YY
Tel: 0131 535 1334
Web: www.nas.gov.uk

ScotlandsPeople Centre
HM General Register House
2 Princes Street, Edinburgh
EH1 3YY
Tel: 0131 314 4300
Web: www.scotlandspeoplehub.gov.uk

National Library of Scotland
57 George IV Bridge, Edinburgh
EH1 1EW
Tel: 0131 623 3700
Web: www.nls.uk

Scottish Genealogy Society
15 Victoria Terrace, Edinburgh
EH1 2JL
Tel: 0131 220 3677
Web: www.scotsgenealogy.com

Ireland

To ring numbers in the Republic of Ireland from the UK add the international prefix 00353 and omit the initial 0 in the dialling code.

National Archives of Ireland
Bishops St, Dublin 8
Tel: 01 407 2300
Web: www.nationalarchives.ie

National Library of Ireland
Kildare St, Dublin 2
Tel: 01 603 0200
Web: www.nli.ie

General Register Office
Government Offices
Convent Road, Roscommon
Tel: 090 663 2900
Web: www.groireland.ie

Public Reading Room
3rd Floor, Block 7
Irish Life Centre
Lower Abbey Street
Dublin 1

Public Record Office of Northern Ireland (PRONI)
2 Titanic Boulevard, Belfast
BT3 9HQ
Tel: 028 9025 5905
Web: www.proni.gov.uk

General Register Office of Northern Ireland
Oxford House
49–55 Chichester St, Belfast
BT1 4HL
Tel: 028 9025 2000
Web: www.groni.gov.uk

Ulster Historical Foundation
49 Malone Road, Belfast
BT9 6RY
Tel: 028 9066 1988
Web: www.ancestryireland.com

BIBLIOGRAPHY

Key Reference Books

Although the internet in its many forms can answer most genealogical questions, it can often be easier to check out a reference book rather than spend hours surfing the net only to find something that turns out to be only half right. Here is a selection of tried and tested books, which you should have in your library.

Amanda Bevan, *Tracing Your Ancestors at The National Archives* (7th edn, The National Archives, 2006).
This is a comprehensive guide to all the records with genealogical material at Kew. It is well written and well organised.

Paul Carter & Kate Thompson, *Sources for Local Historians* (Phillimore, 2007).
Written with students of local history in mind, this book is still useful for family historians as it has much about nineteenth- and twentieth-century sources at Kew and local archives.

Peter Christian, *The Genealogists' Internet* (4th edn, The National Archives, 2009).
Despite the arrival of a number of rivals, it is still the best and most comprehensive guide. Updates are available at www.spub.co.uk/tgi4.

Bruce Durie, *Scottish Genealogy* (The History Press, 2009).
There are lots of excellent books on researching Scottish family history of which this is perhaps the best.

John Grenham, *Tracing Your Irish Ancestors* (3rd edn, Gill & Macmillan, 2006).
A very comprehensive guide to what can turn out to be a very difficult topic for research.

Mark Herber, *Ancestral Trails: The Complete Guide to British Genealogy and Family History* (The History Press, 2005).

Although increasingly dated, Herber's book remains the most comprehensive guide to family history resources.

David Hey, *The Oxford Companion to Local and Family History* (Oxford University Press, 2008).
The companion contains a mixture of longer essays and shorter entries on most aspects of family and local history.

Cecil R. Humphrey-Smith, *Phillimore Atlas and Index of Parish Registers* (3rd edn, Phillimore, 2002).
Attractive and useful with maps and detailed listings of parish registers and where they are to be found.

Pauline Saul, *The Family Historian's Enquire Within* (5th edn, Federation of Family History Societies, 1995).
All you need to know, simply put! Sadly this book has long been out of print, but a new edition from the Family History Partnership should be available by the end of 2012.

Other Reference Books

Robert Blatchford, *The Family and Local History Handbook* (Robert Blatchford Publishing, annually).
C.R. Cheney & M. Jones (eds), *A Handbook of Dates: For Students of British History* (Cambridge University Press, 2000).
Karen Foy, *Family History for Beginners* (The History Press, 2011).
David Hey, *Family History and Local History in England* (Longman, 1987).
Edward, Higgs, *The Information State in England* (Palgrave, 2004).
————, *Making Sense of the Census Revisited* (Institute of Historical Research, 2005).
Thomas Jay Kemp, *International Vital Records Handbook* (5th edn, Genealogical Publishing, 2009).
Peter Laslett, *The World We Have Lost: Further Explored* (3rd edn, Routledge, 1983).
Evelyn Lord, *Investigating the Twentieth Century: Sources for Local History* (Tempus, 1999).
Lionel Munby, *How Much is that Worth?* (British Association for Local History, 1989).
George Redmonds, David Hey & Turi Hunt, *Surnames, DNA, and Family History* (Oxford University Press, 2011).
Colin Waters, *A Dictionary of Old Trades, Titles and Occupations* (Countryside Books, 2002).
Token Publishing, *The Medals Yearbook* (Token Publishing, annually).
K.M. Thompson (ed.), *Short Guide to Records* (2 vols, Historical Association, 1994, 1997).
John West, *Town Records* (Phillimore, 1983).

The Gibson Guides

It is worth looking out for the 'Gibson Guides', which are small paperback guides to particular types of records held at local record offices compiled by Jeremy Gibson, often with the help of other experts. They were originally published by the Federation of Family

History Societies (FFHS), but now come from the Family History Partnership (FHP) at www.thefamilyhistorypartnership.com. Despite all the resources now available online they remain incredibly useful, as they are very accurate and they often list very obscure resources and indexes. The following are still in print:

Bishop's Transcripts and Marriage Licences, Bonds and Allegations (2nd edn, FFHS, 2001).
Coroner's Records in England and Wales (3rd edn, FHP, 2009).
Electoral Registers and Burgess Rolls (2nd edn, FHP, 2006).
Hearth Tax and later Stuart Tax Lists and the Association Oath Rolls (FFHS, 1996).
Land and Window Tax Assessments (2nd edn, FHP, 2004).
Local Census Listings 1522–1930 (3rd edn, FFHS, 1999).
Local Newspapers 1750–1920 (3rd edn, FHP, 2011).
Marriage Indexes for Family Historians (9th edn, FHP, 2007).
Militia Lists and Musters 1767–1876 (4th edn, FHP, 2004).
Poll Books 1696–1872 A Directory to Holdings in Great Britain (4th edn, FHP, 2008).
Poor Law Union Records (2nd edn, FHP, 2005).
Protestation Returns 1641–42 and Other Contemporary Listings (FFHS, 1995).
Quarter Session Records for Family Historians (5th edn, FHP, 2007).
Tudor and Stuart Muster Rolls (FFHS, 1991).
Victuallers' Licences (3rd edn, FHP, 2009).
Wills and Where to find them (Phillimore & Co. Ltd, 1974).

Key Websites

There are a number of very informative, and generally free, websites that can be of great use in your research:

www.agra.org.uk – Association of Genealogists and Researchers in Archives with lists of professional researchers. For Scotland check out www.asgra.co.uk.
www.archive.org – this internet archive takes snapshots of many websites on a regular basis. It also provides access to millions of old books, photographs, films and other resources.
www.british-history.ac.uk – some of the core printed primary and secondary sources for the medieval and early modern history of the British Isles.
www.britishnewspaperarchive.co.uk – contains many British newspapers up to the twentieth century.
www.cwgc.org – Commonwealth War Graves Commission website with details of all British and Commonwealth service personnel whose graves the Commission cares for.
www.connectedhistories.org – useful to search various other history databases (see Chapter 2).
http://thefamilyrecorder.blogspot.com – Audrey Collin's blog about family history resources.
www.deceasedonline.com – details of burials in local authority cemeteries.
www.genealogyintime.com – updates about new resources going online.
www.historicaldirectories.org – a selection of trade and street directories mainly from the 1850s, 1890s and 1910s.
www.askaboutireland.ie – has many Irish resources, including Griffith's valuation and some maps.

www.census.nationalarchives.ie – the Irish 1901 and 1911 censuses.

www.londonlives.org – resources about Londoners in the seventeenth and eighteenth centuries.

www.oldbaileyonline.org – records of trials at the Old Bailey between 1678 and 1913.

http://rootsweb.ancestry.com – the largest (and oldest) genealogical community on the internet.

www.scan.org.uk – lots of resources for Scotland, including links to Scottish archives and online catalogues.

www.slq.qld.gov.au/info/fh/convicts – a free database of about 80 per cent of the criminals transported to Australia from the State Library of Queensland.

www.surnamestudies.org.uk – an excellent introduction to the study of surnames.

http://ukbmd.org – links to many indexes of birth, marriage and death records in local registry offices and elsewhere.

www.unionancestors.co.uk – a guide to researching trade union ancestors.

www.workhouses.org.uk – detailed information about workhouses and the working of the New Poor Law.

Specialist Titles

Chapter 1 Adventures in the Stacks

Peter Clark, *British Clubs and Societies 1580–1800* (Oxford University Press, 2000).

Mark Crail, *Tracing Your Labour Movement Ancestors* (Pen & Sword, 2009).

Patricia Hollis, *Ladies Elect: Women in English Local Government 1865–1914* (Oxford University Press, 1987).

Roger Logan, *Friendly Society Records* (Federation of Family History Societies, 2000).

Liza Picard, *Dr Johnson's London* (Phoenix, 2001).

Stuart Raymond, *Occupational Sources for Family Historians* (2nd edn, Family History Partnership, 2010).

Flora Thompson, *Lark Rise to Candleford* (Penguin, 1981).

Websites

www.freemasonry.london.museum/family-history – introduction to Freemasons' records.

http://hharp.org – a selection of hospital registers and related records for hospitals in London and Glasgow.

www.hiddenhistories.org.uk – a website based on the records of the Church of England Children Society.

Chapter 3 Printed Sources

James Beresford (ed.), *The Diary of a Country Parson* (Oxford University Press, 1978).

William Plomer (ed.), *Kilvert's Diaries* (Jonathan Cape, 1964).

Websites

http://grubstreet.rictornorton.co.uk – Rictor Norton, *Early Eighteenth-Century Newspaper Reports: A Sourcebook.*

www.london-gazette.co.uk – the *London Gazette* online from 1665 to the present day.

www.pepysdiary.com – the online edition of Samuel Pepys' diary.

Chapter 5 Distant Ancestors

Pre-nineteenth Century Genealogy

Paul Chambers, *Medieval Genealogy: how to find your Medieval Ancestors* (Sutton, 2005).

————, *Early Modern Genealogy: Researching your Family History 1600–1838* (Sutton, 2006).

Jane Cox, *Tracing Your East End Ancestor* (Pen & Sword, 2011).

Jonathan Oates, *Tracing Your Ancestors from 1066–1837: a Guide for Family Historians* (Pen & Sword, 2012).

W.E. Tate, *The Parish Chest: a Study of the Records of Parochial Administration in England* (2nd edn, Phillimore, 1983). There is also a third edition published by Cambridge University Press, 2008.

David Underdown, *Fire from Heaven* (Pimlico, 2003).

Amanda Vickery, *Behind Closed Doors: at Home in Georgian England* (Yale University Press, 2009).

Maureen Waller, *The English Marriage: Tales of Love, Money and Adultery* (John Murray, 2009).

Michael Wood, *The Story of England* (Viking, 2009).

Other

Anthony Adolph, *Collins Tracing Your Home's History* (Collins, 2006).

N.W. Alcock, *Old Title Deeds* (Phillimore, 2001).

Nick Barratt, *Nick Barratt's Guide to Your Ancestors' Lives* (Pen & Sword, 2010).

Eileen Gooder, *Latin for Local Historians* (Longman, 1998).

Karen Grannum & Nigel Taylor, *Wills and Probate Records* (The National Archives, 2009).

Richard Hoyle, *Tudor Taxation Records* (Public Record Office, 1995).

Alf Ison, *A Secretary Hand ABC* (Berkshire FHS, 1990).

M. Jurkowski et al., *Lay Taxes in England and Wales, 1188–1688* (Public Record Office, 1998).

Hilary Marshall, *Palaeography for Family and Local Historians* (Phillimore, 2004).

Lionel M. Munby & Steve Hobbs, *Reading Tudor and Stuart Handwriting* (British Association for Local History, 2002).

Dennis Stuart, *Latin for Local and Family Historians* (Phillimore, 1995).

Websites

www.medievalgenealogy.org.uk – a superb and comprehensive site devoted to medieval genealogy.

www.tackbear.co.uk/index.htm – an interesting study of seventeenth-century genealogy with lots of examples from the key documents, mainly for Devon and Cornwall.

http://mhf39.modhist.ox.ac.uk/original-documents/chronological/medieval-1 – an easy
guide to using medieval records primarily for local history.

Chapter 6 Deep Roots: Genealogy in the Wider World

Eric Ehrenreich, *The Nazi Ancestral Proof: Genealogy, Racial Science, and the Final Solution*
(Indiana University Press, 2007).

Deborah Hertz, 'The Genealogical Bureaucracy in the Third Reich', *Jewish History* (11),
1997.

Michael King, *The Penguin History of New Zealand* (Penguin, 2003).

Sally Magnusson, *Dreaming of Iceland: the Lure of a Family Legend* (Hodder & Stoughton,
2004).

Beate Meyer, Hermann Simon & Chana Schütz, *Jews in Nazi Berlin: From Kristallnacht to
Liberation* (University of Chicago Press, 2009).

Michael Sharpe, *Family Matters: a History of Genealogy* (Pen & Sword, 2011).

Anthony Wagner, *A Herald's World* (Author, 1988).

INDEX

Other titles published by The History Press

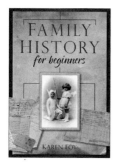

Family History: for beginners
KAREN FOY

Family history is a pastime anyone can enjoy, but the massive proliferation of websites, magazines and books can baffle a would-be genealogist. This book will help you research beyond the simple facts of birth, marriage and death, with chapters on occupation, emigration and military service. Showing you how to get the most information from relatives, to negotiate census data and catalogue and present information.

978-0-7524-5838-0

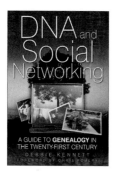

DNA and Social Networking
DEBBIE KENNETT

The first decade of the new millennium has been an exciting time for the family historian. This book looks at all the latest advances in DNA testing from the Y-chromosome tests used in surname projects through to the latest autosomal DNA tests. Debbie Kennett explores the use of new social media, including Facebook, Twitter, blogs and wikis, along with more traditional networking methods. *DNA and Social Networking* is an indispensable guide to the use of twenty-first-century technology in family history research.

978-0-7524-5862-5

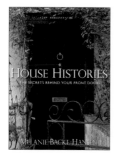

House Histories: The Secrets Behind Your Front Door
MELANIE BACKE-HANSEN

In *House Histories*, Britain's leading house historian uncovers the hidden stories and secrets of ordinary and extraordinary houses across the country. The wide range of houses, from workers' cottages to aristocratic mansions, offers a unique insight into our social and architectural history. Tudor farmhouses, Georgian town houses, modernist twentieth-century designs and converted factories all have a tale to tell. Beautifully illustrated, *House Histories* helps readers get started by outlining the main research sources and how to use them.

978-0-7524-5753-6

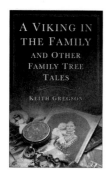

A Viking in the Family, and Other Family Tree Tales
KEITH GREGSON

Genealogist Keith Gregson takes the reader on a whistle-stop tour of quirky family stories and strange ancestors rooted out by amateur and professional family historians. Each lively entry tells the story behind each discovery and then offers a brief insight into how the researcher found and then followed up their leads, revealing a range of chance encounters and the detective qualities required of a family historian. *A Viking in the Family* is full of unexpected discoveries in the branches of family trees.

978-0-7524-5772-7

Visit our website and discover thousands of other History Press books.

www.thehistorypress.co.uk